HOW TO MAKE IT IN THE MUSIC BUSINESS

HOW TO MAKE IT IN THE MUSIC BUSINESS

SIÂN PATTENDEN

Virgin

First published in Great Britain in 1998 by
Virgin Books
an imprint of Virgin Publishing Ltd
332 Ladbroke Grove
London W10 5AH

A catalogue record for this book is available
from the British Library.

ISBN 0 7535 0235 6

Designed and Typeset
by Roger Kohn Designs

Printed and bound by Mackays of Chatham

To Felix
whose paw prints show the way

Thanks to:
Everyone in the book, plus the people
who were invaluable, in a completely
non-ironic sense:
Ian Gittins, Gillian Porter, Chloe at
Heavenly, Polly, John and Melissa,
Martine, Murray Chalmers, Caffy,
Andy Ross and all at Food, Josh, Will,
Brendan, Sue Miles, Mel at London,
Anne at Virgin, Kate at Polydor,
Sylvia, Moran, Jeremy Fowler, Nicky,
Jane, Leesa, Elspeth, Esther, Andrew
and The Afternoon Shift (RIP) –
especially with Laurie Taylor.

CONTENTS

THE MUSIC BUSINESS: HOW IT WORKS

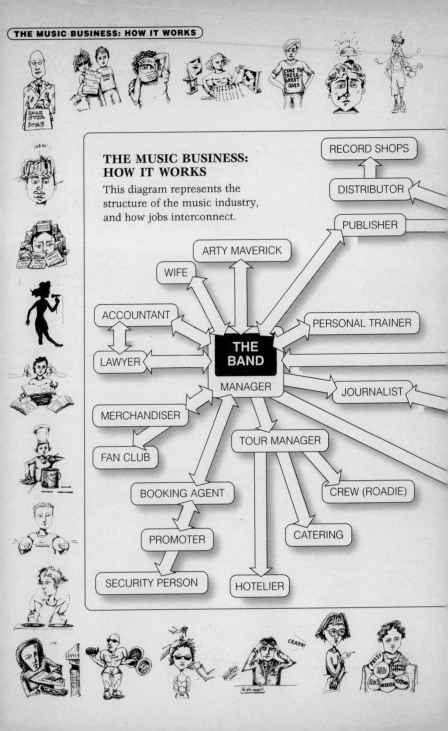

THE MUSIC BUSINESS: HOW IT WORKS

This diagram represents the structure of the music industry, and how jobs interconnect.

RECORD SHOPS

DISTRIBUTOR

PUBLISHER

ARTY MAVERICK

WIFE

ACCOUNTANT

PERSONAL TRAINER

THE BAND

LAWYER

MANAGER

JOURNALIST

MERCHANDISER

FAN CLUB

TOUR MANAGER

BOOKING AGENT

CREW (ROADIE)

PROMOTER

CATERING

SECURITY PERSON

HOTELIER

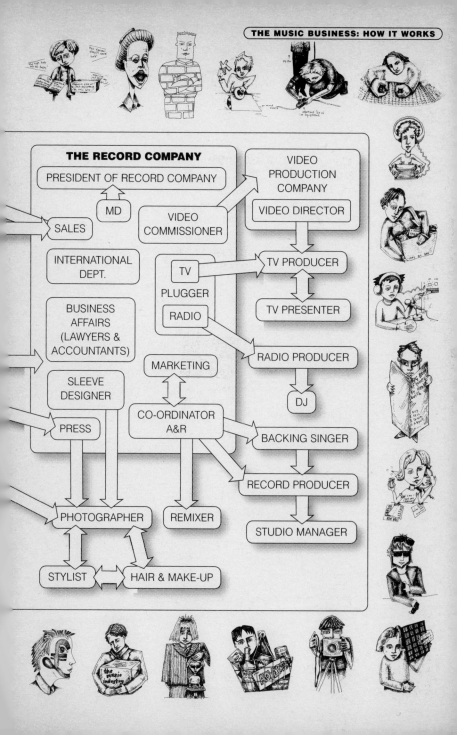

THE RECORD COMPANY

PRESIDENT OF RECORD COMPANY

VIDEO PRODUCTION COMPANY

MD

VIDEO COMMISSIONER

VIDEO DIRECTOR

SALES

INTERNATIONAL DEPT.

TV PLUGGER

RADIO

TV PRODUCER

TV PRESENTER

BUSINESS AFFAIRS (LAWYERS & ACCOUNTANTS)

RADIO PRODUCER

MARKETING

SLEEVE DESIGNER

CO-ORDINATOR A&R

DJ

PRESS

BACKING SINGER

RECORD PRODUCER

PHOTOGRAPHER

REMIXER

STUDIO MANAGER

STYLIST

HAIR & MAKE-UP

INTRODUCTION

The world of pop music and its satellites are strange and singular, primarily because the industry seems to have made up its own peculiar rules. More than any other business, the music world frequently appears to be one in which nobody at all has any idea what will happen next, and its internal machinations can appear arcane and extraordinarily impenetrable to outsiders. Sure, money and sales figures dominate the business, as all others, and yet the ground rules for success are more than just a matter of who's shifting the most records this month: the whole shooting match is as fickle, maverick, unpredictable and fascinating as pop music itself. The music business is not for those who crave safety and security in their career. The only certainty is that anything can happen and normally does.

The majority of the clichés surrounding the industry are essentially true, for better or worse. Sadly, most of the industry *is* based in London. There is a network of labels, promoters, distributors and venues spread throughout the UK, but the majority of graft is done in the capital – all the major record and publishing companies and most of the magazines are based there, and there's a wealth of venues for A&R people to stand at the back of. You don't *have* to be in London to survive in the music world – independent labels like Factory, in Manchester, and Warp, in Sheffield, have bucked the trend over the last two decades - but you'll certainly find a lot more possibilities in the capital.

The idiosyncrasies and foibles of the music industry are truly legion. It won't take you long to notice that, at parties, far more people than is healthy will call you 'dude' or 'babe' while simultaneously craning over your shoulder to see if there's anybody more famous or interesting for them to talk to. They will also ask you whether you 'have any drugs' in much the same way as ordinary folk will discuss the weather. The music business is not a 'normal' calling like estate agency or accountancy, possibly because it's staffed almost exclusively by young people. Oh, and everyone *has* got a mobile phone. How annoying.

Thousands of people long to work in the music world, and the main reason is that it's a lot of fun. Despite how it may look from the outside, it's *not* impossible to get that first foot in the door. However, a recurrent theme of this book is that, whatever sector of the industry you want to work in, you will have to be prepared to work for very little – or even nothing – to get that initial break.

It doesn't matter if the first post you're offered isn't your dream job: with application and skill you'll be able to change tack later on, and many major figures in the music industry started off working in their spare time while holding down 'straight' jobs or living with their parents. And, remember, despite the extraordinary amounts earnt by its top dogs, the music business isn't all baroque decadence and peacocks in the lobby – or not at first, anyway.

How To Make It In The Music Business is a guide to taking your first tentative steps in the most exciting, glamorous and compelling industry in the world, whether you want to be a rock star, label bigwig, A&R person, make-up artist or roadie. I talked to the people who know best – those who've made it to the top of their chosen vocation, whether they be Zoë Ball, Ronan from Boyzone, the guy who designs all Oasis's sleeves, the *Top Of The Pops* producer, or Stephen Street, one of the nation's top record producers. I hope this book is a good read and gives you some vital tips, but also that it shows that the industry isn't so intimidating and nepotistic that a keen individual with a genuine passion for good tunes and several ounces of enthusiasm can't leap in there and start shaking up the fat cats. If you love music, despite what the cynics may tell you, that's the most important thing of all.

So, off you go, then. I'll see you at Wembley.

Siân Pattenden
March 1998

All illustrations by Siân Pattenden

A&R PERSON

A&R people are in charge of searching out, signing, and developing acts for a record label. They go to gigs and listen to tapes of new bands all the time, and never stop looking for The Next Big Thing. And, when they've found that, they have to look for The Next Next Big Thing. And then The Next Next Big Thing Who Wears A Hat.

The **A&R** department of a record company is responsible for the future of music, no less. They sign new bands to the record label they work for, all of which they hope will create great tunes for years to come, while pushing back the boundaries of rock 'n' roll and **shifting units** in the process. They don't just sign bands, but also act as the link between the band, the band's management, and the record company. They are, according to your view, either the human face of the big machine or the evil colossus of the corporate rock industry.

The A&R person's job is very simple – sign a couple of bands that you like a year, then get them to put out a record. It's not hard, surely. Listen to a tape or two, meet a couple of people down the pub, go to a gig, and *voilà*! 'Here, Mr MD, this is the future of rock 'n' roll!' Of course, the reality is much more complicated, because this is the music industry and no one gets away with having an easy life.

In major record labels you have scouts, senior A&R people and a head of A&R; in smaller companies you may have just one or two A&R people. Scouts, er, scout for bands. They go to see as many gigs as they can, which can range from one to four gigs in a given evening, in any part of the country. Scouts listen to tapes that are sent in – sometimes – and are generally the first to meet the bands they like and show their interest. Senior A&R people will get involved once a scout has raved about a band nonstop for hours. They'll come down to the gig and check them out – they have greater decision-making powers than the scouts. Ultimate decision making is down to the head of A&R,

who hears the excited braying from the department and either gives the nod or shakes their head. Already-established acts who want to move record label would really go straight to the head of A&R. That's how the hierarchy works.

David Laurie is head of A&R at Nude Records, home of Suede and Geneva. When he moved down to London about six years ago, David started going to lots of gigs and trying out for A&R vacancies over a period of two years. He decided jobs were going to people the department already knew, and thought there must be another way in. He helped organise gigs in a couple of indie clubs in London and chose top indie names on the brink of being signed, together with just-signed names – well aware that A&R people would flock to his gigs. After three months, he got the job at Nude. Promoting gigs is an A&R exercise in itself – choosing live acts that the punters want to see takes a similar skill. The good thing is you don't have to pay them a huge advance or release their records, so it's a smaller gamble.

'On my first day in the office I was given a £200 advance for expenses, a telephone, the *Music Week* directory, and told to find some groups,' he says. '"Off you go to Manchester," I was ordered. "Get there early to visit some studios, see loads of bands and a local promoter – make the most of your time and get to know as many people as fast as possible."'

Before band tapes reach A&R, they're often given out to local promoters, friends, studios (small **demo studios**

where new bands record will certainly have a lot of stuff lying around) and local journalists. You have to go out and find these people. You have to be cheery and kind, talkative and interested – because you are a Frightening Record-Company Corporate Whore and you won't be trusted just because you've bought someone a shandy. Especially up north. On both counts.

One of the problems of A&R is keeping things secret. You want the band to yourself, to give you all their best tunes, and to kiss you. If you let on how much you like them, every other label will be standing next to you at their next gig, whispering things down their mobile phones and sending the band little cards: A&Rmanship is like courting, once you've found some talented musicians. You have to get on their side, smile, buy them a round (you'll get it paid back as expenses) and express deep love for all of their

A&R MAN

tunes. Except the one with the rap in the middle. Sometimes you'll be expressing deep love for all of their tunes, except the one *without* the rap in the middle, for that is the unpredictability of A&R.

What A&R people do when they meet other A&R people – because they are sly and weaselly creatures – is to say how much they love a band they only *like*, to check whether the other person has heard of them. There goes the peculiar language of the beast. They'll sit for hours talking about some band they can't even remember the name of, trying to gauge whether the other person really does like them, while keeping mum about who they're really after. It's all a very, very silly game.

'It's very difficult to keep your trap shut if you like a band,' says Rick Lennox, senior A&R man at Polydor who has the name of one of his signings – The O – painted on to his short, peroxide hair. 'A lot of scouts do swap information, but I've had to learn not to tell the world.'

And then there's lunch. A&R people are renowned for taking long, boozy lunches with anyone who can hold a microphone. It's all on expenses, you see: the record company pays for it all. And then they turn round and say they haven't signed anyone for nine years and does anyone know if the new Duran Duran single is coming out yet. Pah!!

You do get a fair few iffy A&R types who don't sign up very many acts and can't be bothered to see new bands but instead spend the A&R budget on demoing acts they probably won't sign. Demoing is a very convenient way for a rubbish A&R person to stall hopeful

artists. You get The Tawdrid Antelope into the office, take them for a beer, and promise you'll give them £800 to demo four songs in a cheap studio. Then you don't sign them but instead um and ah (the traditional sarky shorthand for A&R) and keep them wondering about your intentions. This you do repeatedly until you have absolutely no choice but to sign someone. Then, if you A&R for a major record company, you can offer The Nearly Next Big Thing (who you've heard about through the grapevine, or read a live review of in *Melody Maker*) a mountain of money for a deal and see if they accept.

However, it is inappropriate to be utterly cynical about a whole, very important, arm of the music industry. Good A&R people are passionate about their job, and this shows primarily because they tend to sign better bands, and even if they offer a smaller deal cash-wise they will have gained the band's trust from the start. Also, a band's lawyer will generally caution against merely accepting the biggest record label's cash offer: so such simplistic A&R tactics certainly aren't guaranteed to work.

A&R people don't just spot and sign promising acts: they also work closely with them for the length of their career at the label. Problems can therefore arise when you find that you love the music, but possibly not the people who are making it.

'That happened to me quite recently,' says David Laurie. 'There was one particular band who were really hard work. The first time I met them we went out and got really drunk and ended up having a laugh. Then, the next time, they acted like I had

AT A GIG, EVEN IF THEY KNOW EACH OTHER, A&R MEN DO NOT GIVE THEIR SECRETS AWAY.

Laurie. Rick Lennox agrees: 'There are a billion bands out there who have one really good song each. But you can't sign a band because they've got one good song – they need a whole set of them. I won't sign ten bands per year because, if I'm lucky, I'll fall in love with only about two a year.'

It is a fact that fewer bands than ever are signed every year because the music industry has recently witnessed a sea change. There is no longer any alternative, 'leftfield' middle ground as the new, democratic Radio One playlist and the changes wrought in the UK industry by the Britpop explosion mean that acts like Embrace, who would once have been thought 'difficult', now routinely score top-ten hits as easily as Eternal. This means that deals are now signed for a great deal more money than previously – so there are fewer deals to go round.

never met them before. I thought: Oh, I just can't be bothered with this.'

A&R persons can come up against snotty managers who render a band unsignable simply by being pig-headed and impossible to work with. On other occasions, the bands themselves have the big attitude problem. 'I had Embrace in the office, a long time before they signed,' says David. 'Their songs were all over the shop with orchestral bits all over the place. They weren't that good – it's no good having a horn section if the song itself isn't much cop. I told them this, gently, and they got quite pissed off with me. They never phoned me back after that ...'

A&R people constantly stress that, no matter what hair or which trousers they sport, the band must always have *songs*. 'A nice tune and a nice chorus, with proper singing, as a rule,' confirms

It generally costs around £250,000 to 'break' an album, even without allowing for recording costs. A&R people are thus under more pressure to sign the 'right' people, i.e. artists who will have hits. Occasionally, though, A&R execs still get manna from heaven, and a great example was White Town's number-one hit 'Your Woman', which simply arrived in an A&R man's in-tray after being recorded for a pittance by a bedroom musician in Coventry. However, such good fortune comes along maybe once in an A&R career and is very much the exception, not the norm.

Most A&R people agree that not many good bands come along in a year – 'maybe a dozen' is the general estimate. And you can't sign a heavy-metal act to an indie label, because Ver Kids would notice and think something was up. Some dance bands fare very badly when they sign major-label deals, because their audience have a very precise idea of what is cool and what, quite frankly, is not (the latter category very much containing Corporate-Music-Biz Pig Whores).

98% of the tapes sent to Nude are 'dreadful', according to Mr Laurie. 'At the moment it's all Oasis, Radiohead and Verve types. Two guitars, five-piece bands. And, basically, only 2% of them are any good.'

Record companies will try to sign a band for as little as they can get away with. This can be from £50,000 to £100,000 for a small band and between £100,000 to £200,000 if there's a degree of interest from other labels, but the figures can rocket far, far higher. This initial sum is paid out when the band actually sign their contract, and goes towards their living expenses, business costs (lawyer, accountant, etc.) plus buying equipment and everything else. Then they receive a recording budget – for studio time and producer costs – and are allocated press, promotion, and marketing budget. But this is money lent to them, that they have to **recoup**, which is why it is known as an advance.

The A&R department also organises the artists' recording process. The budget for an album is usually around £60,000–£100,000 for a small band, or £100,000–£300,000 for a more established group. This includes the producer's fee. These figures don't apply to megastars: obviously, Celine Dion or Mariah Carey can spend as much as they like. As the recording sessions progress, the A&R person will listen to each new track and give advice as regards which song to choose for a single and which should be album tracks, etc. These hints sometimes clash with the band's and manager's own ideas, so diplomacy needs to be one of the A&R person's talents.

A good A&R person will, therefore, have a thorough musical knowledge and be able to spot a stolen riff or nicked lyrics, or generally contextualise a band's sound, man. You'll see gigs, meet bands and proffer advice. Only when you are very very sure will you sign someone. So it sounds like a good sort of life, roaming free around the country, enjoying power and control, with future pop stars as your mates?

Well, it's not all fun. An all-expenses-paid trip round the country can be dull on your own. A&R can be really hard work, and a thankless, almost impossible task. If you are going to do this job you have to be absolutely sure that you want to. A&R jobs are hard to come by and it's difficult to be a success. You will also find that it totally dominates your social life – and not only your significant other but even your friends will forget who you are because they never see you.

'You can't train to be an A&R person,' says Rick Lennox. 'It's very much a matter of you either have it in you or you don't. You learn as you go along, but you've got to have always had the sense that you were made for the job – and the job for you.'

GLOSSARY

● A&R

Stands for 'Artists and Repertoire'. In ye olde days, record companies had artists, who needed a repertoire of songs to sing. Thus the A&R man got tunes in for people with a good set of pipes. It really was as simple as that.

● Shifting units

Selling records. 'Units' is the global term for denoting quantity, a word which lawyers and accountants happily use but which profoundly upsets *artistes* because they don't like to see their creativity being reduced to economics. But that's the nature of the game, chums.

● Demo studios

Small recording studios which may not have as much equipment as the fancier ones, but which are used to record 'practice versions' of songs for forthcoming singles and albums.

● Recoup

The process of returning to the record company, mainly through album sales (singles and tours don't often make a lot of money), the advance which they lent you when you first signed to them. Advances can take years to recoup, and bands are dropped when the company realises that they'll never get their money back.

SKILLS YOU'LL NEED

Musical knowledge, friendliness, a keen ear for hot new sounds, willingness to get in early in the morning and go home late at night, diplomacy, a general obsession with music that borders on the pathological.

TIPS

● Start going to small gigs, getting to know promoters (the people who run club and gig nights) and cadging in for free. You'll soon start to spot the A&R people.
● Ring up record companies and give them tapes of the bands you've seen (just ask any band and they'll willingly bung you some C60s).
● A lot of people get into A&R via promoting – either fixing up gigs at college or else starting to run a regular night at a local club. Speak to your student union or local venue.
● Talk to managers of local bands. They'll want your impressions of their acts, and can give you contacts.
● Writing for the local paper about local sounds is a good way to start.

USEFUL ADDRESSES

● BMG Records, Bedford House, 69-79 Fulham High Street, London SW6 3JW.
TEL 0171 384 7500. **FAX** 0171 371 9298.
● Creation Records, 109X Regent's Park Road, London NW1 8UR.
TEL 0171 722 8866. **FAX** 0171 722 3443.
● EMI Records, 43 Brook Green, London W6 7EF.
TEL 0171 605 5000. **FAX** 0171 605 5050.
● Polydor Records, 1 Sussex Place, London W6 9XT.
TEL 0181 910 4800. **FAX** 0181 910 4901.
● Sony Records, 10 Great Marlborough Street, London W1V 2LP.
TEL 0171 911 8200. **FAX** 0171 911 8600.
● Virgin Records, Kensal House, 553–579 Harrow Road, London W10 4RH.
TEL 0181 964 6000. **FAX** 0181 968 6533.
● Warner Music, 28 Kensington Church Street, London W8 4EP.
TEL 0171 937 8844. **FAX** 0171 938 3901.

ACCOUNTANT

MONEY: Lots. If you embezzle your client's funds you make a mint, but then you get found out and have to go to prison.

HOURS: 9 a.m. to 5 p.m. every weekday, or 10 a.m. to 6 p.m. You rarely have to go down the pub with Ocean Colour Scene.

HEALTH RISK: 2/10. Sitting in an office all day passive-inhaling Tippex isn't too bad at all.

EQUIPMENT COSTS: Nothing if you are employed as part of an accountancy firm, but if you pay your own costs if you set up your own business. Bought ledger book, fancy Shaeffer ink pen, desk, phone, subscription to *What Suit?* magazine, etc.

PRESSURE RATING: 2/10. Unless you've just nicked all of your client's money and the police are on to you and your phone is being bugged.

GLAMOUR RATING: Very low. Unless you find adding up sexy. You may receive a Christmas card from Phil Collins every year. So, er, not at all glamorous then.

TRAVEL RATING: Apart from your own holidays, not much. And travelling to and from your leatherette office swivel chair with smooth-action height-adjustment and bendy-back springs for those casual 'Look how relaxed I am, Mr/Ms Important Client' moments.

Every single area of the music industry needs an accountant to be in charge of its finances. It is a vital role, yet it can be the least involved in the crazy rock 'n' roll madness. You might not even notice you're in the music industry.

Accountants are the Great Unknown in the world of rock. They're not really meant to be there: they wear suits and drink Andrews Liver Salts and complain that the Doberman has just ripped up their prize sofa. Rock accountants rarely differ from the normal type; they've just been trained in the whys and wherefores of record-business contracts and the way the system works. Essentially, they are still talking calculators.

To be an accountant you have to follow the normal route: train for at least three years, and learn how to put off the tax man when he/she comes knocking at the door (he doesn't physically do this – he'll just send you a stern letter, so don't worry, you won't have to tidy up). Some accountancy firms specialise in music; others handle music and different accounts, like merchant banks. Once you've joined a firm, you'll be given accounts to work on, and you'll work wholly on those accounts. There will be a lot of balancing of figures and last-minute rushes to send off **tax return**s. All musicians are self-employed: they are not taxed at source but owe money to the tax person at the end of each financial year. Therefore, pop stars are expected to keep receipts for stagewear (for those *Top Of The Pops* appearances), taxi journeys (to the Ritz), and anything else known as 'allowable' expenses (i.e. *relevant* expenditure: you can't buy a horse and pretend it'll be playing tambourine on the next album.

The accountant's job is to tot up those expenses, calculate gross income per annum and net income per annum (gross minus expenses). You have the task of finding out where that £500 went. A rock accountant may have to be slightly more imaginative with a rock group's accounts as the group may not have collected receipts for all the beers they want to claim back. They pay you for doing this. It is still, however, a dull task.

If you are sensible, like a bit of soft rock and fancy yourself a whizz at sums, then the accountant's life is for you. It's a sure-fire career: every single department in the music industry needs an accountant to sort out its finances. It's ideal if you're not a rock renegade but you are looking for '**security**'. And, once you've had your practice at someone else's accountancy firm, you can take the plunge and start your own! You can make a lot of money with your fancy

adding up, too, but there's more cash in banking, apparently. Major record companies employ in-house accountants to do the books, as part of their business-affairs department. Sting had a problem with his accountant, in that he found that he was stealing all his 'Message In A Bottle' income. He took him to court. That's probably as exciting as Mr Accountant's life gets.

Colin Young works at OJ Kilkenny, who deal exclusively with rock stars and their chequebooks. He trained and qualified in the City, but didn't have much truck with corporate accounts and wanted to do something a little more interesting. He went for a job at OJ Kilkenny and, not being phased by the thought of sulky rock stars coming in and dropping cigarette ash on the carpet, he got the job.

'A large part of the job is collecting cash from various sources,' he says. 'These include the band's recording company, publishing company, live performance promoters, PRS, etc. We pay the bills and account to the client as to where the money is going.'

OJ Kilkenny employ 29 people in London and 20 in Dublin (the Dublin office deals with U2 – what one would call a 'nice little earner'). Each

ACCOUNTANT

accountant deals with a few clients. Basically, they liaise with the band's lawyer on the band's contracts, which range from record-company contracts, publishing, merchandising, tour business and sponsorship, to name but a few. They make sure the artists put their wonga aside for their tax bills, don't spend too much money on sweets, and can advise them to buy property, art, horses or Iceland, whatever is agreeable with their personal cashscape.

They can also deal with the tax implications of working abroad, which the bands invariably do on overseas tours and suchlike. All this nitty gritty is down to nice Mr Accountant, who'll even supervise putting your cheques into your account so you never have to stand in a queue in Barclays. Accountants will handle an artist's chequebook, but it's difficult for the Sting situation to happen: you'd get found out eventually because there is a governing body that oversees all accountants. Bands also form and dissolve companies willy-nilly: they might have their own record label (a lot of dance types do, as part of their major deals), publishing company or suchlike. The accountant has to deal with moneys going in these directions.

Young is a director at OJ Kilkenny, the youngest director there, and he deals with a lot of the newer bands. He enjoys dealing with bands 'in their infancy' and, yes, goes out to gigs. He checks on his own bands, and up-and-coming ones, too.

'It's not champagne and caviar all the time,' he murmurs. 'It's more often a Becks and a cheese sandwich'.

It can be frustrating, seeing how your clients deal with money and what they overspend on. The accountant can only advise the client as to his/her financial situation and make recommendations to spend less, but the ultimate decision rests with the client, whose money it is. However, accountants always make sure *they* are paid.

One of the frustrations of the job could be the repetitious nature of accountancy: every April (start of the new tax year) the same pattern repeats. One compensation might be that you can get too big for your boots, thinking you 'own' the client because you oversee their spending. But oh no, you can't have that attitude. Nor is there room for favourites.

'We deal with every client the same way,' says Colin. 'There's no hierarchy within that, including myself. We try to steward our client's affairs in an orderly manner, pay their tax in a timely fashion, and advise them on their financial position. Our influence ends there.'

GLOSSARY

● **Tax return**

Big form which details annual earnings: a 'return' of information about 'tax'.

● **Security**

Loose term based on the ignoble pursuit of a steady income. You might not bump into such a word very often in the more creative areas of rock 'n' roll. All it means is that you'll have money to go to B&Q after you're sixty.

SKILLS YOU'LL NEED

Being good at sums, organisational skills, suit-wearing, punctuality.

TIPS

● You'll need to get a degree, and then apply to an accountancy firm for a traineeship.

● Do not swindle anyone out of any money.

● Don't get jealous because everyone you do accounts for is having a rare old time swanning off to the Groucho Club and being sick on George Michael.

USEFUL ADDRESSES

● Baker Tilly, 2 Bloomsbury Street, London WC1B 3ST.
TEL 0171 413 5100. FAX 0171 413 5101.

● Carnmores Royalties Consultants, Suite 228-229, The Linen Hall, 162-168

● Regent Street, London W1R 5TB.
TEL 0171 734 0053. FAX 0171 734 4827.

● EAI, 9 Carnaby Street, London W1V 1PG.
TEL 0171 439 3038. FAX 0171 437 3852.

● Nyman Libson Paul, Regina House, 124 Finchley Road, London NW3 5JS.
TEL 0171 794 5611. FAX 0171 431 1109.

● OJ Kilkenny & Co, 6 Lansdowne Mews, London W11 3BH.
TEL 0171 792 9494. FAX 0171 792 1722.

● SRLV, 23 Bridford Mews, London W1N 1LQ.
TEL 0171 255 3525. FAX 0171 436 3037.

ARTIST MANAGER

MONEY: You take between 15% and 25% of your artist's gross income and net of tour income (although this can vary). Promotional budgets aren't included in these calculations. Your salary can therefore range between nothing to many millions.

HOURS: 24 per day, seven days per week. It's not a breeze.

HEALTH RISK: 9/10. The stress means you could be on Lemsip for *days.*

PRESSURE RATING: 10/10. It's your responsibility if it all goes wrong, and the artist (and others) gets the credit if it's a swinging success.

GLAMOUR RATING: 8/10. Some swanky lunches and some posh dinners, but only because you're manager of Missy Famous, not because you're Ms Manager Lovely-In-Her-Own-Right.

TRAVEL RATING: 9/10. You get to travel first class with the band and go around in limousines, once your artists get to a certain level. If not, it's renting a transit van and squeezing in the back with them.

You sort out everything for your band: which record company they're signing with, what tour they're doing, what pants they wear, paying their gas bill (yes, sometimes), and making sure they ring their mum regularly. It is a thankless and often brutal task, but at least you get a percentage of all their earnings for it.

Managers are notoriously scuzzy, unkempt individuals who make low-down dirty deals with people in suits 'on the quiet' and lie to their bands about how they're not ripping them off. Well, that's the image. Some managers are indeed a little on the grim side, but most of them are quite respectable people who like the music and also enjoy getting shirty with bigwigs once in a while.

It's a job that requires absolute commitment. It is the cliché of being the extra member of the band and, while anyone can be a manager, there are very few who are really good at it. Much of the time people start managing because their friends in a band need helping out. Suddenly someone who's not *au fait* with the workings and evil machinations of the music industry is expected to know what gigs to play, what deals are the best kind, what sort of trousers make you look hunky, etc. Managers are always being flung into the deep end. It takes someone very dedicated to do the job.

Some bands don't have managers,

but only for short periods of time. The Spice Girls didn't for a bit when they sacked Simon Fuller. The KLF never had one, perhaps 'cos Bill Drummond used to be a manager himself and didn't like the idea. But these are exceptions. Think of a band as being like a boat with some people in it. They know they're a boat, they look like a boat, sound like one, but they haven't got a paddle. In wades the manager, to help them steer.

There are some really famous managers from history who were just as loony as the bands they managed and hence remembered almost as much as the band themselves, such as Andrew Loog Oldham and The Stones, Brian Epstein and The Beatles and Peter Grant and Led Zeppelin. In those days they did more of the jobs the record companies hadn't invented yet: marketing, promotions, A&R, etc, all rolled into one. Now the music industry is so structured and defined it's hard for the manager to be as creative as s/he would like. Someone else will be paid to do it, or *not* do it, as the case may be.

Alex Kadis manages a Brighton-based group called Rude Dog and a certain Lake District-based singer called Mark Owen who used to be in Take That. Alex used to be a journalist, then fancied going into the managing side after she saw a group playing live, thought they were wonderful, and found out they were in need of help on the managing front. That was Rude Dog. She was already working with Take That,

NOT OPTIONAL.

helping produce their monthly magazine and a couple of books.

'Take That were about to split and I'd said to Mark that I was managing a band,' says Alex, on one of her not-very-many days off. 'On a number of occasions he said that when he got older he would like to do management as well and, because of this, we talked about our theories of management. He liked my ideas, and when Take That split up he asked me to hear some songs he'd written, to get my opinion. For someone who hadn't written any songs before, they were remarkably good.'

Alex spotted Potential. A few weeks later, Mark asked her to manage him, and from then she took on management full time. This was a bit of a shock, she says: having to set up an office, go down to Woolies to get filing folders, pens and paper. She also had to get a new fax machine and another phone line. She had to find an assistant to file and run the office when she wasn't there. She had to find an accountant and lawyer for Mark, and two for herself – truly in at the deep end in a matter of days. She also had to buy a car. 'There's no way to get to Mark in the Lake District other than with a car,' she explains. 'I also realised that, if I pick up the A&R man to take him to the studio, I can't turn up in my sister's Ford Fiesta. For a year everything I did was for the first time. It was a *big* learning curve – really really scary.'

The next problem Alex had to deal

with was the press. Mark had changed his manager, and journalists and photographers stood outside Alex's house for days and rang her constantly. They also made up stories such as that Mark had gone behind former-manager Nigel Martin-Smith's back, which was simply not the case. A record contract for Owen had yet to be discussed formerly and already all this was going on.

Alex had to learn very quickly, she says. She was initially flummoxed by the contracts and their jargon, which you have to translate: no one is born knowing what '**cross-collateralisation**' is. Legal contracts obviously employ a load of curious phrases that can make or break an artist, and it's imperative to know what all these terms mean because something might be overlooked or need amending, and that's where the big mistakes are made. People are trying to scupper you with their special brand of Esperanto left, right, and centre. Then there's creativespeak – all the studio terms which don't exist in the outside world.

'I'd be walking around thinking: I've just agreed to a remix but *what* have I agreed to?' says Kadis. 'I didn't even know what "mixing" was. I remember the first thing the A&R man said to me was, "Shall we put Mark in pre-production?" and I thought: What the hell is **pre-production**? I kind of agreed to it, put the phone down, and then I just rang him up again and asked exactly what it was.'

Honesty has to be the best gambit in this business. If you pretend you know what's going on but have no idea, you'll end up making stupid mistakes. Ask what people do if you don't know (even

after reading this book). Ask what they're talking about. People won't mind. They'll mind more when you make some silly mistakes. You need to understand every aspect of the industry. How important radio is as compared to TV, the demographics of all programmes ... It used to be that, if you played your single on the Saturday lottery-results programme, you'd have a hit single. This is now not such a hard and fast rule. You have to swot up on all aspects of promotion, merchandising, distribution, and the rest, because your artist doesn't want to be bothered about half of it. Some of them can't even pay a gas bill. They have to be left to roam free in the corners of their creativity and come up with some cracking tunes. Being a manager is not only being a paddle; it is like a meal: you go to the shops, they cook up the lovely supper, you wash up.

You simply can't lord it about and get high and mighty. Some managers are tempted to get delusions of grandeur, but the job shouldn't be a power struggle. You have to tell your artists everything, keep nothing to yourself, and make decisions *with* them. The only exception is when they're too busy and not bothered whether their T-shirts are red or mauve, or when the artist has stopped **being objective** and you're the only person who has an overview and can make a rational decision. In the early stages, a lot of **unsigned bands** will suffer knock-backs from surly record companies and be put off. It's your job to keep them motivated.

'The difficult part,' ponders Alex, 'is coordinating people from the record company, lawyers, accountants, musicians and artists – and somehow

ARTIST MANAGER

them round the head." But the old management responsibility taps you on the shoulder and you have to suppress all your own feelings of anger and insult to think: We have ten minutes to resolve this situation.'

Oliver Smallman (manager of Louise) says, 'Our purpose is to serve the artist, and that really is what it comes down to.' Alex says she does shout sometimes, but only when something minor occurs and 'the stress has built up'. She says that all managers hate bad reviews and 'the great moments are hit records; the worst are flops'. And the most frustrating thing is when an artist won't let the manager be right.

'Sometimes you'll say, "That's a bad haircut and you look really horrid. I know you're not here to be a fairy on a cake but, my God, make an effort." They complain and fight against it, then eventually they start saying, "Everyone else looks better than me," they have the haircut and it was all their idea. And you think to yourself: That's four months it's taken you ...

'It's not glamorous. You have to get your hands dirty,' she continues. 'Often you find you might employ other people to do jobs for you, but ultimately the only one capable of getting things done the way you want it done is yourself. It's not swanning about in smart clothes, turning up at the last minute and ticking people off if they're not doing their job right. It's getting in and getting absolutely filthy dirty and doing everyone else's job.'

'You have to like what you're doing, at the end of the day,' she concludes. 'If you're looking at a long-term career for somebody, you can't be their manager without truly believing in what they do.'

making those disparate factions mould really nicely into one effective working whole. Everybody has a different agenda, a different reason for wanting to be involved with your artist. You have to distinguish how much it's for the love of the artist and how much it's because they've got to earn a wage.'

Egos are fragile because in this particular industry the product isn't a car or a spoon; it's a person's own creative personality. It's that deeply embedded. Any hiccups and they get upset; anything good and they think they're the greatest thing in the world. Artists are never very stable when it comes to their Art.

'If your artist has had a really shitty day, they're sulking, and you know they've got to do an incredibly important interview in ten minutes, what do you do?' asks Alex. 'Your very inner being is saying, "I want to smack

ARTIST MANAGER

GLOSSARY
● **Cross-collateralisation**
Concerned with moneys earnt not just from record sales but through other means such as merchandising, tours, etc.
● **Pre-production**
When an artist practises tunes for an album, at a rehearsal room or a demo studio: fine-tuning and reworking songs.
● **Being objective**
Maintaining a logical and non-emotional approach. In pop-manager terms, this means the art of standing outside yourself and saying, 'Hmm, those trousers are actually rather horrible.' Something pop stars don't do that often.
● **Unsigned bands**
Artists who have yet to sign a record deal. There are a lot of these around.

SKILLS YOU'LL NEED
Diplomacy, tact, motivation, discipline, calmness, being good in a crisis, learning to laugh when record-company bigwigs tell jokes.

TIPS
● See as many fresh, new bands as you can, spot one you like, ask if they have a manager ...
● Get to know local promoters and press people who'll give you more of an insight into the way the industry is run.
● A lot of people running record shops get into managing because young bands come into the shop all the time. Record-shop experience is useful anyway.
● Management training courses will give you an idea of the basics. The Brits school in Croydon, financed by

the BPI, is an excellent place to study media, management, business and finance – and also dance, drama and music. It takes on pupils of fifteen and over and provides GCSE, A-level and BTEC courses. It's the only one of its kind in Britain and is great for making contacts.
● Practise on your friends! Go to the shops for them and pay their gas bills, then demand 20% of their Bristol and West savings account. Oh, only joking.
● Sorry.

USEFUL ADDRESSES
● First Avenue Management, The Courtyard, 42 Colwith Road, London W6 9EY.
TEL 0181 741 1419. **FAX** 0181 741 3289.
● Steve Harrison Management, 2 Witton Walk, Northwich, Cheshire CW9 5AT.
TEL 01606 44559. **FAX** 01606 330185.
● Heavyweight Management, 21 Denmark Street, London WC2 8NA.
TEL 0171 379 0038. **FAX** 0171 497 8909.
● Ignition Management, 54 Linhope Street, London NW1 6HL.
TEL 0171 298 6000. **FAX** 0171 258 0962.
● International Managers Forum, 134 Lots Road, London SW10 ORJ.
TEL 0171 352 4564. **FAX** 0171 351 3117.
● Nigel Martin-Smith Management, 41 South King Street, Manchester M2 6DE.
TEL 0161 832 8080. **FAX** 0161 832 1613.
● Principle Management, 30-32 Sir John Rogersons Quay, Dublin 2, Ireland.
TEL 00 353 1 677 7330.
FAX 00 353 1 677 7276.
● The Brits School, 60 The Crescent, Selhurst, Croydon CR0 2HN.
TEL 0181 665 5242. **FAX** 0181 665 5197.

ARTY MAVERICK

MONEY: From living off gruel to thousands of pounds a week.

HOURS: 24 per day, seven days per week. It's a lifestyle, man.

HEALTH RISK: 7/10. Can be pickly if you want to follow tradition and cut off your ear.

PRESSURE RATING: 2/10. It's art, isn't it?

GLAMOUR RATING: 10/10. Again, the art is in the glamour, not the glamour in the art.

TRAVEL RATING: Irrelevant. All art is travel of some kind.

The arty maverick helps bands and does arty things around and about the music business. S/he also promotes the idea that the music industry is still fun and spontaneous and cross-cultural, etc., etc.

There have always been arty mavericks floating between the avant-garde and **popular culture**, taking in a bit of pop along the way. If it wasn't for such cross-fertilisation, half the good ideas that have ever happened in pop wouldn't have. There once was a time when everyone who went to art school was also in a band. Art rock was the music-biz cliché. The cultural world of rock involved everyone, not just musicians.

Yoko Ono met John Lennon because she was an influential art person of the sixties and involved in the Fluxus movement and similar extremist projects. Seventies 'I am mad' singer Captain Beefheart was a noted artist. In the eighties, Duran Duran keyboardist Nick Rhodes decided he'd take Polaroids for a while until he, and everybody else, got bored of that. The tradition has been brought up to date with Damien Hirst directing the Blur video for 'Country House', and Sam Taylor Wood working with The Pet Shop Boys for their live shows in 1997 by filming her pals getting drunk for ninety minutes. The KLF straddle the line between art exhibitionists and popular, yet weirdy, music makers. You could even say that Rolf Harris has been one of the most successful artists/performers/vet voyeurs in history. But only if you were drunk.

Pop stars are often spotted at exhibition openings quaffing **Chablis** with the poseurs of the year. They love the thought that they can transcend the banalities of rock by associating themselves with more profound and elevated artistic disciplines. Jarvis Cocker will happily turn up for the opening of an art gallery, an exhibition or – some have said – an envelope in the cause of cultural cross-pollination.

Jeremy Dellar is less pretentious than most arty mavericks, but still highly successful. He began his career by making T-shirts which said 'My Drug Hell' on them, which he sold in trendy shops around the country, and his last project was the hugely successful Acid Brass idea. Like many a great notion, Jeremy had the idea in the pub, but unlike most people he did something about it. The Bluecoat

Gallery in Liverpool were asking for ideas because they wanted to commission four pieces of new work which dealt with sound. Jeremy submitted his ideas and they were up for it – mad for it, in fact.

'It just comes out of liking music – that's the basis of my work, as simple as that,' he reflects. 'It's been very straightforward. The idea of the brass band has captured people's imagination.' Acid Brass is essentially a collection of musicians from the William Fairey Brass Band from Yorkshire who stand in uniform and soberly play tunes by 808 State and A Guy Called Gerald, among others. Audience reaction to date has been tremendous. The working-class-liberated-by-brass-band/working-class-people-liberated-by-dancing-to-techno cultural analogy is the main point. It's the kind of arty thing that is a perfect example of the merging of popular cultures and producing something that posh people can paw over.

Possibly the apex of such crossover shenanigans was the KLF 'Fuck The Millennium' performance at the Barbican in autumn 1997. Acid Brass played as the KLF, dressed as old people in pyjamas, whizzed about in wheelchairs, with Bill Drummond holding a dead swan. Fifty sacked Liverpool dockers sang along to The KLF's song 'Fuck The Millennium (We Want It Now!)' and it was chaos. Some of the dockers were allegedly very drunk and no one knew what to make

of it. Now *that's* Art. A few people also said it was a load of risible old tosh, but there you go.

Jeremy thinks the only way to get on as an arty maverick, which is not the most stable of callings, is to do that grizzly thing, 'network'. Go to art-exhibition openings, talk about your ideas in the pub, *and then try to do them*. 'It's **ligging**, basically. That's how you meet people in the arts,' he says. 'It's like meetings. Accountants have meetings with accountants. In the arts it's a more fragile network, more fluid. When you socialise it's like having a meeting. You bump into people and take it from there.'

Dellar has the copyright on the name 'Acid Brass' and the concept, so if the album sells etc., etc. he'll make some money. He also wants to work with Dannii Minogue ('She's brilliant ... unlike her sister, who's lost it') and likes candidates who are 'not the obvious choice'. At the beginning of the year he converted a room in a modernist building in Bexhill into a recording studio in which he got OAPs to make techno records. He is that rare thing – a successful, self-sufficient, fringe-dwelling arty maverick.

Many such, erm, 'visionaries' find it a lot harder to survive, however. Arty types don't mix with the real world too well and some of them sneakily sign on or have to work in chip shops to pay the rent. Art-music is not at its height at the moment – these are the days of

ARTY MAVERICK

19

the Gallagher brothers and Ocean Colour Scene, not Roxy Music, David Bowie and Berlin. However, quite obviously, art-rock will return.

'I think there'll be more of this sort of thing in the next few years,' says Jeremy, of the sort of projects he involves himself in. 'Whether it becomes commercially viable is another matter. But I want my stuff to be as popular as it can.'

The job is tricky. Prankster dreamers get paid sporadically, and either not very well or far too much. You have to come up with the initial concept, working on your own, and then put it into action. And, in comparison to the arty-farty seventies and early eighties, the nineties aren't so inclined towards the aesthetic.

'It's not a job; it's a ball and chain,' concludes Dellar. 'But it can be a lot of fun. My advice would be: if you have an idea it's always better to go to an independent record company who are more interested in originality and what hasn't been done before, intellectually or philosophically. The thing about the music business is it does a lot of things it says it's going to do. Eventually.'

GLOSSARY
● **Popular culture**
What pop stars are obsessed by. It's the new classicism, you know.
● **Chablis**
A white Bordeaux that people who read books, go to art galleries, or pretend not to be pop stars drink.
● **Ligging**
Hanging out at other people's events for no other reason than you want to be 'there', because it's so 'now'.

SKILLS YOU'LL NEED
Guts, wild ideas, the ability to be totally yourself, a thick skin, more luck than you can shake a forest of sticks at.

TIPS
● Nurture all the above qualities, then go out and do it, friends!
● Hang out at pubs opposite gig venues. The band playing will often drink in the pub closest to their show after the soundcheck. A bit obvious really, but this is where you can introduce yourself.

BACKING MUSICIAN/ SINGER

💰 **MONEY:** Musician's Union rates are about £100 for a three-hour session, with extra money for overtime. This is a guide, and often musicians get paid a competitive rate instead. This can be around £2,500 for a few sessions with the Spice Girls but it can stretch to £5–6000 a week if you're working for someone like Sting. Or God (is there a difference?).

⏰ **HOURS:** From one or two hours a week to every single day. Very variable.

➕ **HEALTH RISK:** 6/10. You might get poked with a drumstick if you're not singing right.

〰️ **PRESSURE RATING:** 5/10. Because you're in the background, in all senses, the pressure isn't so great. The freelance nature of the job can be more stressful.

🍸 **GLAMOUR RATING:** 6/10. You see studios and backstage dressing rooms. You might be able to pat George Michael on the back, sometimes.

✈️ **TRAVEL RATING:** 8/10. Lots of gigs, up to Elstree for *Top Of The Pops*, and looking surly on video shoots. Then there's foreign touring and exotic climes and papaya skins with cocktails in them. Oh, and being able to take home those shower caps and fancy sewing kits from top-class hotels.

The backing musician provides extra musicianship and vocals for artists who may not have a virtuoso saxophone player in their band or may want a nice harmony to go along with their warbling.

Not every band can play all the instruments they'd like to, or sing all the harmonies which are bouncing around in their head. Some of them can't sing at all. Session musicians and singers can do these things, and are thus used all the time to augment the sound of recording artists from indie to rock and pop to dance music. When a band is recording, or preparing to tour, they'll find out who they need to fill in any musical gaps. The A&R coordinator at the record label will then go to the agents of the session people and see who's available.

A lot of musicians get work through word of mouth: a producer will recommend someone good s/he worked with the week/year before and then ring them when they're needed. Most session people have an agent to negotiate fees and help get work. The gigs will vary from album work to commercials and film scores. It's not just rock 'n' roll in this game. The session person confirms that they can come in, goes into the studio when needed, and records exactly what the band and producer want. The more established they are, the more input

BACKING SINGER/MUSICIAN

lots of things,' says Beverley. 'One bit of work will lead to other things. A producer heard what I did, and asked, "Can you do **harmonies**?" I happened to be in the right studios at the right time.'

Beverley has since worked with trillions of folk, including M People, Jamiroquai, Jimmy Nail, Chaka Khan, Take That, and Gary Barlow and Robbie Williams when they went solo. She thinks the key to a good backing singer is to be as flexible as possible. A wide vocal range is needed – 'the bigger the better' she says. To be successful you probably have to have what she calls a 'nondescript' voice which won't stand out too much, because you have to blend in: you can't intrude with throat-throttling gusto when the lead vocals are being sung by some lily-livered sort who couldn't blow out a birthday candle.

'I *can* do nondescript, but I get hired because of how I sound as well,' says Skeete, who also does lead-vocal athletics on house records. 'But the skill is mostly in learning how to take a back seat.'

A lot of backing singers want to be lead singers and get frustrated when Ms Lily Liver can't reach beyond three notes and *they* could sing everyone into buying swimsuits at Christmas. Sometimes you have to lay down the track so the singer can sing over the top, you fill in the cracks, as it were – you ape the singer's voice. A bit of a cheat, eh? Even though your part might be harder, doing harmonies and **multiple tracking**, you have to be humble.

they can have. When the session's over, our chum goes home. Easy as that: no having to look hunky on a record sleeve or anything. Smashin'.

Beverley Skeete started doing trainee accountancy when she left school, for she thought that a life of sums would be for her. Singing was an accident. Her sister-in-law mentioned that she was a great friend of a singer who ran a record shop. He was making a single, asked her to sing, and thought she sounded pretty good. She sang backing vocals on his record.

'It's like when you go to a shop to buy one thing, and you end up buying

However, this anonymity has its benefits. Yes, it really does. When you're on stage nobody is looking at you and thinking the B flat was a bit iffy. You can do those funny backing-singer dances, giggle a lot, and wear something saucy. Backing singers always look like they're having a lot more fun than the stars, anyway. Some backing singers were lead singers once upon a time, and enjoy the pressure-free 'ba-ba-ba's much more than spotlight duties.

Session singers have to have a good ear, so playing an instrument helps. The job involves making up harmonies at the drop of a hat, because no one else has a clue. You have to get to places on time, smile, and be prepared to go over things again and again. Having said that, you *can* go into a studio and do twenty minutes' work. Skeete is used to this: 'Sometimes with house music they'll sample one "Yeah baby!" and that's all they want.'

Backing singers are often replaced by fancy models on video shoots. It happens all the time, and it can be annoying if you see someone else there doing your job. It's not exactly truthful, is it? 'I used to get annoyed,' says Skeete. 'But I recognise if you're making house records you're selling to a certain type of audience. If you want to sell records to five- or six-year-olds, then it's very unlikely they're going to use you. And, with videos, you're escaping a fate worse than death. You get paid a pittance and you have to stand there at six o'clock in the morning, half-dressed and freezing. I'd rather they get models.'

The most stressful part of being a freelance session musician is the erratic nature of the work. You can

have no work for weeks or find yourself involved in risible and farcical projects (a *Teletubbies* song, for instance). You get no sick pay or holiday, and often don't know what job is coming up next. Just to make things even better, basic rights, like being paid every time your video is shown on the telly, are also slowly being eroded by the new contracts coming in for session work. This is the toughest part of the job: not having a regular wage, and having the rights that you *did* have taken away.

Session earnings now are much lower than they used to be and, when a band uses more than seventeen musicians on one session, the record company pays no more in total than the Musician's Union rate for seventeen persons. However, this is balanced out by a change whereby the rules on the use of samples are getting tougher, which means that vocalists are more likely to be paid when a band nicks a line or two from an old song. Such minute shifts in the balance of power are watched like hawks by session people – to them it can mean the difference between a living wage, poverty and riches.

As a session musician, naturally, the amount of work you receive will also depend largely on the instrument you play. Guitars rarely go out of fashion, but trumpets are hip only every other decade, and didgeridoo players may well find they need a back-up instrument for those lean spells when Rolf Harris is out of the studio. You will also find competition fierce – many session musicans were previously in signed-up bands and moved into session work when their major project failed to make it big.

It's a difficult area to get into unless you have contacts. Bands employ people whom they know, or who are recommended by people they know. Over the years you'll find you get more and more work, and steadier jobs. Once a band does like you, they'll take you on tour worldwide, treat you to the finest hotels, invite you to cheese 'n' Chablis parties, and remember your birthday. You get to the stage where you can be choosy and decide not to work for some types, or take time off because the money you make is good when you are working.

One well-respected session man, who prefers not to be named so he won't get in trouble with any bigwig employers, played trumpet in a chart band in the eighties. He was spotted playing live by someone who needed a **brass player**. The band were sliding down the ladder of success, and Mr Anonymous got two good sessions. 'Once you get one good job, more follow,' he reckons.

Our Mr Anon is paid a retainer by his major employer, which means they reserve the right to use him whenever they like, and he is given a minimum weekly wage so he doesn't swan off with some other group. He used to play with loads of bands, mainly pop acts, but is now restricted to one thing. He's doubly in the pink because the band he works for have a fair few members, who are often off making solo records and need his trumpeting skills for their

IF THE BAND LIKE BEER, YOU DRINK BEER.

IF THE BAND LIKE HAMBURGERS, YOU EAT HAMBURGERS.

work. They like him; he likes them. A good situation to be in. However, he does find that he has to play the game and fall in with their rules.

'You have to be reasonably tolerant,' he says. 'Some bands want to do certain things like getting you to go out clubbing with them, for instance. Others want everyone in bed by ten o' clock. You have to suss that out because, if you don't, then you can get into trouble. You're there to please the artist.'

Bands might like you to look smart, or they might like you not to wear the chicken costume because it overshadows their prawn get-up. The main trick is getting on with people. If they don't like Marmite backstage, you don't like Marmite backstage. When you do bond, the job is obviously much more satisfying, both personally and professionally. Playing live is the musician's most enjoyable buzz and you may even get the chance to do a couple of super guitar licks. You've seen those gigs when someone simply announced as 'Mr Funkeee Leeroy on the AXE!' plays some Godawful guitar solo while grinning like someone who's got a lemon in his mouth. It's quite an embarrassment, but session musicians live for those moments. That's **jelling**, man.

Mr Anon also believes things have changed. The record companies don't pay session stars as much as they used to because they don't respect the session musicians, he claims, unlike bands and their management. However, our friend loves the job. It has many pluses.

'It can be a long career,' he says. 'And you can jump ship at any time. If you're with a band that's going down, you think: Crikey! It's going pear-shaped – and you leave that artist. The lifestyle is quite privileged, though – you get the good bits of being a pop star but you don't get recognised.'

GLOSSARY

● Harmonies
Playing or singing a musical phrase which tonally complements the main melody line. Standard harmonies are three or five tones up or down from the melody.

● Multiple tracking
When more than one vocal line is recorded. You can record as many as you want, including harmony lines, and it sounds like a choir. Often used in pop records.

● Brass player
All trumpets, trombones and bugles are brass instruments. The saxophone was possibly the most common brass instrument on eighties pop records. Trumpets are very common now.

● Jelling
Bonding, all coming together in a musical way. Yes, it's often live when this happens.

SKILLS YOU'LL NEED
Being able to play an instrument or sing, not having too much ego, discipline, good time-keeping, being friendly.

TIPS
● Learn an instrument properly if you want to play; invest in some singing lessons if you want to sing.
● Offer to use your skills with local bands.
● Playing on friends' demo tapes will get you heard by producers and the like.
● Equity, the actors' and singers' union, has legal guidelines session people should follow.

USEFUL ADDRESSES
● Icon Agency for Session Musicians, Ducie House, Ducie Street, Manchester M1 2JW.
TEL 0161 236 3735. **FAX** 0161 236 3735.
● Musicians Union, 60-62 Clapham Road, London SW9 0JJ.
TEL 0171 582 5666. **FAX** 0171 582 9805.
● Royal Philarmonic Orchestra, 16 Clerkenwell Green, London EC1R 0DP.
TEL 0171 608 2381. **FAX** 0171 608 1226.
● Session Connection, 110-112 Disraeli Road, London SW15 2DX.
TEL 0181 871 1212. **FAX** 0181 877 1214.
● The Singers' Agency, 48C Hutton Grove, London N12 8DT.
TEL 0181 343 7929. **FAX** 0181 349 9150.
● The Vocal Agency, 43 Windsor Drive, East Barnet, Hertfordshire EN4 8UE.
TEL 0181 440 8773. **FAX** 0181 364 9258.

BOOKING AGENT

MONEY: £10,000 to loads, if you are head of your own company.

HOURS: 10 a.m. to 7 p.m. and out to see bands in the evening. It just never stops, basically.

HEALTH RISK: 2/10. Unless you fall over at King Tut's Wah Wah Hut.

PRESSURE RATING: 6/10. If you book Oasis into the Dog & Duck in Doncaster you may have a few problems. Tempestuous artistes are often a bit picky.

GLAMOUR RATING: 2/10. Unless you're helping out The Rolling Stones and become their mate and they invite you on their cruiseliner with Jack Nicholson.

TRAVEL RATING: 3/10. Yes, it's the Bath Moles Club again, or perhaps Leicester's Princess Charlotte. Hmm.

A booking agent gets the right gigs for individual bands and deals with the smooth running of tour schedules in venues from pub rooms to stadiums.

A band plays the Badger and Pineapple a couple of times. They've had a single out and had several letters from Warrington revealing a small army of fans. They've got a new single out soon, which contains a dead ace recorder solo, and they want to shout about it.

What they need is a tour.

Booking agents are the people responsible for booking a band's dates at the right venues on their whirlwind exploration of the glamorous sites of musical history. You can help fledgling, excited new artists spend every night playing the 'toilets' of Great Britain. Or the stadiums, obviously. All depending on what you, as their booking agent, deem suitable.

There are around five major booking agencies who 'sign up' bands they think will be **hot to trot on the live scene**. A lot of bands are relatively experienced in the trotting business and may not have a record contract. Agents are getting into bands earlier and earlier, and thus have to court managers etc. because there's so much competition. Usually the booking agent will provide the band with an income that is separate from the income that a record-company advance gives. However, the record company are the bigwigs who decide how many dates should be played and all that malarkey.

If the job is done properly, say booking agents the world over, a tour will always be tied up with the marketing process. This means that there'll be an album to promote, a single out, and someone will have actually checked that the band aren't just playing cover versions of wildlife-programme themes (unless that's what they usually do, of course). A tour can also coincide with **in-store appearances**, local-press articles and, erm, other stuff that the record

BOOKING AGENT

money, it is vital to ensure that any bands taking part have a contract with the promoters and that everything is above board. In virtually every case, if artists don't sign a contract they don't get paid, and issuing these is something that only the very professional booking people can do really well.

Booking agents also scout for bands, by attending gigs and standing at the back with people like lawyers and journos. There's a lot of competition to get the top new acts, and so you need to have an idea of what people want to go and see, as well as **how to make the hi-hat less toppy**.

Many people who become booking agents, or get into the touring side of the music industry in general, come from student unions. Being entertainments officer is good practice for all this sort of thing. The pressure is less, because colleges have a budget to put on gigs and don't necessarily need to make a profit on every one – although, with the current political climate, there's no guarantee that this situation will continue.

There is one exception to the above way of working: when trying to break a new act, the record company may pay to get the artist a support slot on a tour. They'll fork out up to £5,000 to ensure that their new band gets to play to a large audience first time around, and bypass the whole booking agents' talent-spotting procedure. This is rare, though, and only a pop idea. Genuine indie types have no truck with this. Agents have to understand that indie, pop and rock all appeal to different people, and book the tours

company makes sensitive artists do which makes them turn to heavy drinking.

'We're the bit in between,' says our person from a booking agency, who is shy and doesn't want to reveal her name. 'There's always some debate as to whether a booking agent is superfluous. If you're a smaller band it's vital to have an agent. We can wangle them a **support tour**.'

A booking agent also protects young bands from 'dodgy promoters and ropey venues'. Not every promoter is a nice, smiling chap in a Windcheater who'll give out free crisps. Some are money-grabbing scumbags who'll try to charge bands a load of money for gracing their wobbly stage with their presence. As booking agent, you'll send such wide boys off with a flea in the proverbial ear.

As an agent, you'll ensure that bands get paid for each gig they play, then take 10% of their gross fee for all your bother. With the many summer European festivals, wot pay a lot of appropriately. A successful tour is congratulation enough. And you might get to stand in the same room as Maxim from the Prodigy at an aftershow party.

GLOSSARY

● **Hot to trot on the live scene**
Rather good at wowing an audience – making them dance, sing or clap along. Many bands build up a loyal 'live' following after only a couple of singles – and sometimes even before they have a major release (e.g. Suede, Oasis).

● **In-store appearances**
Whereby a band goes to an HMV store, sits behind a wobbly table and signs copies of their new release. Either that, or else the odd midnight 'gig' at which a band plays three songs off a new album on the day before it's released, and all of the drunken people in the audience get to appear on *Sky News* the following morning.

● **Support tour**
A tour – nationwide or worldwide – by a band playing as 'special guests' of the headlining band. People spill lager over each other during their set as the band flail sensitively but are generally and tragically widely ignored.

● **How to make the hi-hat less toppy**
One of the profoundest conundrums in the realm of recorded sound. The hi-hat – a cymbally-drum thing – either sounds 'toppy' or 'bottomy' and absolutely never 'right in the mix'.

SKILLS YOU'LL NEED

An eye for the next live sensation; organisational abilities; an understanding of the current live scene, man; a mistrust of promoters (in case they're dodgy); obliviousness to standing in a pool of cider while watching some losers try to play their instruments.

TIPS

● If you're at university, approach student-union entertainments and offer to help out.
● Managing a local band might help you get to know the local venues and the art of booking a good night.
● See as many bands as possible. Writing for a college magazine/local paper helps with getting freebie tickets.

USEFUL ADDRESSES

● Asgard Promotions, 125 Parkway, London NW1 7PS.
TEL 0171 387 5090. **FAX** 0171 387 8740.
● International Talent Booking, 27A Floral Street, London WC2E 9DQ.
TEL 0171 379 1313. **FAX** 0171 379 1744.
● Leighton Pope Organisation, 8 Glenthorne Mews, 115A Glenthorne Road, Hammersmith, London W6 0LJ.
TEL 0181 741 4453. **FAX** 0181 741 4289.
● Primary Talent International, Africa House, 64-78 Kingsway, London WC2B 6AH.
TEL 0171 405 4001. **FAX** 0171 405 4002.
● Solo Agency, 55 Fulham High Street, London SW6 3JJ.
TEL 0171 736 5925. **FAX** 0171 731 6921.
● Value Added Talent Agency, 1-2 Purley Place, London N1 1QA.
TEL 0171 704 9720. **FAX** 0171 226 6135.

CATERER

MONEY: From £9,000 to loads if you run your own catering company. Especially if you run it from home and have no office overheads.

HOURS: If you're on tour or at a video shoot you can start at 6 a.m. and go on through the night providing bacon butties for all. Even if you're preparing a posho meal for an awards ceremony, you'll be up the markets at dawn with your string bag.

HEALTH RISK: 8/10. You could scald yourself, set fire to your hands, poison yourself, or fall into a freezer. So very dangerous, really.

PRESSURE RATING: 7/10. Getting grub to the table on time in cramped conditions, for people who think their basslines are the best thing ever, can be a little tiresome.

GLAMOUR RATING: 4/10. You do a lot of washing up, even if it *is* for Paul McCartney.

TRAVEL RATING: 10/10. You never stop! Those smashing European tours, holed up in a tour bus for days. Those thirty-date British tours, holed up in a transit next to a portable fridge. Mm-mm.

Cooking food for band and crew is ever such big business nowadays, and there are specific companies that cater solely for the entertainment business. Everyone needs grub, after all.

C atering can be as impossible as it is rewarding. It can be impossible to satisfy the demands of the fussy pop star, who to all intents and purposes is five years old and has decided not to eat anything beginning with the letter B. It can be rewarding, consequently, to see said pop star tuck into a large plate of bananas 'n' beans.

Caterers are employed by the band management to provide food for the artist and crew during video shoots and on tours. There are 35 companies who deal exclusively with the whims of the music and TV/film industry. So, if you like food and enjoy hearing people discuss how bottomy the hi-hats are on the single or during the encore, this could be your pigeon.

Catering firms employ chefs who've already had some training. Colleges provide basic catering courses which give you a shiny City and Guilds qualification if you get through the rigorous egg-boiling exams. Finding work at a restaurant or a local catering company will help a lot. Ringing up Rock Scoff Ltd and getting your mum to tell them how good your bubble and squeak is will *not* do the trick. These people want a proper CV.

Tony Laurenson is the MD of Eat To The Beat caterers – one of the first music-business catering companies to spring up, eighteen years ago (before then your John Lennons had to run to the corner shop to get a pie before a sell-out arena show). People do apply for jobs at his company thinking they'll be drinking Hooch with Jarvis instead of cooking up a mean gnocchi.

'It happens on occasion,' he says, 'but we're quick to discover them. We don't put people out on tour before we know what they're like. We try them out for a few weeks here first. Being on tour you're with the band all the time and become part of a family. Personality is almost as important as being able to cook.'

But it's not all fun with lentils. You also have to wash up, buy the food and cart around portable hot cupboards and fridges. Eat To The Beat also deal with the band's **rider** and so have to lug cans of Hofmeister up to dressing rooms. Plus, you have to deal with pop stars. Some of them are vegan, some macrobiotic, some only want halal food and others want three portions of everything. Some don't like eating at all. Apparently, Heather Small from M People only eats fruit and hates rice, but likes **sushi** even if it has rice in it. Mark Owen, ex-Take That, is a vegetarian but has admitted he 'doesn't really like food'. Robbie Williams obviously doesn't have that problem. You have to deal with this sort of caper on a daily basis and it ain't easy.

Catering companies send two or three chefs to accompany a band on tour. Eat To The Beat also carry their own equipment with them, including cumbersome fridges, etc., as **venues** have notoriously poor facilities and sometimes don't even run to a sink. Washing up has been known to take place in the shower.

As a music caterer you'll have to know your crème caramel from crème anglaise and keep abreast of current cooking trends. 'When we started we made things like shepherds pie, because it was about quantity rather than quality,' says Tony. 'It was a success just to get a meal out. Now, in this marketplace, it's far more competitive.'

You need to be able to produce a cut-price tuna swirl that's accessible to both the lowliest roadie and the poncey guitarist who is getting into fine cheeses. Eat To The Beat provide mushroom cassoulet and veal peppercorn terrine to the likes of The Spice

CATERER

Girls, Whitesnake, Mansun and Suede. They also deal with supplying **aftershow** party drinks, and cater for festivals and all the hungry crew there. It's nonstop – breakfast, lunch and dinner. Plus snacks. And drinks.

Tony Laurenson says it's worth paying the cash for a caterer because the band stays 'fit and healthy and can perform six shows a week, rather than three, which pays for the catering'. This means there'll always be a job for a good chef – Eat To The Beat receive one CV per day and try out all promising people. So that's OK, then.

GLOSSARY

● **Rider**

Order of food and booze for the artists' dressing room. All bands have a rider per night when they go on tour. They all complain it's not big enough, then their so-called friends come into the dressing room and nick it all for themselves. You'll never get any peace where riders are concerned.

● **Sushi**

Japanese version of a scotch egg, sort of. Rice and raw fish wrapped in seaweed, and eaten by people who wear bright mountaineering clothes but have never been near a National Trust park, let alone a Peak. All pop stars like sushi.

● **Venues**

No, you don't have a special place to cook in: you have to make do in a back room near the electricity meters. You don't have a banqueting hall to eat in, either.

● **Aftershow**

Party after a gig and usually a byword for free beer and top gossip. People go to aftershows and talk about other people in the room without wanting them to hear. Then they fall over and 'go on' somewhere else. 'Going on' is very music business.

SKILLS YOU'LL NEED

Being able to cook; being able to cook under pressure; being able to cook for people who'll have tantrums if there's anything red on the plate; being able to stand all that bacon that the road crew will want every mealtime (and for snacks); being fit – to carry all that grub and bottles of booze; not getting car sick.

TIPS

● Go to catering college to learn your trade.

● Try working at a local restaurant.

● Practise on your friends – invite thirty around and see how you get on.

● Practise with your mum or dad.

● Don't become a caterer just because you want to poison Ocean Colour Scene. You'll be found out and go to jail. Even though you may feel it's still worth it.

USEFUL ADDRESSES

● Any Time Any Place, Unit 1A, Riverside Road, London SW17 0BA. **TEL** 0181 944 1022. **FAX** 0181 944 9434.

● Eat To The Beat, Studio 5, Garnet Close, Greycaine Road, Watford, Herts. WD2 4JN. **TEL** 01923 211702. **FAX** 01923 211704.

● Eat Your Hearts Out, Basement Flat, 108A Elgin Avenue, London W9 2HD. **TEL** 0171 289 9266. **FAX** 0171 266 3160.

● Saucery Catering, Watchcott, Nordan, Leominster, Herefordshire HR6 0AJ. **TEL** 01568 614221. **FAX** 01568 610256.

CLUB DJ/REMIXER

MONEY: Bundles. Although fees can start at a few hundred quid, they leap to around £10,000 for one single remix, or even more if you're a dead swanky, 'name' remixer. DJing also pays very well at the top end of the scale.

HOURS: 12 midnight to 6 a.m. – that sort of nocturnal living.

HEALTH RISK: 6/10. You might accidentally scratch yourself with a stylus.

PRESSURE RATING: 6/10. Making sure the floor is full of jostling torsos … That's about it, really.

GLAMOUR RATING: 6/10. You get to sit in dank clubs with other DJs.

TRAVEL RATING: 8/10. Nipping up the country, to Europe and Japan and wherever else, to DJ those stormin' beats.

The top club DJ swizzles round other people's tunes, plays tunes to people in tight tops and writes his/her own stuff a bit.

Remixers are a new breed. Time was, back in the early eighties, when a swish US producer from the New York or Chicago House scenes might dabble with a chum's tune and give it a porkier beat. This was rare, or reserved for very special releases. By the mid-eighties 'extended version' 12" singles were quite common, and white soul bands and fluffy pop groups commissioned fancy types to extend their records by putting a drum solo in them. Then the **indie-dance crossover** revolution made dancing more mainstream again, and types like Paul Oakenfold remixed records so he could play them at his DJ nights. The record companies of the original artist would get wind of this and ask him to release them. Now remixes are the norm. No single is complete without some trendy type in bangin' trainers cutting 'n' pasting, swizzing 'n' switching different bleepy sounds and making the hi-hats, that were once so very toppy, very bottomy indeed.

Remixers can make a mint, quite frankly. For sitting in a studio half the night eating chips and talking about the football, then just removing the guitar bit from a chorus, they rake it in. They're famous and respected and people recognise them at parties, yet they're cool and trendy and the tabloid newspapers don't know who they are. Cor! What a job!

'Most of us are quite ugly, boring people,' counters Rollo, the man behind Felix's massive anthem 'Don't You Want Me', who regularly remixes the stars and is also the guiding light of dance band Faithless. 'You sacrifice a huge amount when you're a DJ remixer or producer. You drive to DJ at three or four gigs at the weekend then see loads in the week, and spend the rest of your time in the studio. You don't get to see films, read books, or see people. The idea that we're supercool human beings is rather misguided ...'

Rollo went travelling the world seven years ago and met up with a keyboard player in Australia in late 1991. They made a series of demos together then met a producer, Martin Thomas, at a party by chance and 'hassled him till he just said "Ring me" to fob us off'. Rollo rang him four times. Mr Producer had just started going out with a model who wanted to be a singer and said that he'd help them record their tunes if she could sing on them. They soon found out that the lass just couldn't sing. Nonetheless, Rollo and chum got a record deal from the vocal-less tunes they made. If you're involved with a name producer, someone whom record companies have heard of, they tend to lazily assume that you're the tops – whether you are or not.

Rollo got cold feet after he landed his Australian deal and decided to move back to London with his **advance money** and set up a studio with another mate. They got together a sampler, a module, and a couple of keyboards, and hoisted the lot into Rollo's bedroom. From that came Felix's 'Don't You Want Me', which sold two and a half million copies worldwide.

This, however, is a rare case. Most remixers are studio boffins who've been hanging around sequencers for years making hip-hop sounds and getting very little recognition. Roni Size, for instance, the 1997 Mercury Music Prize winner, has been going for several thousand centuries and remembers Pompeii before it was cast in lava.[1] However, once you do have a big hit around the world, and

penetrate the upper echelons of the US charts, you need never worry again – you can become a millionaire by getting one number-one US single, as long as you hold the publishing rights.

Dance music has obviously caused a mini-revolution in the music world, with many people setting up their own home studios cheaply and creating their own tunes. Play them to someone friendly at one of those vibey, independent labels that are called things like Bangin' Trainers and wahey! If you're good enough you can release stuff! And, once people have heard your name about, you'll be asked to remix stuff for all and sundry.

After the Felix hit, Rollo was immediately besieged with requests to remix this and twiddle with that. The general procedure is that the record company will ring you, the label, or your management up, and pop a tape in the post for you to hear the original song to see if you're interested in making a remixed version. Many record companies try out people they think will be good producers for up-and-coming bands by giving them test remixes – in the dance world, even when artists have already had a massive hit, there's still the danger it could have been just a one-off.

Remixers are normally given the song they have to remix on DAT, a midi file (basically, Apple Mac programming for music) or a 2" tape. You sample the bits you like, add some more sampley treats yourself, completely restructure the song, and away you go!

'When we agree to do a remix,' says Rollo, who works closely with fellow

1. Not strictly true in the literal sense.

Faithless member and DJ, Sister Bliss, 'it's because there's something about the track which we like. It can be the vocal, or just one sound. With Olive's "You're Not Alone", there was a lovely sound on it and a good vocal. Sister Bliss played the record as the last track at the end of a night in a club and we just saw the reaction.'

Rollo says remixes take about three days 'and never more'. He and Ms Bliss remixed the huge Faithless hit 'Insomnia' in just one day. In this peculiar nether world of dance music, remixing merges with production – most remixers are DJs and producers as well, and often diversify further into songwriting and even singing. Most remixers nowadays start by making music in their bedroom; the traditional way was for engineers to be trained through studio engineering up to production.

'I think there are two kinds of producer,' says Rollo. 'A technical producer, and, at the other extreme, people with untrained ears. Technical producers are hired for groups like The Spice Girls and are employed to make a sound for a particular market. I'm the other sort of producer: I don't have the patience or the knowledge to make a

track fit into a specific **genre**. I go with what I like.'

That can be the difference between your more underground sounds, **man**, and your professional dyed-in-the-wool producer. The latter tend to work with bands they like, and often work with engineers who do the fiddly bits so they can be more personally friendly with the band. Rollo, on the other hand, finds bands 'problematic' because the process is far more diplomatic and the drummer is always having to have her/his say.

'What's great is I now have my own label. I can produce what I like and have the last word,' he says. 'Sometimes if I'm remixing, say, Black Grape or Simply Red, they want to get involved and have a say. I don't like that. It's so cheap now to lay down tracks that you can be a highly successful producer and never work with a band again.'

There can be situations in which problems do arise. Rollo and Bliss started on a Spice Girls remix but two days into it realised that they couldn't get it right and it just wasn't working. They had to go back to the

DJ REMIXER

record company and say it wasn't happening and waive their fee. In other instances, remixers will complete a track and demand a lot of money for it but the band don't like it, which results in wrangles over whether anyone should get paid or not. It can be a difficult business.

A lot of groups hate remixers. Record companies can try to push bands to spend money on fancy re-jiggling when they don't really want to. There's a little bit of resentment from bands who don't think a 'name' will help boost their sales or club exposure, and are envious of the seemingly 'easy life' of the remixer who may get paid a whole heap of cash for a couple of days' work. Rollo was offered £22,000 to do a remix of a Naomi Campbell tune. He thought long and hard then decided against it, because credibility is all in this game and, anyway, he didn't like the tune. The money can get very silly, comparing it with the £300 it cost him to record his initial biggie 'Don't You Want Me'.

Beavering away in a home studio is a good start. People often club together to get equipment because once you start you can't stop wanting the latest gear. Around £6,000 spent on the right equipment can get you hit-record-making potential. Another way is to loiter around friends' studios, or friends of friends' studios. Sister Bliss first met Rollo when she came down to a studio where he was working. She 'criticised everything', mentioned she played keyboards, then the next time Rollo was stuck for a keyboard player she drove from Cornwall to join the session. Such dedication can pay off. Rollo has likewise signed to his label a chap called Skinny who hung about

and was able to prove his drumming skills when someone didn't show up for another session.

Rollo's ultimate dream is to semi-retire in five years' time (when he's 35) and produce two albums a year. As long as sampling hasn't been replaced by trout-tickling as the nation's coolest pastime/career, he could be in with a chance. The opportunities are there on every level.

'If you're a DJ, your whole job is to find a hot new record and play it, and that's how you get kudos,' says Rollo. 'Kids in their bedroom are producing stuff all the time and dance music is essentially self-perpetuating. If you're good at what you do,' he concludes, 'you *will* get discovered and bankrolled, whether you're from Essex or Nigeria or wherever. You only need to make one good record and everyone starts talking about you. Oh, and the other good factor is that you can make lots of money after years of suffering.'

GLOSSARY
● **Indie/dance crossover**
Early-nineties movement which is also called 'baggy'. Lots of surly indie types decided that dancing was good again and got matey with DJs. Sometimes good: The Stone Roses, The Happy Mondays, Flowered Up. Sometimes bad: **Paris Angels**.
● **Advance money**
The money which bands are paid when they sign a record deal. It is effectively lent to artists by the record company.
● **Genre**
A certain style. Techno and country and western are, thankfully, two very separate genres.

● Man
Contrary to what you might think, musicians and producers still use this term of affection/punctuation in everyday speech. Especially if they 'smoke'. Ahem.

● Paris Angels
From Manchester, surly, indie, dancey ... but *awwwfffulll*.

SKILLS YOU'LL NEED
Initiative and a bit of guts, perseverance, patience when the hi-hats are still too toppy, the art of looking slightly aloof, a vague bit of technical knowledge.

TIPS
● The Prince's Trust can provide grants for arts projects if you're under 25. It may be worth contacting them for studio time and/or equipment money if you're serious.

● Magazines like *Future Music* explain new developments in studio technology and have details on home studios and good equipment on the market.

● Potential DJ-types will spend a lot of time in record shops listening to the latest imports and meeting useful contacts.

● Hang around mates' studios and try to meet up with people who have bedroom studios to get tips from them. Perhaps you might try slyly mentioning your great keyboard/mixing skills.

● Start DJing at friends' parties. Practice is always essential, and your name will get around. No, it *will*.

● If you're cool and have already done all of these things, remember to walk around looking a bit surly.

Propagate that mystique. *Man*.

USEFUL NUMBERS
● The Prince's Trust, 18 Park Square East, London NW1 4LH.
TEL 0171 534 1234.
● Musicians Union, 60-62 Clapham Road, London SW9 0JJ.
TEL 0171 582 5666. **FAX** 0171 582 9805.

DISTRIBUTOR

MONEY: Around £7000 a year for telesales or £6000 if you work in the warehouse. Can zoom up to £60,000 if you're high up. There is a lot of room for part-time staff.

HOURS: 9 a.m. to 5.30 p.m. in telesales, really early and really late if you work in the warehouse, and then there are gigs and things.

HEALTH RISK: 5/10. You could end up trapped in the warehouse under a pile of cassettes, or in the pressing plant by accident. Argh!

PRESSURE RATING: 7/10. If pressed-up discs don't arrive at your warehouse in time, things can get sweaty.

GLAMOUR RATING: 4/10. You *might* have Aretha Franklin come and check the hole in her new CD is in the middle, but it's a fairly remote possibility. You may meet some lesser lights, though.

TRAVEL RATING: 5/10. Up to Manchester to have a cup of tea with a little label and discuss the product, if you're an indie distributor.

This is the actual 'getting the product into the shops' job, from liaising with record companies to making sure that Our Price has enough copies in all of their stores to sell.

Glamour! Excitement! Swanky high-rise living! These are *none* of the things that people associate with being in distribution.

Yet, obviously, distribution is a completely vital part of the 'Let's sell records' process. Without distribution, the records that you like (and also the ones that you hate, granted) would be sitting in a cold warehouse with nothing to do. They're not going to the glittering world of shop lighting, in-store displays and listening-posts if no one's there to put them in the shops. Distribution is vital, and the way that it's done is precise and calculated. The job is far more interesting than putting a CD in the back of your car and driving around with it. It has creative elements to it like any job. It's really down to you to make it interesting.

Record companies are in charge of recording and pressing their artists' wonderful tunes, on CD, vinyl and cassette. They are also in charge of experimenting with the new formats that come out from time to time, such as DAT, DTT and minidisc, which have thus far failed to make any deep inroads into the market, but that's as maybe. Once a tune has been pressed, the major record companies get their own distribution department to ring up **HMV** etc., tell them about the hot new product, and get it to them pronto. Independent labels and indie, record-company subsidiaries speak to their independent distributor, who will deal with many other indie companies.

Dominic Jones is the business development manager at Pinnacle Records, a sales, marketing, and distribution company that has been operating for twelve years in its present form. Dominic finds new business, and deals with six labels on a regular basis. Some of his colleagues work with thirty. He is the main point of contact between the labels and the sales team, who get the record into the shops. He makes sure the records are scheduled properly: for instance, there should be no debut singles by wee garage skiffle bands released at Christmas – they would simply be swamped by all the Mariah Carey releases and thus never see the right end of the charts.

The loveable non-corporate distribution company will treat a new release as follows. Imagine that a new band, The Grantham Cauliflower, has scheduled a release date for their single 'It Ain't Big But It Goes Well With Cheese' on Bakin' It Records in nine weeks' time. The record label inform the distributor and supply advance copies of the product, and all the boring information about what the title is, the correct spelling of the artist's name, plus what gigs are coming up, what press they're doing, any telly appearances, etc. The distributor makes sure this information gets to the retailer. The retailers then pore over this sales note, consider the facts, and decide whether they want to put the record in their shops. Believe it or not, the shops can be as fussy as that. If they think a record won't sell very much, for whatever reason, even if the artist is breaking all boundaries of conventional thought and has produced the Theory of Relativity in record form, Mr Important-Record-Shop Owner will still umm and ahh.

The national account manager at the distributor's deals with national retailers: HMV, Our Price, Virgin, etc. S/he gauges what the retailers make of a record, and reports back to the label. More information is then fed to these retailers over the next few weeks: if there's additional TV and press lined up, any radio interest, if the artist is turning on the Christmas lights in Bolton, etc. Three weeks before release, the final promotion details are given. Then – *then* – the independent record shops nationwide get a promo CD of the new release.

Pinnacle work with Network, around 250 privately owned record shops which sell more indie tunes than they do Celine Dion records. These are the key indie stores that Pinnacle target their campaigns through (e.g. sometimes bands are lovely and want to give away a special coloured vinyl album). Pinnacle's **strike force** will drop off promo CDs at these friendly stores so they can all hear the release properly, tap their indie feet while reading the pertinent information on the sales note, and then order a whole load to sell to smiling revolutionaries who like their rock on the bone. All through this process, Pinnacle will report back to Bakin' It Records (marketing department, label manager, etc.), who need to deliver stock to Pinnacle ten days before the release date. Release dates shift about like nobody's business, so this is always a sticky point.

On the Monday before the week of release, the computer at Pinnacle collates orders – some of which are placed in person and some of which are dealt with over the phone via the telesales staff or ordered electronically via the EROS (Electronic Record Ordering Service) system. Retail shop staff tap in their orders, which the computer sends directly to the relevant distributor. From Tuesday morning it's picking and packing: a team scurry around the warehouse, packing the new releases into boxes which then go to the Securicor regional warehouses for in-store delivery on the Friday before the release date. This gives the retailers two days to price up the new product. At that point, the strike force also bung a load of releases on all formats in their cars and hop around to the smaller shops to boast about the **presale** figures and ask whether these stores need any more. They report to the field sales manager (in charge of the sales team) who in turn reports to the sales director. He completes a report which is given to the label manager, who reports to the label. Blimey.

The dealer price for a single, such as the Grantham Cauliflower's debut, is a minimum £2.45 as set by the BPI, and yet the price of singles can vary between £1.99 and £2.99. Hmm. How so? This is currently a touchy subject with the majors. In a bid to sell! sell! sell! and power singles into the charts, the major distributors have started doing sneaky things like two-for-one deals – in which retailers pay for one single and get two. They are essentially giving records away to lure retailers into stocking singles, which don't generate much income and are known in more cynical record-business circles as 'adverts for the album', since albums *do* make everyone a lot of money.

All record labels want their singles to compete price-wise with releases from other record companies, so the indie distributors have to play the subsidy game, or else fight very hard for the retailers to take their records at the proper price – which the stores are loath to do as they'll make less money, having been spoilt by the majors. If you do sell your record at full price, then some wee indie charlie might come along to the record shop with two purchases in mind, but come out with the cheaper one because wee indie charlie can't afford the pricier one as well. It's a hard and really quite unfair game.

Pinnacle receive around fifty tapes and CDs per week from labels seeking distribution. If a label manager thinks the project worth following, they suggest the proposition to other label managers. If they like it and feel they can do something with it, they offer a distribution deal to the label.

A label needs to sell around 2,500 **units** across the counter to get into the top 75. 'We know to sell 2,500 we have to put around 6,000 in the shops,' explains Dominic. 'You can only expect 50-60% of the intial records shipped out to sell through in the week of release with decent promotion and an activated fanbase.'

Dominic finds that not only do labels frequently fail to deliver the stock in time, but some are unrealistic about sales and blame the sales force if their record doesn't go to number one. Breaking new acts is a bugger, too. The retailers want to have full confidence in a record, and if they've not heard of the act they get sniffy about stocking it. This is where the indie shops come in – they're far more likely to take a chance with new groups because they read *NME* and *Melody Maker* and know what's what. If they stock a fine new band who the big shops don't, more cool kids will go to hang out at their funky dive. And no one has to wear a corporate sweatshirt either.

There are a handful of other independent distributors, such as Vital, SRD, Total, and Shell Shock, to name but a few. Pinnacle deal with music right across the board, from Peter Andre to Skunk Anansie; The Backstreet Boys to 2 Pac; The Levellers to Björk. They also sign labels and give them either one- or two-year deals or sign them on specific releases. They take a percentage of every unit sold to the shops.

Some unscrupulous majors set up indie subsidiary labels and approach indie distributors about distributing their product through them. This means the 'pretend indie' label will get its releases into the indie chart, because the distribution is independent, even if the label is not. This makes the band look cool, a bit less Corporate Whore, and thus the band grows from the wee fanbase level.

You can make a career of distribution. Dominic started working at Our Price in Croydon as a sales assistant, back when such employees had the power to buy singles to sell in the shops themselves, which isn't allowed any more. He was talking to someone in telesales at Pinnacle who said there was a job coming up as a rep. Dominic applied. He didn't get the job because he couldn't drive, but they liked him and invented a job for him: West End merchandiser going round the London megastores and telling them what items they weren't stocking or have sold out of and taking orders from them. Dominic soon learnt to drive and became a sales rep on the South Coast of England, then a West End rep after a year, which is the best rep job in the country since there you find a mystical haven of presales. After one year, he was promoted to head of label management, then business development manager. This kind of career progression is fairly exceptional – but attainable.

'There are other jobs I could be doing within the industry,' says Dominic. 'But I love it. I suppose I've got an anti-major mentality – I'm very indie through and through. It's a great feeling of achievement to see a small act or label you've worked on become successful.'

Distribution is a great tool

To SHOPS

through

DISTRIBUTOR

FROM POP STAR

DISTRIBUTOR

in the fight for Proper Music in shops (not that we want to sound too revolutionary, or anything). It's not just about the nasty things in life, such as godawful, myopic, national, mainstream chains who won't stock The Grantham Cauliflower, or labels who forget to give you their finished sleeves on the right day. It can be an engrossing, stimulating, and creative job.

GLOSSARY
● HMV
The HMV shop, His Master's Voice, as owned by the EMI group. (Yes, all the majors have fingers in many pies, rather like Birds Eye or Nestlé. It's a multinational-dominated world out there.)
● Strike force
The people who drive around the regions of Great Britain, taking orders from shops. They are better paid than telesales because they have to do lots of legwork.
● Presale
The number of records bought by a shop before the record's release. These figures give an indication of how well the record might do eventually.
● Units
A single record is referred to as a unit. 'Shifting units' means selling a lot of records. Sounds heartless, which the industry often is.

SKILLS YOU'LL NEED
All-round knowledge of the industry; firm bargaining skills; communication skills; a car, normally; organisational ability; tidy desk, that sort of thing.

TIPS
● Try working in a record shop to get

to know the distribution side. You can meet reps and strike forces and see how they work.
● As in all trades, work experience can be a good way in – call a few distribution firms and see if they need office help. Practical experience is more important than a degree. Know your tunes.
● Being able to drive is a bonus.

USEFUL ADDRESSES
● Beehive Trading, 1 Warple Mews, London W3 0RF.
TEL 0181 742 9540. **FAX** 0181 749 1608.
● BMG Distribution, Lyng Lane, West Bromwich, West Midlands B70 7ST.
TEL 0121 500 5545. **FAX** 0121 553 6880.
● Caroline International Ltd, 56 Standard Road, Park Royal, London NW10 6ES.
TEL 0181 961 2919. **FAX** 0181 961 1873.
● Pinnacle, Electron House, Cray Avenue, St Mary Cray, Orpington, Kent BR5 3JR.
TEL 01689 870622. **FAX** 01689 878269.
● RTM, 98 St Pancras Way, London NW1 9NF.
TEL 0171 284 1155. **FAX** 0171 284 2211.
● Sound And Media, Unit 3, Wells Place, Gatton Park Business Centre, New Battlebridge Lane, Redhill, Surrey RH1 3DR.
TEL 01737 644445. **FAX** 01737 644443.
● THE, Rosevale Business Park, Newcastle Under Lyme, Staffordshire ST5 7QT.
TEL 01782 566566. **FAX** 01782 566511.
● 3MV, Eastern Office, 81-83 Weston Street, London SE1 3RS.
TEL 0171 378 8866. **FAX** 0171 378 8855.
● Windsong International, Electron House, Cray Avenue, St Mary Cray, Orpington, Kent BR5 3RJ.
TEL 01689 836969. **FAX** 01689 890392.

FANCLUB ORGANISER

MONEY: Either from £4 to £10 per hour, approx., or a full-time wage, if there's a lot of work to do.

HOURS: From a few afternoons a month to full time: again, it depends on the size of the band.

HEALTH RISK: 5/10. Impaled by stapler? Poisoned by the glue on a stamp? Could do too much photocopying and go blind perhaps.

EQUIPMENT COSTS: The band's expenses should generally pay for all printing and manufacturing costs.

PRESSURE RATING: 6/10. The fanclub magazine has to be out on time and you have to think of interesting things to write in it, try to keep membership figures up, and get the band to be involved when they'd rather be lazing around swigging pints of cocktails etc.

GLAMOUR RATING: 2/10. You do spend time with the band but far more on your own, stapling fanclub mags and licking envelopes.

TRAVEL RATING: 2/10. To the post office, to some gigs.

Runs the club that the fans of a particular band join! Sorts out membership, postage, newsletters, nice badges and baubles and things.

There are many routes to becoming a fanclub organiser. You might be just a friend of the band, or an experienced administrator. There are both official fanclubs, and not-so-official ones. Anyone can start one up, and charge any sort of price for overenthusiastic fans to join. However, if you run a crummy, expensive outfit people will wise up to it, won't renew their membership, nor recommend it to anyone else. You've got to be quite good. Few fanclubs make extra cash for the band. Most membership fees cover costs and that's it. It is for *fans*, after all.

You've got to be prepared to put in a lot of effort and lick a lot of envelopes. Alex runs Pulp People – the Pulp fanclub – from her home in Sheffield. She began by helping out her friend Mark Webber, who was running it in 1992 when it cost £2 to join. Mark hung out with the band and then helped out at concerts, doing roadie work and whatever else he could. He used to make gig flyers with Russell from Pulp (who left at the beginning of '97) and it all graduated from there. Alex took over when Mark joined the band full time, in '95.

Alex enlists new members and puts together newsletters and news-update sheets. She also deals with merchandise orders by mail and replies to any reader queries – or gets the band to answer them in the magazine. She does all this from home and also holds down a part-time job. Pulp People now costs £12 to join, for which each fan gets six issues of the newsletter, a badge and a postcard. Alex gets paid by the hour and Pulp make no money from it at all – everything goes on the service they provide.

Sam works at the Suede fanclub, and has done so since 1995. The £10 fee guarantees four newsletters, including a signed photograph, and a special fanclub-only gig at the end of every year. Sam wrote a couple of Suede fanzines, went to their gigs and hung around till the band all knew what she was like and reckoned she wouldn't nick the office stapler if given the fanclub job to do. She now works full time at the band's management office.

Fanclubs start up after there is a sufficient number of people on the band's **database** who've already written to the record company asking for information on the band. As well as fanclubs, there are now people employed to design and write a band's **website**, which has really up-to-date information on which band member is snogging which film star (actually, it's never quite as frank as that, more's the pity). The more corporate fanclubs become, the more they're likely to rip you off. Anne Robinson at *Watchdog* knows who the scoundrels are.

A PHOTOCOPIER. ESSENTIAL.

Pulp People is full of Alex's ideas – every issue, fans can ask questions of 'Dr Pulp' and Jarvis will write articles on events such as his co-opting into the Rock Circus. 'Sometimes the job does get to me,' says Alex. 'I do it *all*. Invariably I'll be doing it late at night – I sometimes spend all weekend doing newsletters. It is tiring. I've only just got a computer and a phone. It's not always very businesslike, but we're not just selling merchandise, and people appreciate that.'

Suede's Sam also comes up with ideas, interviews members of the band for the mag, collects queries for the 'Dear George' column (George is Suede drummer Simon Gilbert's dog) and has to deal with answering readers' queries by post.

'Most people who write to fanclubs are reasonable,' says Alex, 'but a few just want to complain about not getting free things.' Then there is the occupational hazard of cranks who send horrible things by post – Pulp People still receives letters from Michael Jackson fans complaining about Jarvis Cocker's behaviour at the Brits. Then there are the more ardent fans. 'You do tend to get people who think you're their best mate, which is a bit of a strain,' says Alex. 'Someone once found out where I lived and turned up at the back door. I knew who she was immediately, strangely enough. Of course I had to invite her in and she stayed all afternoon, talking. She turned up again a month later, having brought across a photocopier on an old pram from Northern Ireland! I was staggered. She thought we needed one.'

Alex hastens to explain that such bizarre events don't happen too often, but says she does get sent letters that take an hour to read, from people who desperately want to meet her. Sam says she gets people following her home, or fans writing in asking where and when Brett Anderson gets his catfood, and what brand it is. 'They want to come over to England and spend their holidays waiting for Brett to walk into his local corner shop,' she says. She normally tells fans that she buys the catfood herself, at a distant Sainsbury's.

— FANCLUB PERSON

There are perks, however. Sam gets sent luxury Belgian chocolates – but she doesn't eat chocolate (she gives it to Brett's cat, probably). She gets to go to all the Suede gigs she wants to, and Suede are so good about their fans she sees 'at least one of the band every week' to discuss fanclub issues. The worst part of the job, she reckons, is getting the band to sign the photos: 'You'd think from his reaction it was the most difficult thing in the world to sign the letters B R E T T.'

Some pop fanclubs are run by a person employed on a more formal basis. In this instance, the band and management decide upon a membership price, the services the fanclub will provide, and any special offers. Then they employ somebody that already has a track record in organising such entities – ex-journalists, administrators or **PA**s.

Alex says she's not 'in this for the money' (well, there's not much) and doesn't imagine doing it for ever. Neither does Sam. You don't really get to hang out with pop stars or go to swanky parties: your time is taken up typing out penpal lists and sending out keyrings. And some fanclub people (not Alex or Sam) are completely mad, absolutely barmy, even more besotted about their charges than the most besotted fan. It's a labour of love.

GLOSSARY
● **Database**
Now that computer technology is in full swing, every person who writes asking for information, a photo, or where Brett buys his catfood gets their name and address put on to

computer for future reference. Once there are a couple of hundred names, it's time for a fanclub to start.

● **Website**

A little home in the vast global village that is the Internet.

● **PA**

Personal assistant. All top dogs – MD, manager, head of department – have one.

SKILLS YOU'LL NEED

To be organised; ability to file things; ability to write – the newsletter and reply letters; friendliness towards fans that are a bit barking; firmness with the band so that they will sign things and answer readers' queries.

TIPS

● Get to know up-and-coming bands who don't have a fanclub.

● Get to know the people at fanclubs and offer to write articles for them. Large fanclubs have more than one member of staff, or need people to help a wee bit once in a while.

● If you work for a management company you might be asked to help out with such matters. Managers set up fanclubs which are completely independent of record companies.

● Running a fanclub shows you how the music industry works. It is good experience and can be a stepping stone into other things.

● It might even get you into a pop group. (See Mark Webber.)

USEFUL ADDRESSES

● Pulp People: PO Box 87, Sheffield S11 8WJ

● Suede Information Service: PO Box 3431, London N1 7LW.

HAIRDRESSER/ MAKE-UP ARTIST

MONEY: From helping out for nothing to the likes of £1,000 per day if you're a snoot person who works on adverts.

HOURS: From a couple of hours a week to a twenty-hour day at a video shoot starting at 6 a.m.

HEALTH RISK: 8/10. You may be murdered by a pop star whom you inadvertently made look ugly. Or inhale too much Studio Line hairspray.

PRESSURE RATING: 6/10. Rivalry being the main stress – the world of the lipliner being very competitive.

GLAMOUR RATING: 6/10. If you like trying to remember what the drummer's called and then trying to tell him he's got a shiny chin.

TRAVEL RATING: 5/10. Mostly studios around London. You might be asked to go to Birmingham, but you have to be really in with a band for them to take you anywhere further than Glasgow.

Make-up artist and hairdresser are responsible for your pop star looking good in photographs, videos and on telly. The job entails standing around a lot, waiting for a stray hair or a shiny forehead to pop up.

Apparently, if you floss your teeth regularly it has such a beneficial effect on the gums that your face doesn't droop so much when you're older. Already knew that? Then you must be a make-up artist. For make-up artists aren't just a dab hand at putting on blusher. They, and their fellow cosmetic compadres, hairdressers, are a fount of knowledge on all things around your head.

There are make-up courses up and down the country which train people to put on mascara properly. They also teach the basics of beauty training: plucking eyebrows, manicures and applying false eyelashes. A good course teaches day make-up, evening make-up, catwalk make-up and bridal make-up. You also get taught 'men's grooming', which is really just make-up for men.

Magazines like *Vogue* advertise these training courses, and they can be very expensive: from £1,500 for two months to £8,000 for a two-week course. However, many further-education colleges provide similar training.

Fay Leith is a top make-up artist to the stars, working on photo shoots, videos and record covers. She started on a two-month course when she 'saw a make-up artist and heard how much she got paid'! Her teacher, a professional make-up artist herself, would take her students on jobs she was doing during the course as practical training. The day after the course ended, Fay went up to *The Clothes Show* Live exhibition in Birmingham with her teacher and was paid £1,000 for the week. This success continued and Fay got to know a lot more people who needed an assistant to bung on the foundation.

After completing training, many cosmeticians ring up model agencies, who make a habit of 'testing' new models – i.e. taking their picture with lovely make-up on to show around prospective **clients**. Make-up artists often do need assistants – fresh-faced youngsters just out of beauty school. Often all parties do these shoots for nothing, just because they can each get a nice picture out of it to show other people in order to get more work – i.e. it's good for the **portfolio**. The more work you do for these agencies, then the swankier the models get and the better the photographers get, etc. There are also make-up agencies you can approach when you've got more experience. These are the people who will want to see your portfolio, and if you sign up with them they'll haggle for the best rate for you while also taking between 10% and 20% of it for themselves.

Once you get a job with a pop band – either assisting somebody else or on your own – word gets around about your eyebrow-plucking skills. Like most jobs, you don't start earning lots of money immediately.

HAIRSTYLIST/
MAKE-UP PERSON

You may initially find it hard to get work, so £500 for one job might sound a lot but you could have to make it last three weeks.

'I've been lucky,' says Fay. 'I knew a couple of people in bands, and when they started to get into a position where they could recommend me they would give me a ring. I don't know what it would be like if you didn't know anyone. I'm afraid you have to make it your business to know someone.'

Fay did the make-up for some press shots, some album covers, and then videos. 'It's not that easy,' she says. 'You might be in with an artist one week and out with them the next. There's a famous girl band whose mood swings I can't really cope with. You want to have artists you can rely on to get steady work from and it's very hard to get them. Other people try to poach them off you.'

So make-up artists end up having to suck up to people a bit. You always have to force yourself to be nice, even if you have surly bassists insisting they don't need any powder when they have the shiniest nose this side of a copper kettle. You can earn a lot of cash when you're the regular eyebrow-plucker of a star – press shots, TV promotion and **international promotion** all keep you busy. But sometimes the management come in and ask you not to get 'too involved'. There have been instances of make-up artists getting 'too close to the artist', as The Powers That Be see it, and then you're not allowed to go to the pub with the stars afterwards. So you also have to suck up to the management in case they don't like you any more. It can be a bit sticky.

Pop stars are notoriously picky. Fay says, 'Some boys really like the attention. If there's a girl singer too, she doesn't usually get a look in.' This is a game where everyone gets at least moisturiser put on them, just so that it's all fair. You have to placate people, and must remember to ask whether they are allergic to anything in case their skin swells up and you get sued.

The world of make-up is also quite snooty. Some make-up artists like to have poncey rucksacks that cost £150, plus all the latest fancy brushes from whichever cosmetic company they think is trendiest. It goes with the territory.

'The music world is so fickle,' says Fay. 'If a record company is deliberating between two make-up artists for a shoot, they'll go for the most expensive one. You can't undercharge yourself or people think you're useless. You can't be afraid to say what you want.'

Hairstylists work in a similar way to make-up artists. After training as a junior in a hairdressers, some hairdabblers follow a similar route in that they help model agencies to do test shots of models in order to get experience and work with a make-up artist. The make-up agencies also deal with hair folk, and once you're established someone will take you on, upping your fee (as agencies do) and taking their percentage.

Ben trained at Vidal Sassoon and met Madonna's hairdresser through a colleague. They got on straight away and he assisted her on a shoot with a new model called Kate Moss. Around this time, Ben also got a call to go down to MTV to help with Michelle Gayle's hair. Ms Gayle thought he was great and rang him up a couple of days later to ask him to fix her barnet for a photo shoot. As soon as you start to get to know someone in the music biz you find they know someone else who knows someone else – and everyone has a split end or a flyaway fringe to be seen to in this business. As ever, **networking** is the way that a lot of people get on. You can be the best hairdresser in the world, but if you're shy or only want to cut hair in a revolutionary, anti-centralised-government sort of way, then you're a goner.

As well as Michelle Gayle, Ben has worked for pop types such as The Spice Girls, Olive and Catch. He loves his job and finds that nowadays he can do many varieties of interesting haircut because everything is so 'diverse'. Ben does actually have a £150 Prada rucksack, but is likeable nonetheless.

'It's a bit like cutting hair in a salon,' he says. 'You talk about everyday life, but you ask what someone's been up to and they answer "Oh, just been to Acapulco" because that's their everyday life. Plus, sometimes you do a great haircut in a normal salon and it walks out of the door and you think: No one's going to see it! On shoots, I know someone's going to take a picture of it and everyone will see it, which is great. I love my job. I couldn't think of doing anything else.'

GLOSSARY

● **Client**

Posh word for the person employing you, in this case advertising agencies, pop stars and record companies. Note: in our denationalised age, hospital patients are called clients as well. Funny that.

● **Portfolio**

Collection of your work, which you can show to prospective employers.

● **International promotion**

If a band really likes you, they'll take you with them to make them look pretty for overseas appearances.

● **Networking**

The art of talking to the right people at the right time. Takes place at industry parties and you can also spot it on the streets of Soho, London. You used to be able to spot networkers because they wore puffa jackets. At the time of going to press, it's 'big' shoes.

SKILLS YOU'LL NEED

Being able to cut hair, being able to do make-up, talking about hair and make-up, patience when someone blinks and you're trying to put mascara on them, communication skills.

TIPS

● For make-up, try to take a course – either at a local college or a well-established independent course. Look at *The Stage* or health and beauty magazines for details.

● For hairdressing, ring the best local salon, and train as a junior.

● Get in touch with other make-up artists through make-up agencies – model agencies have the number. They will give advice, and maybe

take you on to assist. The same goes for hairdressers.

● Practise on your friends – it's a good way of getting experience, even though it sounds a bit naff.

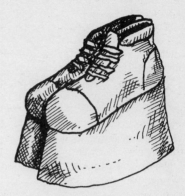

AN EXAMPLE OF
'BIG' SHOES

INDIE-LABEL BOSS

MONEY: From zero or minus figures if you 'own' a flexi label and are funding everything yourself, to lots of casheroo when you've just sold your label to Sony or someone for a couple of million quid.

HOURS: All hours. All the time. Even weekends.

HEALTH RISK: 9/10. Wining and dining The Casual Trout in order to woo them onto your label is fair rotten for your liver.

PRESSURE RATING: 7/10. Not too bad: you can do things under your own steam for a while, until all your acts get lured away by the prospect of 'proper' money and you have to consider selling out to The Man.

GLAMOUR RATING: 6/10. Well, fanzine writers will quite like you. At first.

TRAVEL RATING: 7/10. Mostly to the Powerhaus in Finsbury Park.

A label boss runs their own label and started absolutely from scratch. Running a label was actually a tremendous idea they thought of in the pub one night and slowly it has turned into a 'serious concern'.

Being an indie-label boss is a different job from being an MD of a major record company, although the principle is essentially the same – you are the boss of a company that produces records. However, major-label MDs have to report to all the bigwigs who virtually own the world. You, on the other hand, are either starting out with a few bands or you're at the stage where you might have sold some of your company to a major in order to keep afloat, but you are still in charge of most of the financial and creative decisions. There are less departments to walk around and nod to. Sometimes there are none at all.

It is no exaggeration to say that most indie-label bosses start out as passionate music fans who like hearing tunes so much they decide that the world needs more, and will sign artists they like in order to release the idiosyncratic collection of notes which float their personal boat. Ivo Watts-Russell at 4AD, Daniel Miller at Mute, and Alan McGee at Creation all began this way. However, every single label runs in a different way. Some labels release one single by an artist and then move on to the next act, while other bands might stay loyal for years. Some deal exclusively with dance music; others are across the board. Some last a few months; others years. It's a bit like discussing taxi firms. Yes, they carry people about for money. Other than that, there are no rules at all – the music business in microcosm.

In my youth, I once co-founded a record label, Trolley Records. We released one **flexi-disc** single and it cost us about £100. The band we'd released went on to be signed by Creation in another guise, but we couldn't find any more acts we liked after that, so we gave up. However, the thought that Trolley could rise again is forever in our hearts – for better or worse.

On a rather more elevated level, Alan McGee started Creation with a couple of mates who were in bands and ended up signing The Jesus and Mary Chain, Primal Scream and Oasis – and making a mint. Sony bought 49% of the company from him a few years back, but McGee still makes all the top-dog decisions. A lot of the well-established smallish labels were started in the mid-eighties and have been sniffing around the feet of the music industry since then. The newest labels are mostly dance labels, and their independence provides credibility. A lot of hardcore dance-music fans wouldn't even glance at a club cut released on EMI.

As stated, each smaller label is run in a different manner and it's somewhat hard to generalise about their modi operandi, so we'll begin by focussing on an indie-guitar-style label. Fierce Panda Records is run by Simon Williams, who has written for *NME* for over ten years both as a freelance and staff writer. He started the label with two fellow journalists at the beginning of 1994, when they were all **drunk in the pub**. They wanted to release an EP featuring their two favourite bands at the time, who were yet to sign proper record deals. These bands were termed 'New Wave of New Wave' – they had songs with three chords and they looked a bit punky and went on about smashing the system and lager. Suddenly, Fierce Panda had six bands – people find out about such ventures quickly in this business – and a DAT of each song they wanted to put on the record.

Simon had a friend at Damaged Goods Records, who is now his business partner, and he was able to sort out distribution fairly sharpish. Distribution is one of the hardest things to get when you're trying to set up your own company. If you don't have a track record, or anyone really famous on the label, then distributors won't put out your records. Or they might try, but find it difficult to get the record into the shops because the bigger stores deal with major releases only. But more of this anon.

Fierce Panda held a launch party at the Powerhaus in London, at which all their bands played. They soon sold out of the initial thousand vinyl singles they'd had pressed – not a bad start, as some singles on major labels never even reach that mark. Five months later they released their next record, an EP with all the young bands that seemed to be swamping the scene at the time.

'Then it got addictive,' says Williams. A couple of EPs later – new girl bands, new mod bands – and Simon thought he'd take the process a stage further: 'It was time for proper releases.' That meant finding new bands and paying for them to go in the studio. First release was by a band called Scarfo in the spring of 1995. It sold a thousand singles. Press was relatively easy to get (they had a foot in the *NME* for a start) and Williams's close buddy Steve Lamacq liked the bands and played them on the Radio One *Evening Session*.

Fierce Panda still find it difficult to get their records in the shops, however. Most major record companies employ creative marketing and do discount deals when they're selling singles to retailers. They give them a quantity of records for nothing, or at a tiny price, so the shop can sell them on cheaply and the record can go into the chart. Unfair, but true! Devastatingly true!!! Obviously, small record companies can't afford to do this, so The Kids are tempted into buying major releases and albums because they're cheaper, which is ultimately what makes the money for the majors.

'We can't give singles to retailers at a special price because we lose money on a lot of releases anyway,' moans Williams. There are ways to survive, however. A lot of younger record labels make money through 'Best Of' compilation CDs of previous releases. These sell to Japan and other fancy **territories** abroad. Or, you can press a thousand vinyl singles which then sell out, then reissue five thousand or more CD copies of the single a few months later and make some money that way.

Fierce Panda have, to date, released early recordings by Kenickie, Ash, Gorky's Zygotic Mynci, Placebo, Three Colours Red, and all sorts of other guitar-tastic types who have since been snapped up by major companies. Panda knew that these were one-off singles, but the big fear of some indie bosses is that artists they want to keep will leave their lovely little label, lured by the big £££s that major record companies will invariably offer once

they've seen that the band sell records. If you're strapped for cash, you can't afford to offer groups long deals that tie them to the label – so they can up and go when they wish.

The indie label is essentially doing a **free A&R job** for a lot of majors, and this is difficult because you never make any money *at all*. One fanzine writer wrote that Fierce Panda was The Devil because it was subsidised by IPC magazines, publishers of *NME*. Of course it wasn't subsidised directly, but *NME* paid Williams's wages, which enabled him to keep the thing afloat. Running an indie label full time, without the help of a major record company buy-in or other external funding, would be nigh on impossible. You need great ears, business suss – and the luck of The Devil.

However, when a small label like Fierce Panda has a very good track record, people in the industry know that it can often break a new band, and so canny press officers and pluggers will often donate their services free to help promote a release. It is a gamble, but they know they could be in with the band after they sign a cash-plenty deal with a major.

Williams doesn't really bother much with artwork and at the moment Fierce Panda, a bastion of the indie industry, is still run from his living room. Simon 'doesn't have time' to listen to tapes, preferring to see bands play live. He turned down Bush when they asked if they could be on Fierce Panda, as well as one chap whose demo tape was entitled 'Richey Manic is Dead'. One bod got so excited at the thought of being on the label that he pressed up his own record and turned up with it in a pizza box, at a pub where he thought Williams would be. The record was cut and ready to be copied up and pressed into thousands. He'd even given it a **catalogue number**, which actually clashed with another record. Tragically, of course, the disc was never released.

Other problems indie-label moguls will encounter are bands going into the studio and **running over time** or some piece of equipment blowing up and causing the project to balloon over budget. You have to get used to people messing up. Williams had to learn quickly: 'I used to think, It's my fault! The sleeves aren't pressed in time! The man who prints sleeves must be a very professional person and *he* wouldn't ever make a mistake. Then you realise they're all flaky old tossers like yourself, and you learn to anticipate there'll be some sort of problem with every release.'

Mark Jones runs Wall Of Sound Records, who put out jazzy dance stuff, electronic music, and what everyone was calling Big Beat in 1997. He started up the company when he was working at an independent distributors, Soul Trader. 'We had no master plan,' he says. He would hear tracks by trendy types working in bedroom studios, which were released by Soul Trader. Jones thought the tunes needed to be heard by a wider audience, so got his favourite tracks and released them as a compilation album, *Give 'Em Enough Dope*.

Six years on, Jones is doing well and maintaining his independence despite being offered a fair few tantalising major deals. He's also managed to keep his acts to the label. He reckons that, if a band wants to stay credible, they will stay with their UK indie label, then sign major deals in other territories in order to stay afloat. Mark was able to start

LABEL BOSS/LABEL MANAGER

the label on a practical level because he knew about distribution – the 'unglamorous' side of the business.

He started running Wall Of Sound from home, then set up an office, and now employs three people, as well as a part-time marketing consultant. He's made enough money to keep the business alive by releasing singles *and* albums. Jones made a host of knowing and astute early moves. He made sure that a talented and 'proper' designer gave the label an identity and that Wall Of Sound releases were visually conspicuous and distinctive. He also found acts through being sent tapes, and via friends of friends – following the normal A&R route is pointless, he says, because you can't compete with major labels' chequebooks.

Mark also ran regular club nights, and now does one-offs to keep up the profile of the label. All this is very important. 'It helps to know people. It's good to get out to gigs and try to get as much help and advice as possible. Be yourself, don't be anyone else: that's the key.'

Simon Williams has other tips. 'You have to have a complete and utter belief in your own tastes and never listen to anyone else. So many people will say, "I think that's shit," but 90% of those people will eventually say, "You were right," and the other 10% will never like them anyway – so why try to convince them?'

A BIT ABOUT LABEL MANAGERS

Label managers work for smaller record companies, sorting out the general day-to-day running of the label, and any bits the boss has forgotten. Small labels do need a lot of help, and this job can often develop from a work-experience posting or it can suit a new person starting out on the ladder.

Stephanie has worked for St Etienne's label, Emidisc, for a couple of years. She used to write to Etienne band members Bob Stanley and Pete Wiggs when they wrote a fanzine. Stephanie kept in touch as the duo became pop stars, and, when Bob noticed the band manager was overworked, nearly jumping out of windows and singing Northern Soul songs down the phone to pensioners, he asked Stephanie to come into their office and help. Once Stanley and Wiggs had formed their own label through EMI and had signed up bands such as Kenickie and Denim, Bob and Pete needed help to run their label, too.

'I do general office work: answer phones, send out post, file press clippings, and all that stuff,' says Stephanie. 'I arrange the St Etienne diary and keep things ticking over. I also look after the band when they do gigs, and sort out their transport and guest lists.' Stephanie mails out the St Etienne fanclub parcels, and organises parties as well. It's full time and a lot of work, but she's been to Tokyo, Paris and Sweden among other places as part of the job.

She likes working at a little label. 'I wouldn't be keen about the major-label option,' she says. 'You're working primarily with people who aren't music fans. I like working with friends. If I get pissed off I can tell them so. It's not like a normal job.'

GLOSSARY

● **Flexi-disc**

Vinyl disc that is pressed on such thin plastic that it is flexible. Very cheap to produce. Loved by fanzines and 32-year-old fans of The Wedding Present.

● **Drunk in the pub**

A time-honoured ritual and a breeding ground for great ideas, especially for journalists. The pub is traditionally the best location known to *Homo sapiens* for creative brainstorming and lateral-thinking sessions.

● **Territories**

All the countries of the world split into sales target areas called things like 'Germany' and 'the Far East'. America is the biggest territory, and sells a lot of records. Then it's Japan and Germany, Britain, and fast-emerging areas such as South East Asia.

● **Free A&R job**

In essence, you are finding new talent and nurturing bands until they are 'ready' to be signed by major companies. All major-label A&R people know what the small labels are doing.

● **Catalogue number**

Every release on every record label ever is given a catalogue number. You can also give catalogue numbers to all sorts of daft stuff. Factory Records gave its office cat a number, for instance. However, they didn't remix the cat and re-release it in extended formats.

● **Running over time**

If you take longer on a track in the studio, you will be charged by the hour. Williams pays for all Panda recordings: thus he gets disgruntled when this happens.

SKILLS YOU'LL NEED

Diplomacy, a long-term view, single-mindedness, staying awakeness when it's 2 a.m. and the band still haven't come on, organisational skills, friends to give you a hand, lots of time.

TIPS

● Speak to people with labels to see what advice they can give, as they might know people to help you.

● Fanzines often produce flexi-discs. Buy some copies (there are always ads in *NME* and *Melody Maker*) and weigh up the competition. Bear in mind that some major-ish labels started this way. Then start your own.

● Decide if there's a gap in the market – if you or your sister have a great band with a moose on trombone and your dad is head of a distribution company, then it may be time to release a record. Use all the opportunities you can spot.

● You don't have to have an 'industry' job to start your own label. Many people have more 'normal' occupations while releasing vibrant tunes from an office in their kitchen.

JOURNALIST

MONEY: A staff writer on a magazine or newspaper earns £12,000 to £25,000 a year. Freelance journalists are paid a word rate and so get more money for writing long features and interviews than short reviews. A freelancer who works a day in a newspaper or magazine office will be paid a fixed, agreed day rate.

HOURS: 10 a.m. to 6 p.m. for a staff job, more or less. Freelancers working from home may have spells of intense activity followed by long periods without work, and will also find they have to sacrifice a lot of their weekends.

HEALTH RISK: 9/10. All journalists are in the frontline as far as supping too much free ale at ligs is concerned.

EQUIPMENT COSTS: You need a tape recorder, and perhaps a couple of pens. Magazines will provide the rest of the equipment in the office. Freelance journalists working from home will also have to get themselves a computer, biros and a notepad, as well as a phone and a liver of steel.

PRESSURE RATING: 8/10. Deadlines. Brr. The dreaded word. Deadlines are revered and hated – they make your life a misery, but if you didn't have them you'd spend your life polishing the fridge. Trying to ask, in the name of public interest, whether Ms Pop Star's just snogged Mr Film Star, or else your editor will fire you, is also a bit tricky.

GLAMOUR RATING: 8/10. You may meet the hunks of pop but they're the ones who are having their toenails buffed and ordering the bubbly while you have to sit meekly and tape their words of 'wisdom' and are lucky to be offered a Tizer.

TRAVEL RATING: 8/10. Leicester! Perth! Holland Park! Yes, journalists scoot all over the nation in the search for that story. You may also go abroad reasonably often and be treated to the sights and sounds of foreign climes. However, bear it in mind that most pop stars tend to adventure no further than McDonalds, the Hard Rock Café and the hotel bar.

The journalist is perhaps one of the most high-profile music-industry jobs, second only to pop star. As long as people can read, journalists will be able to write their frothy, often dreadful, prose about Liam 'n' Patsy and Noel 'n' Meg till kingdom come. And then they can write about kingdom come, and what The Spice Girls will be wearing when it happens.

Being a music journalist is one of the greatest jobs known to Man. You get to write down what you think about music: a privilege that most people would give their knees for.

Unfortunately, no one who writes for a living holds this view after six months of being in the job. Journalists are always complaining about something or other, and this is probably because they meet pop stars for a living and hear *them* complaining. Also, because they're always trying to write that semi-autobiographical first novel but end up having to write live reviews of German family bands for a ha'penny (or less) instead. There is, after all, rent to be paid.

A journalist's job is to report the latest music news, interview pop stars and review music, all for the delectation of the **readers**. In the days when writers joined the National Union of Journalists, a union which in this day and age is not really very well recognised by magazine publishing, there was a strict code of conduct which you agreed to by joining. No making up 'My mother's a herring!' quotes, no malicious comment upon the silliness of your interviewee's hair, or other such cruelty. Needless to say, many journalists of the tabloid-paper profession failed to follow these rules by the letter. Or the full stop.

So! What happens? Well, most rock writers get a very early idea that music journalism is the sort of thing they would like to do. Very few people simply 'fall into it'. A few rock writers study journalism (the London College of Printing provides a famous course) but are more likely to be doing their homework at the School of the Live Gig and in the HMV shop. Many start by writing fanzines: their own little magazines will interview ropey local bands (and sometimes the stars, or the bassist, of Dinosaur Jr) then get photocopied and sold at gigs. School and college magazines also serve that purpose – they're good practice, and you can do whatever you want. No one's going to tell you to cut the jokes out and you can rabbit on about what you like with a Joyceian sense of the ridiculous.

'When I left university,' says Chris Heath, who's an internationally renowned music writer (*Rolling Stone*, *The Face* and others) and author of two Pet Shop Boys' books, 'I asked the local free paper if I could do a pop column, because I wanted free records. I got £5 a week. Then they announced they couldn't pay me and I did it for nothing, because it was a shameless device to get free records.'

If you ring up most magazines, wanting to write, they'll ask you to send in some examples of your work, including some reviews written in the style of the magazine. You have to know what sort of music the magazine covers and what sort of person reads it to be able to write for it. A *Smash Hits*-style piece won't fit in the *NME*. Editors receive a lot of **unsolicited work**, and the best ones read through everything, no matter how long it takes. Some writers have started this way, but more often than not the best idea is to contact the reviews editor, whose job is to find new writers to pontificate on the relevance of all the guff that's released every week.

Eddie Lawrence was reviews editor for *Select* magazine in 1997. He started

JOURNALIST

features from writers and makes sure the writer knows the **brief, deadline and word count**. Ian had a fanzine before he started writing, then wrote for *Music Week* and the *NME*. He helps decide what's on the cover of every issue and the direction the paper's going in.

'We have to create a balance in the features, so that indie, pop, dance and hip-hop are covered while we keep our core audience happy. We want the features to be different, so I have to come up with ideas that aren't just yet another boring interview with a boring pop star.'

Ian reckons disasters make good interviews – if anything goes wrong it's an immediate story. As an interviewer, he's had indie groups confess all in five-hour-long interviews, such as band members coming out to him as being gay even before they told anyone in the band. He had such a rapport with one guitarist, who shared his life story with him, that the poor fretmaster was too embarrassed ever to speak to him again.

Most writers start freelance, however – which essentially means being self-employed. Chris Heath started at *Smash Hits* as a freelance.

'The first job I was given was to spend a month getting Christmas messages from the stars for a phoneline they were doing. I met the forty most famous pop stars on the planet – Wham!, New Order, Duran Duran, Depeche Mode ... Sade had to say her sentence fifteen times because she was tired. Then, just before Christmas, I went on tour with Wham!. They gave me the job because no one else wanted to do it due to the time of year. George Michael put his back out

by cartooning ('but I couldn't draw') and eventually freelanced for various music magazines. 'I commission reviews by experienced *and* not-so-experienced writers,' he says. 'And it's not always the experienced writers that are the best. You have to keep an eye out for writers who've become complacent – their ideas aren't up to scratch or they're bad at keeping deadlines.'

Next up, on your way through the magazine structure, is to bag a **feature**. To do this, you need to impress a features editor. Ian Watson holds this post at *Melody Maker*. He commissions and they cancelled one date. I was terrified because I'd been meant to cover the two dates. In the end I went back to London with them on the bus, and went to George Michael's mum's house for tea. He was saying, "Another cup of tea, Mum?" and from that moment on I was golden boy at *Smash Hits*.'

If you get on well, your next step is to get a job on the staff of a magazine. Staff writer is a job in which you can find yourself writing everything from the contents page to features, news pieces, reviews, competitions, and editing letters. You tend to be thrown in at the deep end, especially on **'teen' titles** where new staff can be inexperienced and expected to learn the ropes as they go along.

'I remember being in the first editorial meeting,' says Helen Lamont, who works for *Top Of The Pops* magazine. 'I thought it was like *Absolutely Fabulous*. They were saying, "I'm thinking Take That, I'm thinking Boyzone ..."! The first gig I went to was for the man who used to be in Yell!, at the Atlantic Bar [swanky eaterie/bar in central London], and I got a free CD as I left! I thought this was incredible.'

A lot of people aren't told the whys and wherefores of how the system works when they first begin writing. For instance, it's a journalist's job to hear as much new music as possible, in the interests of the magazine. Therefore, journalists are given free records. If you review a gig, the press officer will give you at least one free ticket. Caitlin Moran, author, ex-TV-presenter and pop journalist for *The Times* and *Select*, didn't have a clue how things worked when she started writing for *Melody Maker*.

'My reviews editor never told me I could get in for nothing at gigs, so I used to pay at every one I was reviewing,' she says. 'The other big mistake I made was letting my dad take me to a Smashing Pumpkins gig. I thought that if you reviewed a concert you automatically went backstage to meet the band afterwards. I took my dad and we somehow got into the dressing room. My dad leant over to the singer, Billy Corgan, and said, "You're a tight little combo and your bassist isn't bad looking either." Now *that* was embarrassing.'

Caitlin Moran has conducted twelve-hour interviews with Courtney Love, been sick next to Kirsty McColl while Kirsty was playing acoustic guitar in her bathroom, and has had a Teenage Fanclub song dedicated to her live. 'But I put in a lot of legwork,' she says. 'I promised to buy them drinks for a year.'

Caitlin began her career by winning an *Observer* Young Writer of the Year competition, by sending in an article about her family. She then joined *The Times* and *Melody Maker*. Most writers hop about from paper to paper – as editors change, so do the staff. An editor either comes up from the ranks via being features editor then assistant editor at the same magazine, or else gets drafted in from another publication (often a **rival**).

The editor's job is to oversee every working of the magazine, from editorial through to design and production (the latter being schedule-keepers and spelling-correctors). It also involves lengthy marketing meetings, scheduling meetings, advertising meetings, meetings meetings, and any other discussion where a representative of the editorial side is needed. Some editors like to do a bit of writing too – just to keep their hand in – because they get envious of writers who don't have to go to so many meetings.

A lot of editors, and particularly features editors, take great pleasure in cutting out particularly good jokes or adding phrases which they think may explain ambiguous passages. Sometimes they are very good at this and sometimes they are appalling. As a writer, one must be prepared to accept this, and realise that one is not a pop star and cannot have a tantrum. Bah.

After editorship, the more officey inclined might choose to be promoted to the role of publisher. This involves wearing a suit (you have to meet a lot of other bigwigs in 'em) and making corporate decisions about the overall direction of your **title**, the profile it has, the readership, the advertising, the page thickness, etc. This is only for the steely – it is very corporate, and you rarely get the chance to go down the Dublin Castle and watch The Fancy Lemons.

Publishers like making lots of rules, so the editor can blame the 'no jokes' policy on someone else. Publishers worry only about selling magazines and could often give nary a bat's wink for the content of the magazine and the amount of corking funnies inside it. The most precious sign of a writer worth their salt is that they've either managed to squeeze in a few jokes, or else they've produced a spectacular and imaginative analogy – likening a well-known rock star to an historical figure from the Repeal the Corn Laws Campaign, for example. I don't recommend that you do this *too* many times.

A BIT ABOUT MAGAZINE BIGWIGS

Mark Ellen is editor in chief at EMAP Metro, who publish *Q*, *Select*, *Mixmag* and *Smash Hits*. He started out working for *Record Mirror* in the late seventies, then worked for *NME* before joining the fledgling *Smash Hits*. Ellen was a top pop scribe during the Adam Ant, ABC, Human League and Soft Cell electropop years – but his aim wasn't to become a venerable music writer. 'I wasn't in it to be a rock journalist,' he says. 'I wanted to work on magazines. I was excited by seeing how magazines were put together.'

Ellen presented BBC2's *Old Grey Whistle Test* with his buddy Dave Hepworth from *Smash Hits*, who had been doing stuff for Radio One then 'drifted into editing magazines' mainly because most of his colleagues couldn't be bothered – they only wanted to hang out with Paul Weller. Ellen's success in the role led to him being given the chance to work in a senior position overseeing all new launches. Mark began this new remit by being part of the team that invented *Q* and has also launched *Mojo* and **relaunched** *Select*, *Mixmag*, and various other titles.

Ellen will find himself discussing the dreams and desires of 25-year-old men with hangovers and a strange laydee in their bathroom at *FHM* editorial meetings during the morning at EMAP, then in the afternoon be involved with *Mojo* bods who are excited because The Byrds have reformed. Ellen enjoys the hands-on aspect of his consultancy role.

'Working on magazines that are doing well, the danger is that you can lazily become self-congratulatory, but I find my time is absorbed by what the day-to-day problems and challenges are,' he reflects. 'But ultimately I have to say I have a fantastic job which is very, very exciting.'

A BIT ABOUT TABLOID JOURNALISM

Tabloid journalism works slightly differently from magazine journalism. For a start, tabloid pop hacks wear smarter clothing because they're always going to lunch with press officers and 'a close friend of the band'. They have a daily deadline by which they have to get in stories, and thus the pressure on them is a lot greater. Matthew Wright is the pop columnist on the *Daily Mirror*. His deadline is around 4.30 p.m. every day and he gets into the office at 10 a.m. and leaves at 7.30 p.m. But it doesn't stop there.

'Then I do my "second job", which is meeting people to bring in stories,' he says. 'Three or four times a week I'm wining and dining, being wined and dined, or attending showbiz parties. On Monday last week I was in Grenada for the Spice Girls' single launch; on Tuesday I came home, ironed my shirt and went straight out to the National TV Awards, and on Wednesday I was wining and dining a PR ... They're incredible hours, but I suppose working for the *NME* is the same – there are gigs to go to.'

Tabloid pop journalism relies on getting stories, and there are many ways to go about finding them. Sometimes there may be an initial phone call from a 'stringer' – someone who supplies stories, or leads to a story, for a one-off fee. Sometimes there may be vague industry rumours

to follow up. Often the press officer of the artist in question will try to give the tabloid a story – probably worried that the hacks will simply make something up if they don't. Some stories are blatantly nicked from music magazines, particularly in the summer when there's nothing happening. At other times the journalist will just stride up to a pop star at a function and asks them if there's anything going on.

'There are many ways of doing it,' says Wright. 'I'm out most evenings and I always aim to come back with something. Sometimes you feel stupid talking to people but, generally speaking, 95% of celebrities are charming and they know I have a job to do. It's easier for everybody if they speak to me – they get the publicity and I go home happy.'

Matthew says he has celebrity friends who come around for tea (although he won't name any names). He says he never makes up stories but that he sometimes might make a slight mistake. He makes every effort to corroborate each story from as many sources as possible.

'I don't get a lot of hassle from people. Noel Gallagher once rang me up screaming blue murder because I'd said the Knebworth concerts weren't very good, but I have the right to say what I feel. Noel and I have kissed and made up since. Paula Yates is a professional story provider to newspapers, but she only wants nice stories printed. She berated me when I said she had her phone cut off despite the fact that I knew for a fact she had.'

There is no established route to learning music journalism until you start doing it. Most writers will claim they 'didn't have a clue' before they were published, and felt they were muddling through while hoping that nobody would suss them out. Interviewing styles vary from magazine to magazine, and writers alter their style accordingly, if only very slightly. The best writers are always after something more than they think anyone else will get and a way to find a different side to the interviewee in question.

SOME POP STARS WILL DESCRIBE THEMSELVES AS A PACKET OF BISCUITS. KNOW YOUR SNACKS.

Often the 'worst' interviews are the best to read. Sylvia Patterson is a master of asking highly individual questions of every star she meets. At *Smash Hits* she was renowned for getting the most from top pop stars by asking apparently spectacularly banal questions. Jon Bon Jovi, after being asked posers like 'Can you cook up a mean spaghetti bolognese?' and 'Have you ever thought life is like an ironing board?', confiscated her questions and ran towards his fellow band members, shouting, 'Guys! Guys! You'll never believe what I've just had to go through!' Similarly, LL Cool J put the phone down on Sylvia when she asked, 'Do you have a goldfish?' Such incidents give an insight into pop-star behaviour which 'How long did it take to record your album?' simply doesn't.

Many journalists go on to broadcasting, and Steve Lamacq, Mary

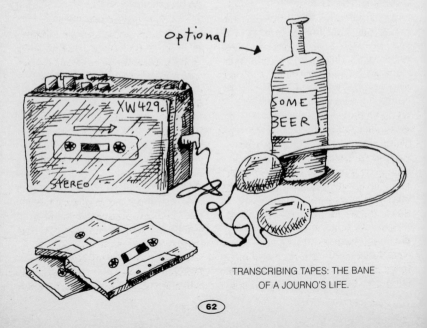

TRANSCRIBING TAPES: THE BANE
OF A JOURNO'S LIFE.

Anne Hobbes, Miranda Sawyer, Andrew Collins and Stuart Maconie are just a few examples of this. Some go on to write books, both fiction and non-fiction. Some even become pop stars, including Neil Tennant, Chrissie Hynde and Bob Stanley from St Etienne.

Very often pop journalism can be deeply frustrating, especially when you have to deal with short deadlines, need to rewrite copy to please the editor, need to transcribe hours of tape (thirty minutes of tape takes over an hour to transcribe), are obliged to write 2,000 words based on a five-minute interview, and – worst of all – need to meet silly pop stars (Sylvia Patterson: 'I don't have a problem with pop stars being stupid. But Sonia took banality into the next dimension.').

Overall, pop writing is just about the next best thing to actually being a pop star. You can sit back and enjoy the travel, the free gigs, the records, and getting to meet hundreds and hundreds of interesting and illuminating people. The very best thing is that, unlike pop stars, you don't get the sack if you're not good-looking enough.

GLOSSARY
● Readers
The people who buy the magazine and dictate what you put in it. They write letters complaining if you don't like Shakin' Stevens or Bon Jovi, and all journalists are obliged to bow down to their infinite knowledge and wisdom. Sort of.
● Unsolicited work
Articles written by a writer without being commissioned. A lot of writers try this and fail because they think a

piece on Jimmy Nail will suit *Private Eye*.
● Feature
All articles, interviews and overviews are referred to as features in the magazine world. Reviews are called 'downpagers' because they run 'down' the page.
● Brief, deadline and word count
These terms are all intrinsic to the awful business of writing a feature. A brief is the angle that your editor wants you to pursue when interviewing a pop star – which line of questioning, which angle you are going in at, which answers the editor wants. The deadline is the day and time of day that the piece has to be in by – and is notoriously rarely observed by journalists. The word count is the exact length of the feature or review. Again, this is often wildly overlooked by the idiosyncratic writer.
● 'Teen' titles
Smash Hits, *Big!*, *Top Of The Pops* magazine and *Sugar* are some of the magazines that have a predominantly teenage audience. Overlooked by pop snobs, teen mags can sometimes contain the best pop stories ever.
● Rival
Melody Maker and *NME* are rivals. So are *Smash Hits* and *Top Of The Pops* magazine. You cannot work for two rival papers: you'll get the sack from one or both.
● Title
Publisher-speak for magazine. Posh publishers always speak of a 'meat and potato' title when talking about a magazine that people tend to buy regularly. They are mad.
● Relaunched
When an existing magazine is given a

severe make-over: redesigned,
different sorts of features, perhaps
different writers and a more specific
content. Sometimes successful;
sometimes not.

SKILLS YOU'LL NEED
Being able to spell, being able to walk
into a room and get on reasonably
well with people you've never met
before, being able to write coherently,
organisation, coping under pressure.

TIPS
● Writing your own fanzine is good
practice in the basic arts and skills of
music journalism.
● Working for student magazines will
give you experience of getting your
work published.
● Reviews editors are the first port of
call for novice freelancers
approaching music magazines. Send a
few examples of your work then call a
few days later for the editor's response.
● Suggest live gigs you can review for
live editors. You have a far better
chance of being given a commission if
you live outside London: *NME* and
Melody Maker are always short of
stringers in Manchester, Birmingham,
Leeds, etc. It's a good way to start.

USEFUL ADDRESSES
● Melody Maker, 26th Floor, Kings
Reach Tower, Stamford Street, London
SE1 9LS.
TEL 0171 261 6229. **FAX** 0171 261 6706.
● NME, 25th Floor, Kings Reach
Tower, Stamford Street, London SE1
9LS.
TEL 0171 261 5813. **FAX** 0171 261 5185.
● Q, EMAP Metro, Mappin House, 1st
Floor, 4 Winsley Street, London W1N
5AR.

TEL 0171 436 1515. **FAX** 0171 323 0680.
● Select, EMAP Metro, Mappin
House, 5th Floor, 4 Winsley Street,
London W1N 7AR.
TEL 0171 436 1515. **FAX** 0171 312 8250.
● Smash Hits, EMAP Metro, 2nd
Floor, Mappin House, 4 Winsley
Street, London W1R 7AR.
TEL 0171 436 1515. **FAX** 0171 636 5792.
● Top Of The Pops, BBC Enterprises,
Woodlands, 80 Wood Lane, London
W12 0TT.
TEL 0181 576 2756. **FAX** 0181 576 3254.

LAWYER

Every aspect of the process of making records and playing live involves contracts, and lawyers are the folk to deal with them. They also sort out the disputes that every band has: mainly fighting the system and each other for cash or credit. They earn a lot of pence for doing so.

'It's all run by lawyers!' Such is the tormented cry of the record industry purist, the soulful individualist who is a bit 'indie'. Lawyers are people for whom 'dressing down' is loosening a tie, or wearing brogues. Lawyers, like accountants, are not known to be very rock 'n' roll. Lawyers like writing things out in neat.

If you fancy yourself as a dazzler in litigation, a sly fox in the world of who owes what to whom, then you'll probably be interested in being a lawyer – or solicitor, as they also like to be known. If you like good tunes and fancy something a bit more exciting than the usual run-of-the-mill suity job, then the music side of the profession is certainly one to think about. In the olden days, musty old lawyers invariably believed that albums always had photographs in them. However, as the entertainment industry grew and grew, some clever firms realised that they could take on these new creative clients *and* get to have a glitzy night out once in a while. Money could be made out of it. And that is, after all, what these types are rather interested in.

To be a lawyer you need to start with a spell at university. You don't necessarily have to plump for the strict law degree as you can always take a conversion course afterwards which lasts a year. Once you've got your law degree, however, you have to do a legal practice course for a year. This covers the practical aspects of the business and subjects like advocacy in court and

EXAM
i lasts hours
ii there's more to come
iii really difficult
iv you won't finish
v it's really sunny
outside
P.T.O.

YOU HAVE TO
ENJOY THESE.

how to deal with clients. You have to enjoy studying in order to be a lawyer, as you can probably gather.

Then you have to do two more years on a trainee contract with a solicitors' firm although, if you've been working on the business side of a record company for a while, the Law Society may reduce your trainee time to a year or so. These two years see you covering the fascinating depths of conveyancing (for buying and selling property know-how), litigation, and company and commercial work. If you've already specialised for your training contract, you'll be taught the intricacies of being an entertainment lawyer. Oh, and there are accounts courses, practice in **client care**, and other practical stuff. Then, and only then, you start looking for a job.

There are now many solicitors specialising in entertainment – and some only deal with music. Bands and recording artists need someone who knows the music industry like the back of their hand and all other parts of their body. This doesn't just involve being able to recite all the Smiths' b-sides in chronological order, including

catalogue numbers. You have to understand the way record contracts are constructed and the way that they change every bleedin' moment depending on whether two-single deals are in, or whether it's ten-album deals. Your job is to get your client – i.e. the band/artist – the best deal possible for them at the time. Knowing who's got what recently, and persuading a record company to give your client the best deal, is imperative. You've got to know your onions, seeing that the current Sony contract is around 75 pages long. It's all *very* grown up.

Harbottle and Lewis are one of the top legal firms in the entertainment business. They deal with, amongst others, Simon Fuller, the Spice Girls' former manager, Robbie Williams, The Manic Street Preachers, Everything But The Girl and Black Grape. The firm deals with film, TV and **multimedia** as well. They also started up an aviation department, dealing with all areas of air travel, when Richard Branson started up Virgin Airlines.

Ann Harrison is a partner at Harbottle and Lewis who did a basic training and then decided after a while that she'd like to work on the entertainment side of things. She started with litigation, which specifically deals with disputes that reach court. She decided to move to the contracts side after six years. Why did she decide to be a lawyer?

'It was the intellectual challenge behind it and the recognised career path. I'm interested in the idea of helping people. You can help a small band who have made mistakes.'

Bands often get the raving hump

with their record companies, their managers, with each other, with famous songwriters who think they've nicked their songs – everyone, really. Up pops a lawyer, making sure no one has to go to jail and ... kercching!! Another five million pounds in the lawyer's pocket!

Most lawyers either work as partners in a company and share the profits and the losses, or as employees of those companies. Some lawyers work in-house for record companies, trying to make sure the record company gets the best deal and that the band can't release twelve mixes of one single whenever they want to – obviously a marvellously creative project, but one that might cost quite a lot of cash. However, record companies are eager that every artist get legal advice, because if the contract they're offering is unfair and the artist signs then gets disgruntled, the artist has a far better case against the cruel record company.

LAWYER

Copyright problems and **sampling** are two of the biggest lawyer headaches. Copyright laws are more complex now that Britain is subject to European as well as UK law. Most record companies have a system for clearing samples, and a standard rate to pay the geniuses who've had their basslines nicked by some goon making a summer snogging record. Again, this is to try to ensure that not many cases end up in court.

Ann Harrison sometimes does put her leather jacket on to go down the Bull and Gate to watch her clients play. She also goes to other gigs to 'see what's happening out there'. She doesn't pick her bands because she likes their tunes. 'If I wanted to do *that*, I'd do A&R,' she says. 'If I knew what made a number one I wouldn't be sitting behind this desk.'

Pop stars are, she warns, a little different from your average client. 'You can't expect them to keep to an 11 a.m. appointment. It'll be 11.30 if you're lucky. But it's good fun. You do get tantrums and egos, and you're not allowed a beer in my office, but I enjoy it. If I'm seeing a client for the first time we may meet in a pub because it's more relaxed. I can imagine it's quite tense for them going to see a lawyer. It's a non-smoking building, but I let them have a cigarette if they want one.'

And so, is the music business really run by lawyers, Ms Harrison? 'Hm ... There are a lot of lawyers at record-company management level – legally trained people. Some companies are more lawyer led than others, but lawyers are, to an extent, indispensable. We oversee contracts for bands, producers, album mixers, publishing, merchandising, managers, tours ... I guess we're part of every single element of the music industry.'

GLOSSARY
● **Client care**
Diplomacy and customer relations. Psychological stuff.
● **Multimedia**
Internet, computer games, CD-Roms. New media involving pictures and sound.
● **Sampling**
The art of nicking other people's music ...

SKILLS YOU'LL NEED
Interest in paperwork and small print, being able to communicate formally and informally with the suits and mohicans alike, interest in money, sense of justice and fairness for all, patience.

TIPS
● A law degree is an absolutely essential first step. There are *no* short-cuts.
● Try to do your training with the entertainment division of a firm.
● You can pick up a nice suit in the high street these days, and it won't cost you an arm and a leg. Arf arf.

USEFUL ADDRESSES
● Clintons Solicitors, 55 Drury Lane, London WC2B 5SQ.
TEL 0171 379 6080. **FAX** 0171 240 9310.
● Denton Hall, 5 Chancery Lane, Clifford's Inn, London EC4A 1BU.
TEL 0171 242 1212. **FAX** 0171 320 6571.
● Harbottle and Lewis, Hanover House, 14 Hanover Square, London W1R OBE.
TEL 0171 667 5000. **FAX** 0171 667 5100.

● Nicholas Morris, 70-71 New Bond Street, London W1Y 9DE.
TEL 0171 493 8811. **FAX** 0171 491 2094.
● David Wineman Solicitors, Craven House, 121 Kingsway, London WC2B 6NX.
TEL 0171 831 0521. **FAX** 0171 831 0731.

MARKETING

MONEY: From around £14,000 for a trainee job at a major company to £30,000 and upward if you've been around for a while.

HOURS: 10 a.m. to 6 p.m. minimum, then a few gigs per week to catch up on the latest vibes.

HEALTH RISK: 7/10. Stressful, and a whole box of posters might fall on your head.

PRESSURE RATING: 8/10. If the whole corporate strategy doesn't work, people seeking a scapegoat often point the finger at marketing, and then laugh cruelly.

GLAMOUR RATING: 6/10. Ringing up and ordering posters isn't exactly the top end of the fancy stick.

TRAVEL RATING: 7/10. Not bad, if you're into going to gigs up and down the country, but you may grind your teeth if you're stuck at your desk while the international executives jet off to Paraguay.

The marketing person plans and coordinates all adverts in the press and on the TV and radio, as well as poster campaigns. Can also be called a product manager.

A h, the wonderful world of marketing! It doesn't exactly conjure up any mental images of vast, spectacular rock 'n' roll excess or high-octane 'Let's stop work this afternoon to play Rummikub!!'-style anarchy, does it? However, music-industry marketing has the potential to be far more involving and stimulating than you may imagine. Obviously it's very important and high-powered and responsible and everything, but it's also essentially challenging and creative. And there are no dodgy greengrocers involved![1]

Marketing, or product management as it's also known, is a job which is in actuality very closely linked to the band or artist it is promoting. The sacred triumvirate who have the task of promoting and exploiting the artist's hot tunes is made up of their management, the A&R person who signs the band to the record company, and the record-company marketing people. These three work together, once the material has been recorded and mixed, and plot a grand strategy. Press and promotions people are then involved further down the line.

The marketing person is in charge of placing adverts in the right places, positioning well-appointed posters around the country, leafleting gigs, etc. With the very top stars and household names, there may be a TV **campaign** to plan. S/he is essentially in charge of **exploiting** the special appeal of the

1. This is a feeble joke about markets and we are very, very sorry.

band and working out how they are going to pick up millions of potential fans – or, if the artist already has a large fanbase, keeping them happy and excited.

There are as many different marketing campaigns as there are types of artist. If the look is geeky, then product managers will geek the band up even more and festoon the nation's buses with the words 'Geeks are cool!'. If the look is ancient-grizzled-old-rocker-croons-the-hits, then the target is all the old rockers who still have an ounce – or a memory – of rock rebellion in their souls, but have to be up by eight on a Monday. Ideally, the marketing exec will love the product they are working with and say, 'Wahey! This band are *great* – but how do I let everyone know that?!'

Jo Power started helping out at the entertainments office at her university and helped to book and promote touring bands. She saw a job advertised for trainee product manager at Sony Records and swotted up all she could before the interview – she went to the library to read **Music Week** and marketing magazines as well as ringing anyone she knew who was even vaguely connected with the business. Jo also found out all the departments at Sony and learnt who the company's main rivals were, and read all the music magazines and watched TV so that she understood which publications and programmes were right for which artists. After one initial interview and a day and a half spent plotting a test marketing campaign for a single release, she was given the job on a Friday – and started the following Monday.

Jo's first major project, after a few months in the job, was Liverpool band The Real People. She also worked with Kris Kross, whom she 'just knew would happen', and Julio Iglesias, which was a relatively straightforward marketing job as old Julio already had a ready-made audience of ardent laydees willing to snatch up his every release. However, she still had to work within a budget to place adverts, talk to the press and promotions people about the campaign and who they would target, liaise with designers about logos and record sleeves, talk to **sales executives**

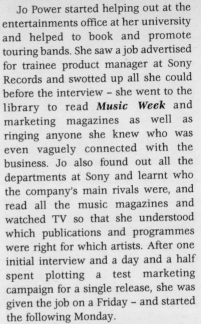

MARKETING MANAGER

about getting the CDs into shops, and place a couple of TV adverts – although television is usually a luxury reserved for only the most well-funded marketing campaign.

Marketing comes with its own built-in frustrations. You have to try and work well with A&R people as it's good to have a vision when working as a team – but, as A&R execs are notoriously opinionated and have their own agenda, personalities can clash. It's also frustrating if you love the band but don't have a big budget to promote them, or if you have to spend your time dealing with American acts who already have *their* people giving *your* people a load of gyp about what they think is right. Then there is the artist's management, who vehemently believe that a full-page colour advert in the *NME* is the right way forward and don't appreciate that's not always the only way to do things. You should also get used to the fact that, when the album's number one and you're feeling jolly pleased with yourself, you get no credit whatsoever – but when the album's not number one you will without doubt find someone poking you in the chest and complaining about the orangeness of the logo, or the fact that the band are wearing deeply unhip Big Shoes on the posters and this was totally your lookout. Oh God.

Marketing people need to have a long-term vision for long-term acts and maintain it within financial constraints. They nearly all work in-house at major companies. Jo Power left Sony after five years to work as marketing manager at Food Records, who are owned by EMI. She thus works very closely with Food's bands, such as Blur, but then has to go through EMI's product-management people. At this smaller, more intimate, company she is far more involved with the A&R people than she was at Sony, and feels far less corporate pressure. As ever with marketing positions, though, she still has a creative job to perform and a lot of people to answer to.

William Higham started out in the press department at Epic Records, then slithered over to marketing and now works for Polydor as a senior product manager. He advises those keen to get involved in music-biz marketing to either take a marketing degree or else get involved in another aspect of the music industry, such as press, so that you form an overview of how the job works before starting it. He cites his marketing philosophy as follows:

'Brian Epstein [legendary Beatles' manager] was once asked how he did what he did with The Beatles. He replied, "I imagined them at number one, and then worked backwards." Ultimately, you have to imagine a triangle. The band is at the top and all the people you can get to and influence are the base.'

Higham has worked with many acts over the years, from The Rolling

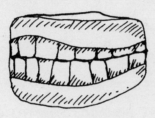

IF YOUR BAND WEAR THESE, YOU HAVE TO MAKE THEM A TRENDY LIFESTYLE ACCESSORY.

Stones to Silver Sun, which was a good example of the marketing process. 'To sell a lot of records you have to present a new band as a gang everyone would like to join,' he reflects. 'It's a package – a lifestyle. With Silver Sun, we thought: Right, there's these guys with skinny ties who are a bit strange, so let's really go for that image. Don't let's hide it. Let's make it cool.' William dealt with Meatloaf, but prefers to work with nippers who've just joined the label because he has the chance to work with them from the start, make their image work, and get them in the charts.

'A number-one album is the ultimate,' he says, 'and the excitement is developing acts from nothing at all to established names. But you can't have an ego, because it's very difficult to quantify exactly *what* it is you do and exactly *how* you help artists. You just have to have a vision and fight very hard, but the reward is that, if you work with a great band who truly understand what you do, and it works, they always say thank you.'

There are also specific independent marketing firms who specialise in arranging for bands to sponsor commercial brands, the obvious example being The Spice Girls putting their name to absolutely everything at the end of 1997. These people liaise with the band and the marketing departments of the companies which make consumer items such as crisps, soft drinks or chocolate. They will also strive to persuade companies to provide tour sponsorship – a growing industry – and so have to organise many, many finger-buffet lunches for surly types from Spot-U-Hate Lotion Ltd who are contemplating putting their name to the next Cast tour. It's a dirty job, but ...

GLOSSARY
● Campaign
The master plan. Every department will have a strategy, a vision. Every single element will combine, hopefully, in getting the artist to the highest chart position possible. Serious business types use this word, and it's also the name of the marketing/advertising trade magazine, too. It will do you no harm to read it.
● Exploiting
All music-business people refer to selling an artist's records as 'exploiting' the artist. A financial term no doubt. A bit dubious, subtextually.
● *Music Week*
Industry rag which details charts, BPI news, industry news, sales breakdowns, management changes, radio play, etc. It is essential to read this when you are starting out.
● Sales executives
The people who work with the distributors in getting the records into the shops. Very important, but not very glamorous.

SKILLS YOU'LL NEED
Long-term vision; diplomacy; to be highly organised and not mind paperwork; keenness to spot the potential in new bands; interest in all aspects of the industry; to be simultaneously inspirational, phlegmatic and self-effacing. Not easy.

TIPS
● A marketing degree might help, but ain't essential.

● A media-studies course will include information on marketing.

● Some business courses feature music-management studies, but do not give you a qualification in music management. The BPI has updated lists of all music courses.

● Start out somewhere in the industry – anything from working at the student-union entertainments office to work experience in a record-company post room will help.

● Practise on your friends by trying to 'market' them to other pals/parents/prospective partners and seeing if it works. You could, however, lose all of your friends because they've gone off with the 'better proposition' of the people you've marketed them to. This, at least, means you are a success ...

USEFUL ADDRESSES

● BMG Records, Bedford House, 69-79 Fulham High Street, London SW6 3JW.
TEL 0171 384 7500 **FAX** 0171 371 9298.

● BPI, 25 Savile Row, London W1X 1AA.
TEL 0171 287 4422. **FAX** 0171 287 2252.

● EMI Records, 43 Brook Green, London W6 7EF.
TEL 0171 605 5000 **FAX** 0171 605 5050.

● Polydor Records, 1 Sussex Place, London W6 9XT.
TEL 0181 910 4800. **FAX** 0181 910 4901.

● Sony Records, 10 Great Marlborough Street, London W1V 2LP.
TEL 0171 911 8200. **FAX** 0171 911 8600.

● Warner Music, 28 Kensington Church Street, London W8 4EP.
TEL 0171 937 8844. **FAX** 0171 938 3901.

MERCHANDISER

MONEY: £9,000 if you've just started helping out, but can rise to £50,000.
Hours: 9.30 a.m. to 6 p.m., with the added option of going to gigs.

HEALTH RISK: 7/10. A box of keyrings may fall on your head, or you could get smothered in promo T-shirts.

EQUIPMENT COSTS: Some companies farm out their work, such as printing, distribution, etc., but the more in-house business there is going on the more money your company is going to make.

PRESSURE RATING: 7/10. If you've got a batch of T-shirts to be done in three days and no one can find the artwork, fairly high. If a band get lured away by a better royalty deal ... hm, well, pretty high stress levels there.

GLAMOUR RATING: 6/10. Some of the wee pop stars might pop in shyly to express concern over a particular shade of blue on their garment.

TRAVEL RATING: 7/10. If you drive the T-shirt lorry, you could find yourself in Basingstoke one day and Norwich the next. If you're big pals of the band, they might let you go to Rome, for example.

A merchandiser deals with T-shirt design, printing and distribution. All other baubles – badges, bags, posters and jackets – will be the responsibility of the merchandiser as well.

L etting everyone know just who your favourite pop star happens to be is not a new pastime. The Beatles had a whole range of merchandise – tights, wigs and figurines are just three saucy items which were sold with the Beatles' name attached. Button badges were very much in vogue in those days, and you can still find little brooches with Ringo on them, but all the John Lennon ones are really rare. Fans have always been proud of their heroes, even if that included The Bay City Rollers. Actually, come to think of it, the more loonish the band, the more lucrative the merchandising opportunity appears to be ...

Merchandising is now big business. Once you have a successful band on your books and are **licensed** to produce all their accessories, you can make a lot of money. There are a handful of major merchandising companies who deal with every stage of the process. The biggest is Underworld, who work with between 150 and 200 bands, including Pulp, Robbie Williams, Ash, Oasis, Embrace and more. There are four A&R people who go around small gigs finding good bands, then talk them into working with their company.

I MADE THIS T-SHIRT

signed a pop star

DON'T LET POP STARS DESIGN THEIR OWN T-SHIRT.

MERCHANDISING

Emma Evans is the A&R coordinator. 'With most bands we do a handshake deal and there's no contract,' she says. 'We're good because we can turn stuff around in three days, whereas most other companies take between five and seven days.'

After a band decides to go with a merchandising company they'll work together on an eye-catching design and decide what sort of shirts they can afford. It's simply no use demanding silk and brocade – artists must have a large guaranteed audience for that kind of finery. There is, however, a very large range of styles nowadays. Fashions vary spectacularly. Trimmed edges were very popular at the height of the so-called mod revival. T-shirts

were once very large; then they got very small indeed. At one stage in the early nineties, 'T-shirt band' was used as an insult. And it was all Carter USM's fault. Well, sort of.

Merchandisers either pay a distribution company to put their T-shirts into shops, or do it themselves. Shops will buy shirts for around £6.40 to £6.90. They then put a 100% mark-up on the shirts so that punters end up paying £13.

'Merch' companies (as they're sort of known) also have to deal with the festivals. Underworld cover Reading, Phoenix, V97, T In The Park and the Fleadh. They make the shirts, drive them up, set up the stalls, handle the official merchandising for the event itself, employ sellers, and then use their in-house accountants to add the whole thing up afterwards. They thus ensure skimpy tops for muddy people, and their own good standing with bands. It doesn't make them much cash; they just like doing it, claims Emma.

The 'profit and loss' deal given to larger artists such as The Charlatans means that Underworld incur all the costs such as manufacture and distribution as well as, when they go on tour with bands, travel, van hire and staff to sell the stuff. They split the profits 75-25 in favour of the band on most occasions, but it can vary. For smaller bands, the company will simply invoice the artists directly for every shirt made up.

Pop merchandising is the sort of job people get into by accident. Nobody wakes up one morning and suddenly says 'I want to get into merchandising!' unless they are a bit loopy. Emma Evans just had a friend who knew that a job was going. 'I said to her, "If you think for one minute I'm making T-shirts, you're dreaming," but then I thought – what have I got to lose? I'd been locked out of my house the night before and I turned up at my interview wearing the same clothes as the day before. The guy who interviewed me asked me who was up and coming. I'd just seen Oasis's first London gig so I told him about them. The next day he rang to say I'd got the job. I'd started working for Oasis by the time they did their third T-shirt.'

There are, however, a few pitfalls. There's often **dead stock** which you can't even give away – in central London there are warehouses full of Boyzone scarves and Big Breakfast T-shirts. Creation band Adorable once produced a respectable range of leggings in an attempt to provide decent merchandising for women.

They sold two pairs, but the upside is that the singer hasn't bought a dishcloth since.

If your merchandising company doesn't sign a contract with the band then another company might nick them by offering better **royalty agreements** or better designs. Some bands have successfully handled their own merchandising. Anthemic baggy pop stars James didn't have the cash to give to a merchandising company in the old days, and thus took T-shirt control. This kept them afloat through the grim times before they got famous, as every single person in Manchester had to have at least one James T-shirt by law. Or so it seemed. James have now signed a merchandising contract with Underworld.

If you're a merchandiser, glamour may occasionally walk in the door in the guise of a pop star pondering exactly what style of sleeve will adequately, if not analogously, define the intrinsic meaning of Boyzone. If you work at Underworld you may well

✔ THIS ONE SELLS.

✘ THIS ONE DIDN'T.

end up swapping fashion hints with Liam Gallagher or Tim from Ash. 'Some of them,' says Emma, candidly, 'haven't got a clue. You show them this colour and that trim but a lot of them aren't very adventurous. They don't understand what sells and what people will buy.'

GLOSSARY
● **Licensed**
Officially allowed by the band to sell T-shirts. Pirates are not allowed to sell, even though they do. You see them outside gigs shouting like fruit-sellers.
● **Dead stock**
Out-of-date T-shirts are common in this whirlwind industry. Tour T-shirts, album-cover designs, etc. all pass their sell-by date quickly.
● **Royalty agreements**
A percentage for every T-shirt sold, rather than a flat fee. Like the record company's points system, the bigger the band, the higher the percentage.

SKILLS YOU'LL NEED
Good business sense – spotting the unit-shifters and deleting the unpopular designs before you lose money on them; a visual eye, obviously; some idea about fashion; a keen eye on the new groups coming up so that you can lure them to your company.

TIPS
● You could try talking to the people who help run the T-shirt stalls at gigs.
● Make friends with young bands.
● If you're a design type, approach companies with ideas – they're always on the lookout for exciting, yet simple, designs.

USEFUL ADDRESSES
● Event Merchandising, Unit 11, The Edge, Humber Road, London NW2 6EW.
TEL 0181 208 1166. **FAX** 0181 208 4477.
● Impact, 137 Devon Mansions, Tooley Street, London SE1 2NT.
TEL 0171 378 0609. **FAX** 0171 378 9559.
● Nice Man Merchandising, Bedford House, 69-79 Fulham High Street, London SW6 3JW.
TEL 0171 973 8585. **FAX** 0171 973 8588.
● Underworld, Unit 6, Princes Court, Wapping Lane, London E1 9DA.
TEL 0171 488 4288. **FAX** 0171 488 3660.

MUSIC PUBLISHER

$ MONEY: Anything between £11,000 and £60,000+.

HOURS: 10 a.m. to 6 p.m. in the office, with evenings and weekends spent seeing gigs in hallowed nightspots up and down the country.

+ HEALTH RISK: 7/10. Signing bands and helping them to develop can be exhausting. Multi-vitamins, please.

EQUIPMENT COSTS: Not a lot, unless you own your own company. It helps if you can drive a car from the off.

PRESSURE RATING: 7/10. The heat isn't on and the competition is slightly less fierce than for A&R men.

GLAMOUR RATING: 7/10. Yes, the stars of today and tomorrow may well come whistling into your office, but you only get to talk to them about Schedule D tax returns on their PRS cheques. And whether they could write a chorus for Dannii Minogue. Sometime. When they get a spare moment.

TRAVEL RATING: 6/10. If the Northampton Roadmender's Club is your idea of an exotic locale, then cheers to you. Otherwise, you may not be roaming very far.

Almost every signed band has a publishing contract. You don't need to have your music published in order to have a top-forty hit, but someone has to collect your songwriting royalties from all over the world, and a publisher will do all the paperwork for you while you can go and try on new shoes for Top Of The Pops.

So you're in a band and a few record companies have expressed an interest. One night, a man in a hairy suit comes up to you after a gig and announces that he is an A&R man from Hairy Suit Publishing, and can he buy you a Campari and soda? You're worried, as well you might be – you've never met his like before.

Publishing is the only branch of the music industry that doesn't manufacture anything. It's thus one of the hardest to comprehend. All publishing companies scout around for new acts in the same way that record companies do. Anybody who writes songs is legally entitled to be paid every time they are played on the radio, or every time someone buys a record. So artists sign a publishing deal, which is a bit like a record contract – they sign up, on average, for between three to five albums. They receive an advance payment, the same as they do with a record contract. Excitingly, they can belong to two different multinational corporations (e.g., a band can sign to Polygram

Island Publishing but release their records on EMI).

Essentially, publishers collect **songwriter** royalties from record companies and TV and radio stations. The recipients are the people who write the music and the lyrics – tambourine players tend not to feature. When bands sign a deal, the money may be split equally but more often than not the main songwriter gets a higher percentage of publishing royalties. Noel Gallagher, for instance, is a lot better off than Bonehead because he writes all those 'mazin' tunes. Louise Wener from Sleeper is the same. Louise from Used-To-Be-In-Eternal *isn't*, because she's happier to trill angelically and leave the **bridge** to somebody else.

Songwriters get royalties from the Mechanical Copyright Protection Society (MCPS) and the Performing Rights Society (PRS). MCPS makes sure that, from every CD pressed, around 8.5% of the **dealer price** is given to the songwriter. PRS deal with TV and radio programmes, which have to pay money to broadcast songs. Pubs and cafés also have to pay the PRS as jukeboxes and radios in a public place count as a 'performance'. However, the PRS may well take ages to wing the 30p round to the artist's door, so as a publisher you'll chase it up for them. For overseas royalties, international publishing collection agencies need to be approached. Tricky, isn't it? There's

YOU DEAL WITH SONGWRITERS WHO MAY NOT HAVE THE RIGHT LOOK TO GET A DEAL OF THEIR OWN. ROBBIE WILLIAMS'S SONGWRITER, ABOVE.*

a lot of paperwork, and that's what publishers are there for.

You *can* get a publishing deal, or get help from a publisher, even before you get a record deal. Mike Smith is Senior A&R Manager at EMI UK Publishing. 'Elastica is the obvious example of this,' he says. 'Justine came to me saying she'd got an idea for a band but only she and Justin the drummer were involved at the time. A guy who worked in our studio knew Annie [who became Elastica's bassist], and Justine found Donna [guitarist] through the small ads in *Melody Maker*. We booked them some early gigs in Windsor under an assumed name to give them practice, then demoed them in our studios, and they got a record deal from that.'

Mike Smith began by managing a band then met some record company A&R people and realised that he'd discovered 'the best job in the world'. He moved to London after university, got a temp job in the post room in the office building which housed MCA Music Publishing, and he got to know the A&R people there.

'I was going out, then telling the guys at MCA what bands I'd seen and who was good,' he says. 'I made a mock card with my name on it and I'd ring venues and blag in. It did get tricky 'cos I started to meet bands and say

* NOT REALLY.

BIG BOOK of tunes to deal with.

BUY.
1. SELL
2. THINK ABOUT

PUBLISHER

them get a manager, an agent, a drummer and bass player ... and a record deal. We have our own demo studio that bands can use. Helping artists to do everything in the early days is possibly the most rewarding part of the job. Publishers are best at launching a band's career, then developing the group until they can go to a record company with a complete package.'

Once a record company is involved they will make the final decision on releases and general strategy, but a publisher can always give advice. Publishing companies also have a soundtrack department, which is essentially involved in pitching music for films and television. The Sneaker Pimps' trip-hoppy single '6 Underground' was re-released after the director of *The Saint* heard it, loved it, and put it in his film. The single was a big hit here and in America as a consequence. Often the soundtrack department will work alongside the director and producer of a film to craft a bangin' contemporary soundtrack which will help the film achieve new levels of youth kudos and help the artists involved sell more of their own records, a classic example of this being *Trainspotting*, which got Underworld heard by thousands more people.

EMI Publishing also deals with individual songwriters, who sign a publishing deal and then sell their songs to singers and bands or work with them in the studio. Paul Lisberg works at EMI Music Publishing handling eighteen songwriters and writer/producers. 'Some songwriters can't get deals because they're not artists. I try to marry their work to any opportunity in which it might get

that I worked at MCA and they'd think "Great!". Before they were signed, the Darling Buds' manager thought it was fantastic that MCA Publishing were interested in them. He didn't know I was just the guy from the post room.'

Smith believes publishers can nurture talent in a way record companies often can't. 'The best part of being a publisher is the chance to work with a band that has no record deal. Sometimes I work with just one songwriter, and then it's my job to help released. Nowadays, you can also get artists working with writer/producers. For instance, producers Stannard and Rowe write with The Spice Girls. 'Wannabe' was co-written with The Spice Girls in the studio – the girls came up with the words and melody and together they built the song.'

Lisberg says his job has got more difficult because nowadays most artists write their own songs and it's regarded as far less credible to work with songwriters, even if you're a pop pancake like The Spice Girls. Paul works with Suggs, Cathy Dennis, Texas, Kavana and Mark Owen and finds them all suitable writers to work with.

Richard Manners is the managing director of Polygram Island Publishing. He began as an A&R scout for Island Records, then hopped over to publishing and worked his way up, with his first hit signing being 'Pump Up the Volume' by MARRS. His signings include Pulp, The Cranberries, The Lighthouse Family and Suede. How does a top bigwig keep a company successful?

'You have to work hard and make sure that, when you have success, you're prepared for it. Don't sit around celebrating that success, then wonder what went wrong. It's like a good football team – having got to first place it actually stays there and builds on that success.'

He trusts his team to pick the good songwriters and to stick with them and encourage them when they're down in the dumps and haven't made it yet. He is still in awe of his acts because he regards them as such good tunesmiths. 'I love them all,' he says. 'I've never lost my passion for a good song.'

When a cover version is released, the publishing money goes to the original songwriter. Wet Wet Wet's 'Love Is All Around' may have earnt them a few bob when it was number one for a billion years, but Reg Presley from The Troggs made a tidy sum as the original songwriter. He then proceeded to spend the entire fortune on investigating the cosmic mysteries behind corn circles, apparently. Ah, well. There you go.

GLOSSARY
● **Songwriter**
The person, or team, who composes the melody, lyrics and chord structure of a song. Songwriter's royalties are often split between the members of a band. They may each get a different percentage of the whole, depending on how key their contribution was. Can cause friction within the band later on.
● **Bridge**
The bit in the song that leads up to the chorus, normally from the verse. It can also lead from the chorus to the verse – hence a 'bridge' between two bits of rockin' tune.
● **Dealer price**
The price at which the CD is sold to the record shop, which varies a great deal, depending on how the record company envisages the product will sell.

SKILLS YOU'LL NEED
Ability to spot a good chorus, irrespective of whether the bassist has a beard or not; communication skills, including being tactful about a ropey verse; sociability; dedication – results aren't often as immediate as in other areas of the industry.

TIPS

● You can get into publishing from a record company; A&R scouting is good practice.

● Media studies courses are invaluable as background training, but won't guarantee a job. Experience counts.

● Take a job in the post room, if you have to, to get a foot in the door.

● Always be aware of different musical trends – whether you personally like them or not. Folk music might come back again. Well, you never know. It *might*.

USEFUL ADDRESSES

● BMG Music Publishing, Bedford House, 69-79 Fulham High Street, London SW6 3JW.
TEL 0171 384 7600. **FAX** 0171 371 7089.

● EMI Music Publishing, 127 Charing Cross Road, London WC2H 0EA.
TEL 0171 434 2131. **FAX** 0171 434 3531.

● Mechanical Copyright Protection Society, Elgar House, 41 Streatham High Road, London SW16 1ER.
TEL 0181 664 4400. **FAX** 0181 769 8792.

● Music Publishers Association, 3rd Floor, Strandgate, 18-20 York Buildings, London WC2N 6JU.
TEL 0171 839 7779. **FAX** 0171 839 7776.

● PolyGram International Music Publishing, 8 St James' Square, London SW1Y 4JU.
TEL 0171 747 4000. **FAX** 0171 747 4467.

● Performing Rights Society, 29-33 Berners Street, London W1P 4AA.
TEL 0171 580 5544. **FAX** 0171 306 4050.

● Sony/ATV Music Publishing, 13 Great Marlborough Street, London W1V 2LP.
TEL 0171 911 8400. **FAX** 0171 911 8600.

● Warner/Chappell Music, 129 Park Street, London W1Y 3FA.
TEL 0171 514 5200. **FAX** 0171 514 5201.

MUSIC-TV PRESENTER

MONEY: From around £16,000, as a BBC presenter starting out, to hundreds of thousands of pounds simply for saying, 'And our next act is …'

HOURS: Ridiculous. Getting up early, staying up late, doing whatever the programme or producer demands.

HEALTH RISK: 7/10. Stress-related: everybody laughs when you make a mistake, and you may have to maintain a rictus grin for hours on end. Will want a face lift by the time you're 32.

PRESSURE RATING: 9/10. You have to get things right on camera, try not to look too hungover, and be reasonably interesting.

GLAMOUR RATING: 7/10. You get to talk to pop stars in exotic locales, go to premieres, be bored by people in suits talking about audience figures, etc.

TRAVEL RATING: 9/10. Hopping about hither and thither, countrywide and abroad, to file on-the-spot reports with Ant and Dec in China or Scarfo in Chingford.

They're in charge of presenting top nuggets of rare insight, hot news, and philosophical interviews on the television – and introducing the bands on Top Of The Pops.

Television is always allowing bands to parade around in moonboots singing songs about traffic cones and doing interviews in which they harp on about the number of raisins you get in Fruitibix. The wibbly wobbly world of the pop star fits like a glove into the bright and breezy world of TV. But! The medium needs someone to translate the genius of the bands for the audience! A presenter! Presenting is like being a magazine journalist for the telly, except you're not allowed to be so bitter and twisted and you have to smile a lot more.

Despite its appearance, presenting isn't something you can have a go at just because you've got good teeth. Most people have to spend years working behind the scenes in television before they get in front of the camera. Some people may appear to be novices, but even they'll have gone for trillions of auditions and screen tests and been subjected to the umming and ahhing of The Powers That Be. You can't just ring up Visio-Tunes Productions and demand that you present *That's My Bassline!!* next Monday, although they may appreciate your gumption and take you on as a **runner**.

Which is how many people first start out on the rocky road towards being a presenter. Runners may spend their time making cups of tea for people, but just being on the inside of a production company will help you learn how television programmes are commissioned and made. Researchers,

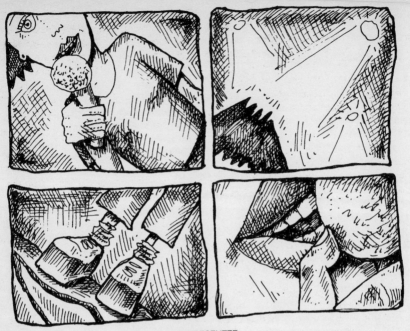

TV PRESENTER

the next step up from runners, are there to liaise with promotions people to get the gen on new releases and who's around for interviews and performances. The final decision on which artists will appear on the programme rests with the producer, and the researcher then books them and gets hold of press clippings, videos, and general info so the presenter can swot up on them. Most presenters will have a huge turnover of very varied guests – but will need to know their onions all the time.

There are many routes into the job. Jonathan Ross was a researcher before he became a TV presenter. Mark Lamarr was a stand-up comedian. Dani Behr was a failed pop star. Dannii Minogue is *still* a pop star. There are a fair few ex-journalists wielding a mean microphone. A lot of presenters on the main four British networks started through cable and satellite television. Zoë Ball was a runner then a researcher, and she believes this is the best way to learn the ropes. Her first break was through 'a friend of a friend of a friend' starting on a kids' show in Manchester which went out on BSkyB (now Sky television). Promoted to researcher, Zoë set about attending auditions and **screen tests** for presenters because that's what she decided she wanted to do (after toying with the rival ideas of acting and journalism – no train driving for this one).

'At first I'd get so nervous that I'd bodge things up,' she remembers. 'I'd speak much too fast and I had to be a lot more controlled – but auditions and screen tests *are* terrifying things.' After a couple of screen tests Zoë 'began to wonder why I was bothering'. She hadn't realised how fierce competition was for this particular line of work. However, she eventually got a job as researcher for *The Big Breakfast*. She is keen to emphasise that she did it all off her own bat: her dad is ex-TV-presenter Johnny Ball, but Zoë was far too mortified to ask him for help and opted not to mention the connection to potential employers. Next up she went for a job on *Going Live!* and her screen-test tape was passed on to a bigwig at Children's BBC who rang her to ask her to join the CBBC team. She was in!

Zoë Ball says the BBC is good at training people, rather than simply chucking newcomers in front of the camera as some channels tend to. The BBC, even today, tends to be loyal, has lots of job opportunities, and is more reputable than some small independent companies who work presenters to the bone for very little cash. Zoë started off doing birthday links and built up her confidence through this small, lower-profile stuff on CBBC. It's good training, and far better than being suddenly plucked from nowhere to be the pressured and high-profile new presenter on *The Word* – anybody remember poor **Huffty**?

Ms Ball had a spell on *The O-Zone*, interviewing surly pop stars and chirpy rock types alike, before moving on to *Fully Booked* and similar youngsters' programmes. She was then asked to present *Live and Kicking* and quickly became the gleeful face of Saturday mornings, happily sweet and kiddy-friendly, while also appealing to chaps who quite liked the fact she wore satiny trousers and looked like she might have had a few too many the night before.

TV presenting is a very hectic job. There are invariably early starts and late finishes, and then there are interviews and promotions to publicise the programme. Zoë spends Fridays working on preparation for *Live And Kicking!*: script meetings, finalising the running order, going through readers' letters, watching pre-taped pieces, etc.

The job can, on occasions, be an endurance and initiative test. It's tough trying to interview someone **live on air** who's got out of the wrong side of bed that morning and can't be arsed to talk. If they're your heroes, it's even tougher – you mustn't get starstruck on screen. 'You might get someone who doesn't know or care who you are and has done sixty-five interviews already so they're bored stupid,' says Zoë. 'And sometimes I'm made to ask questions I don't want to! I'm told, "You *will* ask so-and-so about his private life, you *have* to!" There are things I wouldn't want to be asked, so I hate doing it to other people.'

Jobs on the telly can lead to many other lines of work, with DJing being an obvious example. Jonathan Ross did a spot of turntable twiddling after the telly, and Chris Evans has a sky-high profile on both. Zoë was given the job of co-hosting the Radio One breakfast show in autumn 1997: a job she finds hugely enjoyable.

Overall, the career opportunities for a successful presenter are immense, even more so if you become an intrepid businessperson and start your own production company, Chris Evans/Ginger Productions-style. Obviously, you have more power within the industry, more control over what you do, and loads more cash as head of a company. Buy all the Prada rucksacks you wish! Shout at people in board meetings! Reassuringly, however, not everyone is like that though.

'I'm a realist,' says Zoë Ball. 'I know I don't have a head for business – I'm not manipulative enough. I really have no idea about business and finance – I just push that side of things away and smile!'

Presenting is not something that everyone can do, even though it may seem a wheeze and an absolute doddle from the outside. Some people, however, are naturals – they get in front of a camera and make talking about Radiohead's new promotional pyjamas seem like the most natural thing in the world.

'A lot of people act when they're trying to present, but you have to be yourself,' says Zoë. 'Someone told me when I first started out that I should imagine there's one small child sitting at home on their own and you have to make them feel that you're their friend. You have to be cheerful, no matter how crappy you're feeling or how crappy your life is that day.'

Naturally, appearing on television comes with its own inbuilt pressures. Everyone knows who you are so, when you've got flu and have to go to the chemist, when you're out at a film premiere with a new hunk, or when

PEOPLE HATE YOU 'COS YOU'RE ON TELLY AND TRY TO SPILL THIS ON YOUR TROUSERS.

you're putting out the rubbish in your dressing gown, people will spot you. Inevitably you get called things in the street and people deliberately spill their pint on your trousers because they hate you just for being on telly. One ex-presenter says, 'I'll never do it again. I don't mind being successful, but not on television. It can screw you up if you start young.'

'People expect you to smile and be charming all the time,' says Zoë. 'Sometimes I wish people would leave me alone. The papers build you up and knock you down. You just have to not take it too seriously, or yourself too seriously.'

PRESENTER PRESSURES ALSO INCLUDE:

a) The fact that there are fewer and fewer presenter-led shows. *The Chart Show*, for instance, is a good example of a successful music programme that has no goon in a revolving tie japing around between promos.

b) The fact that presenters go in and out of vogue very rapidly. Whither Keith Chegwin?

c) You can't take loads of holidays and very often you have to work at weekends and Christmas.

d) If you're a woman, you're more likely to get patronised by some colleagues and under-valued by others (although this may arguably apply in every job, ever).

e) Because you're famous, all your mates will think you're loaded and everyone will expect you to buy them loads of beer. Zoë Ball recalls that when she joined *The Big Breakfast* she earnt six times the amount she had in previous jobs (mainstream independent telly pays better then the BBC) but lavished most of it on her impoverished friends. 'And I'm a shopaholic,' she adds. 'I spent a fortune – but I really don't know what on.'

Top presenters invariably have agents. Zoë Ball's agent is Peter Powell, who used to be a presenter and DJ himself in the seventies and eighties. He negotiates deals for her, gives advice, and sorts out good offers from bad. His roster includes Anthea Turner (his ex-wife), Andi Peters, Darren Day, and many others.

Zoë's advice for budding presenters is to get into drama clubs, work on the school magazine, and generally put yourself about a bit. If you ring up TV and production companies and offer to do work for nothing at weekends and holidays, you might be lucky and they might need someone. Even if you have had no experience of telly, the fact that you've done other things, like drama, shows people you have an interest in performing. Follow the charts, watch presenters, and work out why you like the ones you do – what their special bit of magic is. As mentioned above, there are many youngsters doing work experience or working as runners in television who will eventually go on to do other, far more exciting, things – but not without a lot of determination.

Zoë is very honest about her job, which she adores. 'I love my job, I fully recommend it – but at the same time there are other sides,' she concludes. 'It's not always glamorous and you're not always up for it! But you get paid a fortune and it's a great laugh – I honestly don't know what else I'd do.'

GLOSSARY
● Runner
The tea boy/girl position. Runs errands, mails things out, files pieces of paper, rings up other runners when things are needed from other companies. Also, goes out to Prêt à Manger to get the presenter a poncey sandwich.

● Screen tests
When you present a piece of news, gossip or off-the-top-of-your-head nonsense in front of a video camera. You might have to interview someone. Generally, they put you under the same pressure as a TV presenter live on air, to test you out. The director watches all of them afterwards and decides who to employ.

● Huffty
Ill-fated TV presenter who was roped in to present *The Word* because she was deemed 'alternative' (a lesbian in City braces). Didn't quite work out because she was so transparently employed for only this silly reason. She left after one series.

● Live on air
Some programmes are pre-recorded; others go out as they happen. Live TV is very demanding and extremely difficult to master: you have to be prepared for anything to happen (pop stars swearing and the like).

SKILLS YOU'LL NEED
To be natural in front of a camera; to be able to get on with kids, suits, and rock stars alike; to be interested in not just music but the world and people and their pets; to look reasonably cheery.

TIPS

● Get work experience – helping at weekends with independent companies or the BBC is ideal. Ring them up to find out what sort of people they require. Any foot in the door is good.

● Watch other presenters and see how they do it.

● Never try to copy anyone. It'll end in humiliation and tears.

● It's best to realise that you won't be on *Top Of The Pops* next Friday. The rungs of the ladder have to be scaled and there are no short cuts.

USEFUL ADDRESSES

● BBC, TV Centre, Wood Lane, London W12 7RJ.
TEL 0171 743 8000. FAX 0171 749 7520.

● Channel 4, 124 Horseferry Road, London SW1P 2TX.
TEL 0171 396 4444. FAX 0171 306 8351.

● Channel 5, 22 Long Acre, London WC2E 9LY.
TEL 0171 421 7100. FAX 0171 497 5222.

● Granada, Quay Street, Manchester M60 9EA.
TEL 0161 832 7211. FAX 0161 953 0298.

● L!VE TV, 1 Canada Square, London E14 5AP.
TEL 0171 510 3900. FAX 0171 293 2166.

● MTV Europe, 17–19 Hawley Crescent, London NW1 8TT.
TEL 0171 284 7777. FAX 0171 284 7788.

● Planet 24 Productions, The Planet Building, Thames Quay, 195 Marsh Wall, London E14 9SG.
TEL 0171 345 2424. FAX 0171 345 9400.

● VH-1, The Interchange, 32 Oval Road, London NW1 7EP.
TEL 0171 284 7777. FAX 0171 284 7755.

MUSIC-TV PRODUCER

💰 MONEY: From a few hundred quid per show if you're working on cable or after-dark programmes, to thousands and thousands per year on mainstream programmes.

⏰ HOURS: From a couple of days to more than seventy hours a week.

➕ HEALTH RISK: 7/10. Having to work with people 'in television' is enough to give anyone permanent heartburn, at least.

💪 PRESSURE RATING: 9/10. It's your job to make sure the programmes are top quality and have artists that people want to hear.

🍸 GLAMOUR RATING: 7/10. You get to talk to the stars about how they want their close-up, then force a rictus grin if they don't agree with you.

✈ TRAVEL RATING: 6/10. Mainly working from your office, the studio, and perhaps some location work.

Music-TV producers are the people that book all the sumptuous new sounds on to their programme and are responsible for providing a good visual bed for tunes to lie down on, as it were.

Y ou'd think getting a band on to TV would be easy. They have a hit single, you like them, they have a spare afternoon and wooh! They're playing live to an audience of several million with time for a chip supper in the **canteen** before they whizz off home to catch *Brookside*. Not so! Putting pop stars on the box is the job of the TV producer, and it is a lot of hard work. Producers deal with the whole programme: it's their vision; they're the ones who ultimately have to come up with ideas and the feel of the series they're working on. They have to make pop stars either look a bit shiny, or a bit pasty, or ugly – whatever the remit they've invented for themselves is.

Chris Cowey is the producer of *Top Of The Pops*. He works with a team of only two other people – a coordinator and a production assistant. Unlike any other music show, *Top Of The Pops* is on every single week of the year.

Chris started DJing in his local town of Sunderland while he was doing his A levels. 'Television was not something I ever considered,' he says. 'Nobody in their right mind does.' However, some Tyne Tees TV representatives came to one of his disco nights and filmed it, and then their head of children's programmes asked him if he'd audition as a presenter for the station. Cowey began work on a kid's programme called *Check It Out* within a few weeks.

'I decided I liked the look of the whole TV lark,' he says. 'But I thought: Surely this can't be a long-term job! I soon realised that the power and the glory lay behind the camera.' Cowey stopped DJing and threw himself into TV work. He would sit in and watch programmes being edited, and gradually learnt the practicalities of

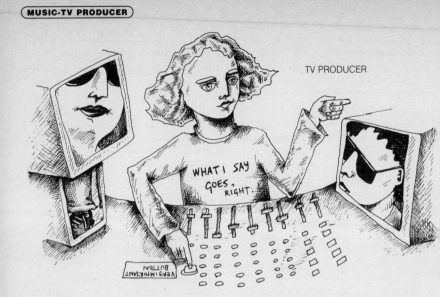

TV PRODUCER

WHAT I SAY GOES, RIGHT.

VERY IMPORTANT BUTTON

how television programmes are made. This was the foot in the door which every aspiring youngster needs.

At the time, Tyne Tees was developing *The Tube*, a seminal early-eighties rock and yoof-culture programme which came out live from Newcastle every week and was presented by Paula Yates, Jools Holland and Leslie Ash. Chris was made trainee researcher in 1982 and in the meantime continued to present local programmes as he worked his way up to becoming *The Tube* producer.

However, in 1987 **deregulation** was the new Thatcherite television mantra and Cowey saw which way the wind was blowing: he left Tyne Tees before the last series of *The Tube* and hopped into the world of freelance production. With colleagues, he invented a whole different kind of toons-based, no-frills show called *The White Room*, which went out on Channel Four. He also turned *The Brit Awards* round from

being the silliest show on earth (the year Samantha Fox and Mick Fleetwood did their no-brainer routine remains a seminal pop-TV moment) to something very good (talented presenters, top bands, etc.). At the start of 1997 the BBC asked him to produce *Top Of The Pops*.

'It took me all of five seconds to say, "Not half!"' he admits. 'With *The White Room* we built it up from the very start. *Top Of The Pops* not only goes out 52 weeks every year but it's been going for 34 years. If it was a ship you'd put it in dry dock for a while. But you can't take the show off the air: the public outcry would be huge. I inherited the existing budget and the existing set, and I hate and loathe the set – it looks like a German kitchen, all stainless steel. I hate the logo and the theme tune. I will be changing *all* of that.'

So far, Chris is proud because he's hidden most of the stainless-steel scaffolding 'in bandages' and made most artists sing live, with their video as backdrop. He's also banished the **camera script** so that it's all more loose and exciting and terribly rock 'n' roll. Hey! A band can wave their hands in the air and the camera might actually catch it! Cowey says his input is total – after all, he doesn't have many staff. He's both the producer and director: 'Basically, I have arguments and meetings with myself.'

The essential difference between producer and director is that the producer comes up with ideas and makes sure things stick to a budget. The director turns the ideas into reality and works within the boundaries the producer has set. 'The rest of the team are there to make the producer and director look good,' reckons Chris. These people do the boring stuff such as booking stars, getting them to the studio on time, and making sure they know what's going on.

Producers and directors are the top dogs, so 'you have to have the common sense not to turn into a dickhead', says Chris. However, he's already enjoyed a very proud moment, when he finally realised the show was *his* baby. A few weeks prior to taking charge, he'd gone to see *Top Of The Pops* being recorded and seen soul singer Rosie Gaines miming to her single. He'd previously seen her sing with Prince and thought she had an 'amazing' voice. Her bassist was a chap called **Tubs** who was equally fab.

'Tubs and I had a beer after the show,' recalls Cowey. 'I said, "Listen, mate, I'm taking over this show – will you come back and do this live?" He said that he'd love to. So a few weeks later we were halfway through shooting Rosie live and the vibe

around the place was wonderful. When it finished, an old guy who I knew was an old member of staff walked over and said, "Excuse me, mate, you don't know who I am, but what I've seen tonight is what the programme's been waiting for for thirty years." I just thought: Yeah, that's it! I've cracked it!'

Producers, and televisual people in general, have a reputation for being loud, arrogant tossers who stamp about trying to be important. They 'do lunch' possibly even more than music-biz types. Or, at least, this is the generally received wisdom.

'There is a huge amount of mythology surrounding TV,' contends Cowey. 'People say it's really competitive, pressurised or hard work. Well, from the first time I walked into a TV studio I've been trying to find the hard bit. To me, it's like being paid for a hobby. I work seventy hours every week but it's so much fun. I'm from a mining family in Sunderland, and true pressure is working a mile underground in a three-foot-high coal seam with six inches of water around you! No, TV is sheer fun.'

Ideas are the solid-gold currency of TV production, and sadly they can prove very vulnerable to exploitation from cynical people. New TV shows have to go through the **pilot stage**, and TV deregulation means you have to employ a production company to pay for the pilot. Now, if they pay you to produce the programme, many such production companies rather cynically assume they've also paid for the original idea. Many people get ripped off in this game and a lot of players are utterly ruthless.

Some TV producers fall into the job virtually by accident while for others it's a mission they pursue devoutly. Lee Lodge, one of the directors of *The O Zone*, engineered his first break by writing hundreds and hundreds of letters to production companies, all wrapped in unusual parcels (the one he is proudest of contained jelly babies) to get attention. He ended up being given work experience as a researcher at MTV and progressed from there to producing – so such lateral thinking can pay dividends when you're first trying to draw attention to yourself.

By contrast, Tim Byrne decided at university that music-TV production was his calling, applied for jobs and attended interviews with gritty determination, and now produces the annual *Smash Hits Poll Winners Party*. Once you've got your foot on to the first rung of that ladder, your ascent may be excitingly swift.

Chris Cowey, after fifteen years in music television, still finds the job stimulating and relatively glamorous. 'There are boring bits,' he concedes, reluctantly. 'You sit in an office a lot and, like any job, have to spend some time dotting 'i's and crossing 't's. But, basically, every week really pleasant and very famous people come down to my studio and we get on pretty well and have a beer in the bar afterwards. I just think: Fantastic! This is my *job*! This must be how footballers feel when they play for Liverpool.'

GLOSSARY
● **Canteen**

All TV studios have a basic canteen which sells cheap food, but is inhabited by the influential and famous at all hours of the day, drinking pop and playing Gameboys.

● **Deregulation**

Independent companies can make programmes for any of the main terrestrial (i.e. not satellite or cable) stations. Therefore, they can get away with paying people what they want, making cheaper programmes, or more populist stuff. It's a free market.

● **Camera script**

Schedule of all the camera angles: at what time, in what order, etc. Rather boring and not very rock 'n' roll.

● **Tubs**

Good live musicians are often called silly things like Tubs.

● **Pilot stage**

Every show on telly has had a pilot made: a practice show to give the TV station an idea of the content, tone and design of the programme. Nothing to do with aeroplanes.

SKILLS YOU'LL NEED

Chris says you need to be: calm, organised, adaptable, have a sense of humour, be a born optimist, be capable of lots of lateral thinking.

TIPS

● Start by getting your foot in the door: do work experience, write lots of letters to TV stations.

● Learning camera technique isn't really necessary. Few people come from the technical side; most come from researching and presenting.

● Journalism courses are good training for researching. A media-studies background is also a good starting point.

● Simply, if you have a brilliant idea and some knowledge of the media, you can approach an independent TV

company with a view to producing a
pilot.
● Practise on your friends by inviting
local bands to their houses and seeing
if they want to hear their tunes or
not.
● Well, it's a start.

USEFUL ADDRESSES
● BBC, TV Centre, Wood Lane,
London W12 7RJ.
TEL 0171 743 8000. **FAX** 0171 749 7520.
● Channel 4, 124 Horseferry Road,
London SW1P 2TX.
TEL 0171 396 4444. **FAX** 0171 306 8351.
● Channel 5, 22 Long Acre, London
WC2E 9LY.
TEL 0171 421 7100. **FAX** 0171 497 5222.
● Granada, Quay Street, Manchester
M60 9EA.
TEL 0161 832 7211. **FAX** 0161 953 0298.
● L!VE TV, 1 Canada Square, London
E14 5AP.
TEL 0171 510 3900. **FAX** 0171 293 2166.
● MTV Europe, 17–19 Hawley
Crescent, London NW1 8TT.
TEL 0171 284 7777. **FAX** 0171 284 7788.
● Planet 24 Productions, The Planet
Building, Thames Quay, 195 Marsh
Wall, London E14 9SG.
TEL 0171 345 2424. **FAX** 0171 345 9400.
● VH-1, The Interchange, 32 Oval
Road, London NW1 7EP.
TEL 0171 284 7777. **FAX** 0171 284 7755.

PERSONAL TRAINER

MONEY: From £15,000 to £40,000 per year – or freelance, paid by the hour, if you're just starting out.

HOURS: Starting early in the morning (you know how people like to jog) to evening time.

HEALTH RISK: 7/10. You may drop a barbell on your foot, or trouble yourself going for that all-important last bench press.

EQUIPMENT COSTS: If you own your own gym, you'll have to pay for the machines. However, freelance trainers do use public gym facilities.

PRESSURE RATING: 5/10. Getting the stars to find some motivation isn't always the easiest thing.

GLAMOUR RATING: 5/10. You see famous people sweat. Not so glitzy.

TRAVEL RATING: 3/10. To the gym. Around the park. Only if you work for someone like Madonna will she ship you around the world with her curling tongs.

Fitness instructors help many pop stars keep lookin' good and feelin' great. There are such a lot of opportunities to eat badly and sit around a lot that many artists are gagging to get on a rowing machine for twenty minutes every day.

Pop stars sometimes get lardy around the middle. One day they'll look in the mirror, or espy a particularly ropey picture of themselves, and realise it's time to slim down. Personal trainers are the people to give them motivation to jog around. Where would Peter Andre be today without his sparkling **chest teeth**? What price Eternal if they didn't go to the gym for their **butts'** sake? And Robbie Williams? Exactly. He didn't shrink because he got left out in the rain, you know.

John Plum has his own company, the London Fitness Consultancy Ltd, and trains pop stars like Sarah Cracknell from St Etienne to get fit and slinky. He started out by getting a sports science degree – concentrating on biomechanical analysis(!). No rugby was played; it was strictly theoretical stuff: how muscle strength affects movement, for instance. The degree course is combined with chemistry and maths, psychology and sociology, and more stuff about exercise.

A lot of trainers aren't all that qualified, and so if you do a tough university course like the one above it should help you to get a good job ... eventually. Most trainers start out being fairly badly paid but working in the leisure industry is attractive and you get free turns on the stair-o-lator, which means that a lot of people want to do the job.

John started at the Champneys Health Club below the Meridian Hotel in Piccadilly, London, as a fitness instructor assessing people and devising exercise programmes. 'The pay was atrocious,' he remembers.

The next step for a muscly type is to go into management – but, again, it's not that well paid and there's lots of paperwork to do. John therefore decided to go travelling and looked around Australia and North America to see how the fitness industry worked there. This turned him into a man on a mission – to become a personal trainer.

Being a personal trainer involves dealing directly with individual keep-fitters and being with them at every session or alternate session in order to monitor their progress and keep their motivation levels up. A personal trainer is neither a nutritionist nor a doctor, but you should certainly know the basic ins and outs of healthy eating and first aid.

Some experts train people in their homes if they have enough room to fit in a rowing machine and treadmill. Other trainers take them out to the park to jog around the ponds. John started a gym in west London with two other trainers by converting an old industrial unit. It's all by appointment only. So what are these stars like to work with?

'Mostly they're nice people,' says Mr Plum. 'I wouldn't treat them any differently from anybody else. I've met some trainers who think it's important to get a few stars so they can then raise their prices. I'm into this to improve people's health. Celebrities are all well and good but we can never view them as long-term clients. They're not easy clients, through no fault of their own. They travel a lot and you don't see them for months.'

John says he never gets free T-shirts or gold discs. He charges £45 per hour but admits it's hard to take holidays and the levels of work are inconsistent. However, seeing plumpies develop glistening pecs and thighs of steel is recompense enough. He also thanks his lucky stars he's never got into too much bother with clients.

'My friend is a trainer in LA. He was hired by a film studio to help a star lose a few pounds. He was going to get $20,000 to work two hours per day for three months. The trainer was pleased

WARNING. SOME CLIENTS MAY
HAVE SHOES THAT ARE PRICIER
THAN YOUR EQUIPMENT.

SKILLS YOU'LL NEED

Ability to get on with people, being
fit, knowing about the human body
and fitness, knowing about how the
expensive weight-trainers work, being
muscly so people think that you know
what you're talking about. Looking
like Charles Hawtrey won't help.

TIPS

● The better qualified you are, the
better the job you will get – and the
better job you will do. A degree in
sports science is a good way to start.
● You have to be interested in
exercise and have at least played a bit
of lacrosse in your time. It's no use
explaining how the abs develop if you
don't possess any yourself.
● Gain experience in a health club. At
least you'll have access to the abs
machine. Some people start as
members and become instructors.

to do it because it was good for his
kudos and it was good money – he got
half the money up front. The star took
a fancy to the trainer and told him, "If
you don't do exactly what I say you
ain't gonna get the money." He didn't
continue with the job. There are some
unscrupulous people out there.'

GLOSSARY

● **Chest teeth**
Or 'abs', as they are also known.
Abdominal muscles are cubey and
bobbly and spring out if you do about
a hundred sit-ups a day. They look
like teeth, a bit, if you hold your head
at a 90° angle. Watch out for them.

● **Butt**
Bottom.

● **Kudos**
Very important in the world of
entertainment. Kudos is the glory that
you'll garner from being involved in
something trendy or well-respected. It
usually does not last unless you've
discovered a cure for a disease, or
something.

PHOTOGRAPHER

MONEY: Varies. Photographer's assistants often work for nothing when they start, and yet top photographers get paid in the thousands for shooting album campaigns and tour programmes.

HOURS: 'About 24 hours a day, every day,' many of them say. You can start a shoot at five in the morning and it can go on until well past midnight.

HEALTH RISK: 8/10. Those developing fluids aren't kind to the system, especially if you start drinking them.

EQUIPMENT COSTS: Fairly high. Camera equipment is being constantly updated and a new lens alone can set you back £1,000. You may have to pay your own film and developing costs for magazines, and these can easily be at least a couple of hundred quid.

PRESSURE RATING: 8/10. If you have two minutes to take a picture for the cover of *Smash Hits*, which is often the case, then the pressure is high. However, most photographers survive on the adrenaline. Man.

GLAMOUR RATING: 9/10. You get to meet top celebrities and have to ask them to 'Please stop doing that with your nose' and so forth. You may go on tour with a band and be mistaken for the bassist's aunt in Ohio.

TRAVEL RATING: 9/10. You go all over the ruddy place. However, you must always remember to complain about how heavy your equipment is and how you don't want customs to scan your bag with sensitive film in it.

Every band needs their picture taken, and they have to rely on someone who won't put their finger over the lens.

There has never been, in the sizzling history of rock 'n' roll, a band who didn't have their picture taken. Well, not one that was any good, anyway. Rock *artistes* are never happy with one little snap. They want rolls and rolls of film: different ones for every magazine article, single release and tour. Hair up, hair down, with a new moustache, dressed as a prawn ... Bands always need someone to press the shutter in new and dynamic eye-startling ways.

There are many courses in photography from GCSE and HND right up to degree level. Some budding snappers start with a course – although many more don't – then graduate to helping out already established photographers in the studio and on location shoots, which is generally known as 'assisting'. John Spinks, who works for *The Face* and various other magazines, rang around the photographic studios he found in *Yellow Pages*.

'Eventually I phoned Metro studios,' he says. 'I spoke to someone there and explained who I was, and he said, "What are you doing next Friday?" So I borrowed money from my mum to go down from Manchester to London for a couple of days. In the end they gave me a job but it didn't pay – they bunged me a bit of cash on the side and I carried on claiming dole money.

'When you are an assistant, you are basically a skivvy,' reckons Spinks. 'You do menial things such as sweeping up, painting **the infinity cove** and doing the washing-up. You're below even the bottom rung of the ladder.' John soon became the assistant to swanky fashion photographer Jurgen Teller, and then started a photography collective called Sixsixfour.

Tom Howard, who's a top *Smash Hits*-type snapper, started out as a freelance assistant then worked full time for lensperson Simon Fowler, who created his own distinctive style of brightly coloured bouncy pop images which every pop band of the late eighties and early nineties wanted.

'I gained confidence from that experience because I felt I had plenty of creative input,' says Tom. 'I reached a stage when I would be standing beside him, thinking: I can do this. After two years I decided to move on and do my own thing, and then I realised how difficult it actually is. Suddenly you are the photographer and the buck stops at you.'

Valerie Phillips also began working at *Smash Hits*, and now has sessions with Tricky and PJ Harvey and swanky fashion shoots in her portfolio. However, she never even studied photography or assisted anyone.

'I was completely unqualified,' she says. 'I studied a foundation course at art school in New York. It was a four-year course, of which I did one year. Then I moved to London and started going to concerts and taking live photos of bands and showing them to people who might know someone who wanted some pictures done on the cheap. I was rubbish, but I had a lot of enthusiasm and did whatever it took to do a job.'

Valerie persuaded the then manager of The Manic Street Preachers to let her take pictures of the band live. He liked the photos, and she was consequently commissioned by the band to do a couple of record sleeves. This led to work for *Smash Hits* taking pictures of New Kids On The Block, Take That, and all the other young nippers on the scene. She was such a novice when she started, having blagged her way in, that before her first studio session – with Van Morrison – she had never even used **lights** before. For another session, she put the film through the wrong process and completely melted it. Luckily she had another few rolls which she processed very carefully and correctly. 'I was mortified, but I never owned up,' she recalls.

Magazines employ a picture editor (see 'Picture Editor' chapter) to commission **photo shoots** for features and other items. And once you work regularly for a magazine such as *Smash Hits* you're strongly discouraged from working also for rival titles such as *Top Of The Pops* magazine. The *NME* and *Melody Maker* still pay photographers according to the size of the picture used on the page, but all other magazines pay a day rate to cover the shoot, cost of film, developing and the pictures.

A few months after the publication that commissioned you has used your pictures, you can sell them on to a **picture agency** who may syndicate them worldwide, mainly to foreign magazines who can't get an exclusive shoot with a band. There is a lot of money to be made in syndication, but top pop bands like The Spice Girls or All Saints will nowadays make you sign a form which promises that you won't syndicate the shots, as this inevitably means that the band lose revenue from their own merchandising sales. Tough, isn't it?

Record companies commission their own photos to send out to the press (for use alongside news stories, small articles or simply for their files) or for album

YOU MIGHT SPEND MOST OF YOUR TIME PERSUADING YOUR POP STARS NOT TO WEAR SHADES.

and single sleeves. After a certain amount of time working for magazines, record-company types will get to know your name and ask you to take a picture for Suzi Quatro's comeback record, for example. If they get to really like your work, you may be sent on Suzi's round-the-world tour to shoot snaps for a tour programme, for worldwide press pictures for the record company to use, or perhaps even eventually for a book of Suzi's *currazy* exploits. This, as they say, rakes in the cash. You'll also see the

world's hotel bars, from Bahrain to Bournemouth. You may, however, find yourself missing your cat at home after a few weeks.

For each job you will be given a brief by the commissioning editor or record company – you are told exactly what sort of shots is wanted. This can get a little complicated, says Tom Howard. 'The worst brief is where there are four or five people involved in a job and they all have different ideas as to what should be happening as far as pictures are concerned,' he says. 'My job is to please all of them *and* the people in front of the camera. The easiest part of being a photographer is taking the pictures; dealing with the egos that are inevitably involved is the hardest part. You can't please everyone the whole time.'

A lot of the photographer's skill lies in bringing out something special in the person in front of the lens, which may well prove tricky if the star thinks he is such a cool hunkin' dude that all he has to do is sit there with his shades and muffler on.

'When I've got someone really difficult and arrogant,' says Tom, 'I take whatever quality is there in them and try to exaggerate it. If someone is really self-satisfied then I play on that and encourage them to be even more so. They should feel relaxed in front of the camera, so sometimes I end up making a fool of myself. I just go twittering on, and sometimes it works and sometimes it doesn't.

'You have to gauge each situation as it arises. You may have only five minutes, so you have to just steam in and see what happens. I always like to create an atmosphere where a) people are relaxed and b) you allow space for spontaneous things to happen and are ready for them when they occur. One of my favourite people, who I think has complete charisma, is Robbie Williams.'

When photographing supertop stars for a magazine, time is very much of the essence. You may well have taken three months at college to complete one project, but MC Hammer rarely allows a photographer to take more than eight frames, and Spike Milligan once famously let a hapless photographer take just one solitary picture before booting him out!

Many music photographers diversify into fashion shoots, which are notoriously badly paid when they appear in magazines but can effectively act as an advert to get you into the high-cash world of fashion advertising, where a single campaign can net you tens of thousands of pounds. The downside to music photography is that you're too often working with someone else's ideas, or else with people who may not even

PHOTOGRAPHER

want their picture taken in the first place and are hell-bent on keeping on the Windcheater which sure as anything will ruin your **chiaroscuro**.

Valerie Phillips soon found that fashion photography could be more creative than working for pop magazines. 'I realised how unbelievably simple a lot of people were when I worked with bands,' she says, in outspoken style, 'and I found it frustrating trying to communicate the things that I wanted to do. I also kept having to go on tours with people I wouldn't voluntarily have spent time with. In the end I simply thought: I cannot suffer another Menswear session. I didn't want to get stuck with the inevitable, never-ending look-it's-a-pop-star-wheel-them-in-wheel-them-out thing.'

Contrary to what you may instinctively believe, many pop stars absolutely hate having their picture taken. Sheryl Crow has been known to cry after some photo sessions, even if they've gone well. Sarah Cracknell from St Etienne has been quoted as saying, 'They say the camera never lies. Well, it does. It's a lying bastard.' Singers are often so vain that they fear the camera will make them look too ugly. Tony Mortimer from East 17 thinks he's so weedy-looking and grim-mouthed that he can't bear to see a picture of himself, and singers playing live only let photographers shoot the first three songs of their set, before they start looking sweaty and knackered. What an odd bunch these people are. And you're the one who has to cope with it.

Once you have a body of work in a portfolio, you can approach magazines that you like and show them your stuff. Hopefully they'll think that David Bailey's got nothing on you, and generously allow you to go and take pictures of The Sneaker Pimps playing Burnley (you will almost certainly have to start this way before you start snapping glamorous front covers). A lot of photographers eventually get agents who show their portfolio around for them, liaise with the bigwig editors, and take a percentage fee accordingly.

Photography is often seen as a loner's trade – but it doesn't have to be that way. John Spinks and his mates started their Sixsixfour company in order to boost each other's morale. 'We pool our experience, money and equipment,' he says. 'We'll only ever have our photos credited to Sixsixfour, rather than our individual names, which originally led people to think we were a bunch of gits – but they came round to our way of doing things. We also share all the payments equally, even if only one of us has done the job.'

Photographic equipment is expensive but it's not an absolute given that in order to be a good photographer you need bucketfuls of flashlights and twenty super-snoot lenses. 'Anton Corbijn [ground-breaking and much revered stylish Dutch music photographer who is first

port of call for U2, REM and Depeche Mode] has two lenses and one 35mm camera and he's enormously successful,' says John Spinks. 'I don't believe in all that rubbish that you always have to have the latest piece of equipment. You don't need very much when you start. You can hire stuff, but the problem is you either have to already have an account with the hiring firm or else leave a deposit which is roughly the value of the gear.'

Tom Howard reckons he has a bag that has £12,000 worth of camera malarkey in it: a lens, a camera, a flashlight, and little else. Insurance bills are naturally very high and, if you drive, your car insurance is higher because insurers automatically expect that rock photographers will be taking Jon Bon Jovi to his favourite Chinese restaurant every evening, whether that's actually the case or not.

Valerie Phillips says of being a rock photographer: 'Never take no for an answer and don't start compromising.' John Spinks agrees. 'There are loads of arseholes out there, so try to be nice,' he advises. 'I once spent seven hours painting the infinity cove red, yellow and green, then when the photographer arrived he just screamed and swore at me in front of the whole crew of models, clients and assistants. Another assistant had mistakenly asked me to do it, but I was in a position where I couldn't start screaming back.'

Tom Howard says he would never have considered becoming a photographer had he known what it was really like to do the job. 'I was blessed with ignorance,' he reflects. 'If I'd known what the competition was going to be like, I would have had second thoughts. But you have started:

your enthusiasm carries you through. The only other thing I have to say about the job is ...'

What?

'It's not a good way to sleep with pop stars. I wouldn't recommend it for that.'

There you have it.

GLOSSARY

● **The infinity cove**

Where the wall meets the floor in a studio. It's all smoothed around so you can't see the line when Mr or Ms Pop Star stands in front of it. It has to be painted (mainly white) every time it's used – which is many times a week. What a job!

● **Lights**

The big tungsten things that burn holes into your brain if you look at them when they flash. A lot of photography is about getting these 'right', i.e. making people look like they're among the golden sands of Tahiti rather than dossing around in a shed. Unless you want them looking like they're in a particularly artistic shed, that is. Very difficult, that one, as it happens.

● **Photo shoots**

A session is booked at a studio, or else time on location allotted, which can be anything from a couple of hours to a couple of days. All hair, make-up and clothes will have to be organised before photos are taken.

● **Picture agency**

These represent individual photographers, from *NME* lenspeople to paparazzi, and sell their work around the world. Shots of Axl Rose coming out of Mr Byrite, for instance, will be bought for a price by a magazine to print in a future issue.

Studio sessions already printed in Britain will be sold overseas by the company, who take a percentage for every picture used.

● **Chiaroscuro**

The treatment of light and shade which make up the composition of the visual image. Very Anton Corbijn.

SKILLS YOU'LL NEED

A good 'eye' for a picture, communication skills (to wake up bleary pop stars who've not been long out of bed), friendliness, organisational skills, a good memory, enthusiasm. Lots of photographers turn into video directors, so it may be an advantage in the long run if you are interested in cinema.

TIPS

● Look at photographic books to see which styles you like.

● The London College of Printing provides good photography courses, as do art schools. You'll need to do a foundation course first.

● Try to assist either at a photographic studio or with a specific photographer to learn the trade – ring them up and sound friendly and confident. Don't try too hard: be honest about your experience, and don't crack any bad jokes.

● Realise that you'll be making cups of tea for people who probably have several grands' worth of hangover.

● You can't make too many blunders. If you forget to put the film in a camera during an average session, you can just shoot another roll – but don't do it *too* often.

● Take pictures of friends. It's good practice and they never insist on wearing sunglasses.

PICTURE EDITOR

MONEY: From £17,000 to £20,000 a year if you're on a magazine's staff. Between £75 and £150 per day for a freelancer.

HOURS: 10 a.m. to 6 p.m. Pretty regular, really.

HEALTH RISK: 4/10. You may die laughing at early photos of Peter Gabriel.

PRESSURE RATING: 7/10. Because getting that snap at the last minute of Mick Hucknall walking out of Woolworths can be a bit irksome.

GLAMOUR RATING: 6/10. You might get to meet some top pop people at photo shoots, but you're likely to be suggesting that they might 'not wear that hat' rather than downing a couple of bottles of Moet with them.

TRAVEL RATING: 7/10. Sometimes you might go on location to do some shots, but budgets don't often stretch to taking the picture editor abroad. Bah.

For magazines, the picture editor ensures that shoots are commissioned for most features and, when this is not possible, that there is a photograph for every piece of editorial copy that demands one. S/he also files pictures in alphabetical order a lot.

Picture editors are at the core of magazine production, and will invariably claim that every reader looks at the pictures first in a magazine. They like to get statistics out to prove this, as they are often much neglected and don't get many of the glamorous bits of being in the music industry.

Almost every music magazine commissions **studio shoots** with a regular team of photographers for the main features. The picture editor will ring up Snotty Snapper and ask him if he is free the next Friday to photograph a particular band. S/he will then have to haggle with the photographer about payment, as there will be a very strict budget for every issue of the magazine. The picture editor's job is to give the photographer a brief: explain what different kinds of shot they might want, whether they need colour photos, black and white, or both, and when the shots need to be delivered. Teen magazines like *Top Of The Pops* often want to do more than one session, especially with a band they may not get access to again in the next year. One shot will be used for a feature, another for a poster, another for a different feature, etc.

Kate Suiter, picture editor on *Vox*, started as editorial assistant on *Premiere*, the film magazine. 'I left college and had a few jobs then did a night-school course in learning to type,' she says. 'Then I became a temp and got the job at *Premiere*. I really wanted to work in music, and preferred magazines to television

PICTURE EDITOR/AGENCY

London Records. After becoming editorial assistant for *Smash Hits* when it first started, she went over to *Just 17* when it launched, as picture editor. Then she returned to *Smash Hits*.

'*Just 17* was the first magazine of its kind when it launched, just as *Smash Hits* had been,' she recalls. 'We didn't have a proper budget and were making it up as we went along. Now there are a lot of rival magazines and I think jobs like that are a lot harder to get.'

Picture editing requires a great deal of organisation. Editors have to schedule shoots, file pictures in big cabinets in such a way that any member of the editorial staff can find them easily, and return pictures to photo agencies when they've finished with them. They are charged a whole heap of cash if they lose **transparencies**, and it is thus essential that they stay firmly on top of the job.

Picture editors need to be stern with photographers who may try to up their day-rate pay, or claim ludicrously high expenses which the magazine simply does not have the budget for: some top photographers are notorious for charging expenses which are four times higher than their agreed fee for the job. You also have to persuade picture agencies to give you exclusive shots, and bargain with them for the best rate. And, absurdly simple as this may sound, you need to choose a photo which is in focus. Transparencies are so small, even on a **lightbox** with a magnifier, that it's also essential that you have good eyesight.

because TV people didn't seem very nice. I was so happy to be in an office where you could listen to music when you worked. It was a beautiful job compared with the real world, even if you did have to do filing.'

Kate then became editorial assistant on *Select*, working with the picture department when they needed extra help or the picture editor was on holiday. She was given a contact book full of the numbers of picture agencies and photographers, and told to get on with it.

Sue Miles, picture editor at *Smash Hits*, started doing work experience at Polydor Records when she was sixteen, through a friend's sister who worked at their sister company,

'Sometimes the best picture from a session may not be the one that's used,' says Kate. 'You have to pick a picture that goes with the text, not just a great picture. You really have to check everything – whether the bass player's got his eyes closed, or the singer's not lit properly.' No magazine likes putting a singer on their cover if he or she is wearing shades.

Different magazines require different skills. An old toad's magazine for ancient music lovers like *Mojo* needs somebody who is good at research – very few photographs are especially commissioned. You will be asked to find a picture of The Greats as they have never been seen before, which can sometimes be a tad tricky. A magazine like *Select*, on the other hand, commissions new sessions for most of its features. *Smash Hits* publishes lots of news stories which are picture led and thus deals with a lot of picture agencies, which are the only places you can get pictures of Gary Barlow coming out of the Mecca Bingo Hall, Oldham.

If the shoot has a curious angle to it, it is the picture editor who will have to find comedy props such as a bunny suit, a large hedgerow or twenty old people for the background. The picture editor works with the **designer** on the magazine, gauging exactly what's required. 'You have to think

YOU MIGHT ALSO SPEND MOST OF YOUR TIME PERSUADING YOUR POP STARS NOT TO WEAR SHADES. HMPH.

quickly and get props even quicker,' says Sue. 'There's always something that's been forgotten. You have to keep coming up with good ideas for shoots to make them different.'

Newspapers rely on agency shots, or pictures which they gather through their team of paparazzi-style photographers. They rarely do studio sessions unless it's with a buxom *Coronation Street* 'lovely' who's doing an interview about snogging. Picture editors are generally regarded as more important than the journalists on the tabloids. Fancy that.

Being a picture editor is very much an office job, but because the agencies shut, at the very latest, by 6 p.m., you can leave work at a reasonable time. And you're still part of the rollercoaster world of pop.

A BIT ABOUT PICTURE AGENTS

The picture editor liaises closely with picture agents. Sometimes photos from previous sessions are needed, or press shots which the editor won't have on file at the magazine. A band may be out of the country or too busy to do an exclusive session, and no one wants to see old pictures when the bassist had long hair and the wrong trainers on. However, band promotion is a worldwide business, so you can always get something from an agency in an emergency.

Idols is a picture agency which specialises in entertainment. Some agencies deal in anything from pictures of livestock to ham sandwiches, but Idols is on the button for pop stars, films stars and the like. 'We look after the interests of photographers while protecting the rights of the artists,' says Simon Kenton, director of the agency, which started fourteen years ago when the use of pictures was starting to become more of a serious business. Bands today are, more than ever before, involved in controlling their image. New photographs are absolutely imperative if you're in a band. You have to feed the press constantly with updated images as they clammer on your proverbial door night and day. An agency like Idols deals with established artists so that the impossible *can* be done and the press can get the pictures they want but would never normally have access to. For instance, a photographer might take a picture of Davey from The Davey Band, and sell it to Germany, a place that Davey hasn't had time to go to recently, through the agency. Likewise, Shula from The Shula Band in Germany can get top photographs seen in South Korea. Magazines and newspapers round the globe commission work through Idols. Nowadays, artists and their management work *with* the agency so the whole process is very official – no coming-out-of-a-chip-shop-with-no-make-up-on shots. Idols functions virtually as part of the band's PR team. Nothing is given to magazines or newspapers without the band's prior knowledge or consent.

Some artists choose to take a photographer with them on a round-the-world tour. This always comes in handy for tour brochures, merchandising, CD/video packaging,

inclusion in the fanclub newsletter, band annuals, and myriad other uses. Other, high-profile, artists need photographers to hang around at video shoots or at special events like turning on Christmas lights. All artists have the right to give their approval, so the chip-shop pictures won't get circulated. Everyone's interests, as they say, are served.

Each magazine has its own rates of payment for shots, and will haggle with agencies. Sometimes publications will ring to tell the agency what they're looking for: e.g., a shot of Davey in Australia. Or the agency may have some good shots of Shula, and will ring magazines who they think might have an interest – many magazines rely on agencies to give them shots for news and gossip pages. A lot of Idols' work is scheduled in advance, while press and promotions dates are being confirmed by the management. This way the bands have full picture control – it's all very regulated.

Idols and similar agencies have a **roster** of photographers who work for them round the globe. The demand is always met. How much you are paid as an agency photographer depends on the type of photograph, the shoot, and the artist concerned, but agencies will always take a commission on every shot they license.

It's also important to note that sometimes a band feels there's been too much exposure, and a need to hold back pictures, so the **market isn't saturated**. Idols, like all agencies, is well versed in strategically refusing to supply photos.

'We're quite an established company,' says Kenton. 'People see our credits in magazines and know we can get material into a long list of publications on an international basis. Also, we can control picture release very carefully. We can do as much or as little as people want.'

GLOSSARY
Studio shoots
A photographic session lasting a few hours in a photo studio. Most magazine features include new studio shots.

● **Transparencies**
These are processed films, a bit like mini-slides, and are used to check all pictures before they are scanned on to the page. They come in big sheets from the photographer or from the processing company.

● **Lightbox**
A small table which lights up from within so that designers, picture editors, etc. can look at transparencies properly through a special magnifying glass. It's not actually a box at all, really.

● **Designer**
Designs the pages of magazines, using computers to plan layouts and scan pictures on to the screen digitally. In the old days they used felt-tip pens, you know.

● **Roster**
Group of regular employees: freelance photographers in this case. Record companies have rosters of acts, as do independent press officers.

● **Market isn't saturated**
The one hope of everyone involved in a successful band, e.g. The Spice Girls. Their extensive promotion of numerous products did lead some to believe that 'saturated' was indeed what the market was.

SKILLS YOU'LL NEED
Organisation, ability to communicate well, responsibility, good eyesight, the ability to haggle and to think on your feet.

TIPS
● You can start at a magazine doing work experience. Ask to go in and help during the holidays.
● Many editorial secretaries help with pictures and become picture editors. Secretarial skills are good. Evening classes and holiday courses teach basics.
● Media-studies courses focus on picture use, and provide good background knowledge.

USEFUL ADDRESSES
● All Action, 32 Great Sutton Street, London EC1V 0DX.
TEL 0171 608 2988. **FAX** 0171 250 3376.
● Idols, Time Place, 593–599 Fulham Road, London SW6 5UA.
TEL 0171 385 5121. **FAX** 0171 385 5110.
● The Kobal Collection, 4th Floor, 184 Drummond Street, London NW1 3HP.
TEL 0171 383 0011. **FAX** 0171 383 0044.
● London College of Printing, Elephant & Castle, London SE1 6SB.
TEL 0171 514 6500. **FAX** 0171 514 6535.
● London Features International, 3 Boscobel Street, London NW8 8PS.
TEL 0171 723 4204. **FAX** 0171 723 9201.
● Redferns Music Picture Library, 7 Bramley Road, London W10 6SZ.
TEL 0171 792 9914. **FAX** 0171 792 0921.
● SIN, Second Floor, 208–209 Upper Street, London N1 1RL.
TEL 0171 359 8181. **FAX** 0171 359 0200.

POP STAR

 MONEY: From owing the record company lots of money to suddenly making thousands for yourself, owning a small record label, publishing company, many golf courses in Surrey, etc.

HOURS: 24 per day, seven days per week.

HEALTH RISK: 10/10. You work all the time and never eat. You stay up late and forget to floss. It is very bad for you indeed.

PRESSURE RATING: 10/10. You can always blame someone else, but ultimately you feel it's your responsibility if it all goes wrong. As it probably is.

GLAMOUR RATING: 10/10. You get to meet other famous people who have heard of you, get snapped leaving 7-11 by paparazzi, see your love life splattered all over the tabloids. Glamorous, huh?

TRAVEL RATING: 10/10. You're always whizzing about somewhere. Trouble is, you forget you have a home and find yourself in hedges of an evening, or trying to order room service in your bedsit.

Pop stars are the people who wear dubious trousers on Top Of The Pops *and appear in the papers coming out of nightclubs.*

Glamour! Excitement! Swanky high-rise living! These are just some of the things that people associate with being a pop star. Just think! To be part of an industry which revolves solely around the product that *you* make, the tweakings of your mind in melody form. To be pampered and preened, lauded and applauded, ridiculed and ripped off, and the ignominy of doing it all in public. It's a rotten job, but lots of people want to do it.

Are pop stars born or are they made? The Darwinians will never provide conclusive evidence, but most people decide they have pop-star potential from an early stage. Once someone decides to be a pop star, and is really rather determined, there are a variety of routes to take. Some of our most shimmering lovelies on the pop scene spent their adolescence at stage school. Stage school is an evil place where four-year-olds who think they can survive on one packet of TicTacs a day chill out with the likes of, um, **Bonnie Langford**. Stage training *can* produce cracking pop stars though: the phwortastic Louise, Eternal, Michelle Gayle and Damon Albarn. However, it also gave us the horrors of John Alford (from *London's Burning*), Chesney Hawkes, Yell! and Darren Day.

Other types – who want to make 'genuine' music for people who don't like homework – play guitar in their bedrooms and hang around shopping centres trying to look pale and interesting (e.g. The Verve). Either way, the ambition is the same and, eventually, if you try hard enough and long enough, you'll at least get to number 68 in the charts and have the local paper coming down to interview you.

So, you have to be ambitious. You have to have a whole bucketful of self-belief and a bit of spare time to practise in front of the mirror. The next thing – do you have to be good looking?

The answer, oddly enough, is no. Some pop stars are good-looking and some have the advantage of fancy make-up and nice lighting. Some have the full complement of features but in no way, shape or form could ever be said to have anything approaching looks. However, this has nothing to do with attractiveness. **Richard Ashcroft** is arguably not beautiful, but his wobbly nose has a charming quality only the greatest surgeons could create. Jimmy Nail, Noel Gallagher, Elton John, and even the lovely Celine Dion aren't exactly God's gift in the forehead department. Nor is Björk.

It's not necessary to be pretty at all, but you do have to have a certain spark which shows up behind your eyes: a magic glow that tells everyone you've just smelt the greatest flower, just eaten the nicest pie, just talked to God and He says your

POP STAR

next single has a ripping good chorus. This is what people like Matthew Kelly call Star Quality. And, if you ain't got that, you ain't got much (or you're a bassist, so that's OK).

As a nascent, wannabe rock star you can go one of two ways. You can decide you're a **pop** act, and therefore need a whole team of people to write songs, cut your hair, buy your socks and laugh at your jokes. In this case, you need to get yourself a manager, or find someone who can get one for you – a friendly publisher, a chum who's in a band, any sort of person connected with the music biz who knows a few names. You can answer adverts in the press (the drama-industry rag *The Stage, Melody Maker*, and top industry weekly *Music Week* have adverts all the time for singers) which are placed by managers looking for top acts.

At this point, however, be very wary. A lot of such managers are sharks. If you take this route, make sure the people you contact are not asking you to put up any recording costs, and find out whether they have contacts and a music-business history. If you meet them at their office and it turns out to be above Toys R Us and one of them's never heard of R Kelly, then *beware*. However, don't despair: Take That, The Spice Girls and En Vogue were all discovered by this method, so it *can* work. In each case, management companies took some nippers who looked nice, could sing,

and had a bit of spark and made them into the loveable superstars they are today.

So how do you go about succeeding by this method? Well, make a tape of your singing, hawk it around, and see what people think of it. Perhaps invest in some singing lessons – there are always local teachers who can help. If you've formed a pop band, try to find out the names of producers, or producers' agents who might be able to help. If a producer likes something, they might help you record a cheap demo, because it means they're getting in on something first and can reap the rewards later. You don't need a manager from day one.

The other way to achieve rock stardom is via **indie** – and indie works a little bit differently. Indie is from the soul, man, and indie bands start when friends start to **jam** together, or else some young pup with a handful of tunes and a head full of a load of rubbish advertises for like-minded cheekboned vibers to jam in a rehearsal space for fifteen minutes then listen to her/him rant on about Sly and The Family Stone in the pub for three hours.

Elastica were formed through the *Melody Maker* classifieds, as were Suede, and a local paper was the birthplace of American indie icons The Pixies. Yer average indie band

YOU'LL NEED VITAMINS TO REPLENISH YOUR FRAIL JET-LAGGED SYSTEM.

forms, rehearses some top tunes, argues about who had the nicest hair in The Beatles, and gets a few live dates by ringing up local venues and sending them a demo tape. Around this point, the band also makes demos and flings them out to local journos, potential managers and record companies. The latter can prove fairly fruitless, as A&R departments tend to go to see bands there's already a 'buzz' about – word of mouth counts for a lot. They don't have much time to listen to tapes, although they get sent hundreds every week. A friendly manager *might* get meetings with different A&R people to play tapes, but it's not easy. Live music is most often the key. And, if you're good, someone *will* start gabbling about how 'hot' you are.

Generally speaking, once any artist is considered to be slightly warmer than average, the record companies will pounce like a pack of wolves on their prey. You get invited out to dinner, to lunch, to breakfast sometimes. You will be invited to make more demos of your songs at the record company's expense. People will listen to you talking about middle eights and even try to stifle their yawns. Suddenly, you may be bumping into Peter Andre on the streets of Soho, where all the media people hang out in London, and he will be looking less happy than you are.

This will be a magic time, but it will not last for long. If the buzz is major you will get a bidding war, when different record companies (a lot of them just copy each other in these matters) will put in assorted bids to sign you up for five or six albums. You can simply accept the largest offer, but this amount is recoupable (i.e., you have to pay it back eventually), so this may prove a very short-sighted move. You have to tread very, very carefully.

At this point, when you are being offered deals by record companies, you will need to have found yourself a lawyer and accountant to assist you. Your manager should be able to help you to obtain these, and the number of meetings with men in suits will increase. However, all companies know what pop stars are like and most will offer you a beer even though it is only 10.30 a.m. They are probably surprised a) that you got out of bed that early and b) that you aren't already drunk. (They will expect you to be the cliché – so why should you disappoint them?)

Once you have secured your record-company deal, you'll have to record some tunes, release them, see how they do, go on tour, do press, telly and radio promotion, see that the business side of things is dealt with by your lawyer etc. There'll be meetings, meetings about meetings: hearing people waffle on about cross-collateralisation, and talk about you as if you're not there or the band you're in is a brand of peas.

Shaznay from All Saints is relatively new to the pop game, although she's been singing for many years. She got a shock when she first became a pop star. 'It's very hard work,' she says. 'It's not what I expected it to be. I only ever expected to write songs, make records, perform on stage, and be on TV a couple of times. I didn't imagine all the rest of it – the politics and the serious business side. You find you're not performing as much as you're caught up in the other stuff.'

In reality, the ratio is probably under 10% singing and playing songs, and 90% "the other stuff". You appear on radio shows and have to record horrible commercial idents for the station: 'Hi! I'm Zac from Hanson and you're listening to Radio Popsnot 86-88 FM. Weeurgh!!' You have to battle with foreign telly producers who insist their pop stars wear chicken costumes while playing. They may also have go-go dancers in the background. Boyzone were sponsored by a cigarette company for part of their Asian tour, which they didn't know about until they got to the first venue. It's a battle, it honestly is.

Toby Slater, singer in new pop band Catch, has already had to compromise his artistic integrity. For his first appearance on *Live And Kicking* he had to change the line in hit single 'Bingo' from '£100 for Diet Coke' to 'A hundred pence for Diet Coke'. He couldn't sing 'piss off' or sing about 'red lights'. This goes against every instinct of pop stars, who generally want to do whatever they feel like and don't give a stuff about what the marketing, promotions, A&R and business people say.

'There's this whole politics around TV appearances,' says Shaznay. 'If you're doing something for one channel, you can't do something for another, because they're rivals. People forget that it's only music at the end of the day.'

Pop stars, of course, throw epic sulks all the time, which is little wonder when the whole shooting match can appear to be so so little about the music and so much about plugging, playlists, marketing, and corporate politics. Or rather, it is until the pop star becomes extravagantly famous and successful and suddenly finds that s/he holds all the power – which can lead to epic legal battles such as those between George Michael and Sony, and The Artist Formerly Known As Prince and Warner.

Pop stars haven't, as a rule of thumb, got any money – not until a couple of years or more after they've had their first hit, anyway. Pop stars live off their advance, **free taxis**, clothes and meals paid for by record-industry sorts. It takes a long time for royalties to come through, and your first few years are spent paying back your record-company advance until you've sold enough albums to cover yourself.

Artists are paid a percentage (known as points) of the money received by the record company for albums sold. It generally varies between 12 and 25 points: the lower figure is poor; the high one fantastic. If you are confident of success, you should negotiate a deal wherein the advance may be small but you receive high royalties (i.e. loads of points). Then, the more albums you sell, the more money you make.

Deals are constantly being renegotiated in the light of your success (or otherwise). If you have had two high-selling albums, on the third one you should be able to negotiate an increase in points and maybe also argue for swifter payment of royalties. Now you are holding the power – but don't forget that your manager is taking 20% of your earnings and there is still a load of lawyers, accountants and other employees to pay.

The typical day for the pop star is a bit gruelling and can start as early as 6 a.m. for photo and video shoots. Photo shoots can involve as many as five costume changes as the photographer will invariably want different 'looks'. You'll have meetings and interviews on the phone and in person before, during and after the shoots. There could be a dinner-date meeting afterwards with a lawyer, and your brain will have to switch to 'I don't think I understand what cross-collateralisation means ... and are bears too expensive to fly with us for our world tour?' mode. You may go weeks, or even months, doing no singing or strumming at all.

When you do record, you have to keep within the budget the A&R department has set you, so the pressure is on not to go overtime or hire too many bassoons. You're under pressure to record a masterpiece

POP STARS ARE ALWAYS PUT IN FRONT OF FRUIT DURING INTERVIEWS.

even if the drummer's dog has just died, you don't get on with the producer, and your manager is asking you to do interviews while you're concentrating on the hi-hat sounds. You spend six weeks or so recording something which you're not sure is any good – some of the time it sounds great; sometimes dreadful. Then you have to wait at least four months till the bloody thing's released.

There are signings at record shops in the week of an album release, television appearances, more interviews ... Overseas promotion

will mean talking to strangers on the phone who're still asking you why you called the band Hanson, even when it's your surname and it's quite obvious why, thank you very much. Or there's flying about Europe on rattling aeroplanes, being served inedible slices of ham and touching down only to talk to people who are under the impression that, if your name is Hanson, you must be related to hip-hop pop person Beck *Hansen*.

'It can be crazy when you're flying around the place and you're not eating at the right times,' says Ronan Keating from Boyzone. 'Your body is used to eating at different times and you're not getting enough sleep because you're working so hard. Glamour factor? Zero. No, I'll give it a two. Out of twenty.'

'You are doing a deal with the devil,' says Toby Slater. 'I haven't met him yet, but you get no privacy. The press just make up what you do and say.'

Shaznay is twenty-two, but 'felt thirty' when All Saints began to have some success. Ronan is twenty, but says he feels 'like forty'. Toby bought himself a trampoline with his advance money, which is perhaps some psychological impulse to revert back to a childlike state when he's not working. As a pop star, the pressure is on you, but the responsibility is not always yours – you can at least farm it out to other people.

Really, being a pop star is a most peculiar state to be in, and one most akin to being a big kid. People are there to do everything for you. You get cars to pick you up and deliver you to where you're meant to be, your manager and record company sort out your diary for up to twelve months in advance: which countries you'll be in, when you tour, when you record, when your mum's birthday is, in case you forget. You are respected for things you didn't do – in the case of singles recorded then remixed by DJs – or things you do by accident. You have to be strong, because pop stardom can drive people to insanity. They go around saying, 'We're the best band in the world, and I can do everything,' when quite clearly no one is the best band in the world and no one can do everything. Like flying, for instance. No one can do that. Not even Richard Ashcroft.

'You've got to believe in yourself and be confident, though,' says Ronan. 'You've got to have a good head on your shoulders and not let people walk all over you because it's a horrible business if they do. You've got to be happy and enjoy it very much, because that's the most important thing, to enjoy it. If you don't it will turn into hell.'

Frightening words – but very obviously the truth, as the number of pop-star suicides, breakdowns, and plunges into drug addiction confirm. The only way to keep your sanity is to resist the temptation to take off on an extraordinary ego trip from which there may be no return. You have to laugh(!) when they make up lies about you in the tabloids. Giggle(!) when they slag off your trainers in *The Face*.

Smirk(!) when you fall over because your daft Spice Girls shoes are too big on *Top Of The Pops*. You must learn to love Jools Holland, even though he doesn't want you on his adult-orientated show because your new single is about lollipops. You mustn't mind getting recognised in the street, or having fans that are, frankly, embarrassing.

'I got recognised in a bookshop,' says Toby. 'It was horrible. I was looking at this book called *1000 Ways To Keep Yourself Sane* and I realised I had been spotted and had to hide the book. Girls do wait around for you when you're coming out of places. You know that there's something wrong with them and that these people have a deficiency they're using you to fill – but it's still pretty weird.'

YOUR PET MIGHT GET GRAND IDEAS.

Nobody is denying pop stardom has millions of perks. You get into clubs for free and never have to queue. You can get a table in a restaurant, no problem. You get free clothes, because you wear them and are thus advertising them. And, once you do make a bit of cash, you can treat your mum to a bungalow by the sea or buy your sister a horse ... or even spend some on yourself. Jamiroquai likes fancy cars. Justine Frischmann was on telly buying fancy art. Others blow it on fancy shoes, fancy houses, or just about fancy anything really. 'We all have our little toys that we like,' says Ronan, who has a fast motorbike. 'Bikes and cars and houses. But there's a big gap between us and George Michael – he's on a different level. He's got millions!'

Shaznay likes the job, but admits she does get concerned that she's not in control of everything that she does and the band could be ripped off. 'You shouldn't worry obsessively, but do bear the dangers in mind,' she reasons. 'It's down to you to be smart and query everything. I am happy. You have your good days and bad days, but overall the job is cool.'

'I don't think I'd advise any of my children to get into this business, but if they really wanted to I wouldn't stop them,' says Ronan. 'It is a crazy business and it's changed my life totally. I've been round the world, I love what I do, I wouldn't know how to do anything else. I eat sleep and breathe the business and it's fantastic. But I can't say I'd go and rush out and tell anybody to do it.'

GLOSSARY
● **Bonnie Langford**

Child star of the late seventies who was born wearing make-up and had a squeaky voice. Time was when all girls were modelled on Langford, who now appears in pantomimes.

● **Richard Ashcroft**

Lanky, 'I am mad' singer with The Verve.

● **Pop**

The world of chirpy, high-quality, radio-friendly tunes. Often described as 'shallow'. It is not.

● **Indie**

The world of meaningful, genuine, soulful tunes by boys with guitars (mostly). Often described as 'dirgey'. It is not. Not all the time.

● **Jam**

Spontaneous music making. Like improvisation but with the key and time signature decided in advance.

Jazz jamming needs neither key nor set signature. And can sound awful.

● **Free taxis**

The greatest mystery of the modern world is why pop stars spend millions of their record company's money using their taxi account. Why don't they use the bus? Some of them can drive, too.

SKILLS YOU'LL NEED

An ounce of talent, a bit of spark, look reasonably interesting, have something to say in songs and interviews, persistence, tolerance, being thick-skinned, humbleness, willingness to wait around a lot, willingness to lug clothes around a lot. All for your mum to tell the neighbours about your hair.

TIPS

● 'If you want to be in a group, I wouldn't advise auditioning,' says Shaznay. 'Go with people that you know. Think about the reasons, delve deep. If you think it's what you see on the telly, you need to think again.'

● Ronan: 'Believe in yourself. Get some tracks together, from your own pocket, to make a recording. Go to a record company, maybe get a manager along the way that you can trust, get some sort of a deal.'

● Don't worry, if you get dropped by a record company you don't have to pay them their advance back.

● Local singing teachers can be found through the local library or newspaper. Ask who they teach and whether they have any qualifications. Recommendation is the best way.

USEFUL NUMBERS

Samaritans **TEL** 0345 909090

PRESS OFFICER

MONEY: £9,000 a year for a junior press officer, to £70,000 for head of press at a major label.

HOURS: 9.30 a.m. to 7 p.m. or later every weekday. Many evenings, including weekends, spent seeing bands play live.

HEALTH RISK: 6/10 A degree of stress caused by having to occasionally pretend that bands who can't hold a guitar the right way up are actually The Future Of Rock'n'Roll.

PRESSURE RATING: 8/10. Trying to break a band can be tricky. Also, people will shout at you – because they can – and you have to be nice back.

GLAMOUR RATING: 7/10. You meet the stars as part of your job, yes, but the novelty value soon wanes when they ring up complaining.

TRAVEL RATING: 9/10. You accompany bands abroad when they have interviews to be done. You may not see a lot of the country you're visiting (sometimes just a venue and a hotel room) and you're often there for less than a day.

The press officer manages press campaigns and tries to maximise exposure and attention for the bands they are working with.

The job of a press officer is one of the most frustrating and rewarding in the music industry. A job in press means that you will spend weeks planning and implementing a carefully thought-out print campaign in which you will try to get as many column inches as possible.

When you join a major record company's press department (each company has an in-house department which represents most of the artists on its **roster**) you'll most likely start off as a press assistant, with a view to in due course becoming a regional press officer or junior press officer.

'The thing is, you just need to get your foot in the door,' says Gillian Porter, press officer with EMI Records. Gillian did a music management course at Bathgate College in Scotland. She got a work-experience placement with distributors Pinnacle and never went back to her college again!

'It doesn't really matter what you do at first: just get into the business somehow and apply for all the press jobs you hear about. You've just got to love magazines and want to do anything you're asked to. Every day I go through *every* newspaper and new magazine. You've got to be very interested in all that.'

'I never *wanted* to be a press officer, but I really enjoy it,' says John Best, now head of his own press company, Savage and Best, who handle press for Pulp, Suede and many other major names. 'I loved music and liked going to gigs. When you start there's no substitute for knowing what you're talking about. Some people start answering phones on reception and are press officers a couple of years later. Be dogged and tenacious, then you'll get somewhere.'

When you start as a regional press officer, you'll deal with the major **fanzine**s, student magazines, and local newspapers countrywide. This shouldn't be too daunting. 'Everyone is generally really enthusiastic,' says Gillian Porter. 'They're pleased you've taken the time to call them. And they often move with you, becoming national music journalists at the same time as you're promoted to a press officer with acts everyone wants to write about.

'As a press officer proper, you will be given a couple of new artists to work on who may never have even had a record out. Your task will be to get them heard by as many journalists as possible, and to write a press release every time your artist has a single, a tour, or breaks an ankle. You may even have to commission a photographer to take some nice pictures of them to send out with your **press pack**. You'll inherit a long list of names, addresses and telephone numbers which will look completely daunting, but in a year's time you'll know who *everybody* is.'

'I thought the job was embarrassing at first and had no idea how to get stories in the press,' says Eugene Manzi, who is now head of press at London Records and became a press officer in 1984 when he was drafted in by a friend who had a fledgling indie record company. 'I said, "What the hell's a PR?" when he said that's what I could do. I just wanted to drive vans,

delivering records to the record shops, because that's the only job I knew existed. The first act I had, I was told to go to *Record Mirror* and get a cover story. I bought the album at HMV, because we hadn't got stocks in, and took it in to the editor. I made him listen to it track by track. He should have said, "Just piss off," because you never make anyone listen to that much but he didn't. I didn't get a cover, but he did do a little piece on them.'

The usual press **strategy** is this: you receive a couple of hundred **advance cassette**s to send out to the journalists on your list. You need to listen to the single and decide which magazines would be interested. 'You don't ring up *Kerrang!* and ask them to do a feature on Pepsi and Shirlie,' says Gillian Porter. A week later, you have to phone and check if any have listened to it. A week later, you have to remind them again.

Most music magazines, when vaguely interested, will run a review of a band in the singles column, and if it goes down well they'll run a small piece. If the single sells reasonably, or they think their readership will love the artist, they run a feature (from half a page to three pages), and usually someone who adores the band will interview them and slobber through a series of tough questions. If you've got a band who have an enormous hit without much backing (like No Doubt did with 'Don't Speak' – the single gained attention through its success in America first) then the band will instantly command large features with **intellectual bits** justifying the fact that no one in Blighty knew they would be huge.

It might be the case that no one

sees the potential of your band or singer – they could very well be ahead of their time. Do not worry, it's only pop music. Press officers sometimes get very upset and shout at journalists for not liking their artists. This is futile: cynics – and musicians – claim that journalists have very little clue as to what is good or not.

'The worst thing is when you love a band and you can't get anywhere with them,' says Eugene Manzi. 'You might have worked really hard but you sometimes feel like you're getting no return. You shouldn't get upset about bad reviews either. Journalists often hate a band who still go on to sell millions of records.'

With a gigging band, whose success grows through the **fanbase**, your job will start when you invite journalists to hear them play live. That way you hope to get interest, and a live review before or just at the time they release a single. 'You *do* get an expenses account,' says Eugene. 'It's a legitimate expense to pay for a couple of drinks for the journalists who turn up for gigs.' Lunch is also a viable expense, if you're inviting people out. Press officers take journalists to lunch (the record company pays, rarely the magazine) to either discuss acts or sometimes just to link up, man.

'You don't get to know that many writers: you speak to them on the phone and they write reviews but doing lunch gives you the opportunity

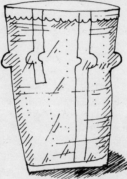

YOU HAVE TO BUY PEOPLE A FEW OF THESE, BUT YOU GET THEM ON EXPENSES.

to match the voice with a face,' Eugene Manzi explains. 'Needless to say, you do need a credit card as part of your job. I used to take loads of cash out with me and I didn't know how expenses worked so I became massively overdrawn. Some press officers get a company car, too.'

Once your act is successful, you'll have to beat off the hordes of magazines ringing up for a quote about anything from your artist's favourite biscuits to their secret love child. You'll also have to attempt to get on the right side of the tabloid press, the most notorious of the media.

'I was working at an office which dealt with Dogs D'Amour's press when they broke through,' recalls Manzi. 'They were a great tabloid band – real rock 'n' roll, drank, trashed hotels, had model girlfriends … clichéd, basically. The band came into the office, looking ridiculous in full-length leather coats, cowboy boots, Stetsons. The lead showbiz story in a tabloid paper that day revealed the singer, Tyler, was in a heroin scare. They came in, saw the paper – they were all drinking – and they were fine about it. Tyler phoned his sister to say he'd be on *Top Of The Pops* the next day. She said, "You'd better not show your face around here, Mum's furious!" This had never occurred to Tyler, who immediately started shouting, "This fucking paper writes lies!" He smashes his bottle on the desk and chucks a table across the room, which knocks a gold disc off the wall. "My family are being affected!" he screams, and storms out. I'm sitting in the corner thinking: So *this* is press ...'

Artists will commonly shout at you for their mistakes – if a bad picture is printed, or they're misquoted. The artist's manager will also put pressure on you to get more or less press, depending on their point of view. 'You are stuck in the middle,' says Leesa Daniels, who moved from music journalist to independent press officer. 'You have to try not to react sometimes, because often you can't win.'

And that goes for dealing with writers. 'There is a sense that you're a kind

of mother to them. You're calling them up, asking their opinions, sending them albums and tickets. You do spend a lot of time flattering people.'

Independent press is different from in-house press in that the former choose their artist, and thus are more involved in the development of the act. Acts (mostly indie, it has to be said) choose independent press because they know they should get results and they are perceived as having more cred. Often a small band can be overlooked within the schedule of a large record company who are worrying about Mariah Carey's hair

PRESS OFFICER

119

all the time. Independent press can also give a flagging established artist some amount of credibility. Gillian Porter moved from independent press, dealing with Manic Street Preachers and Shampoo, to in-house at EMI, dealing with Terrorvision. She notices another way of working.

'You can't choose your own acts. Although, you don't get artists dumped on you, because if you're not into something you're not going to do a very good job on it. You do a lot of meetings for the sake of doing meetings.'

'The good thing about independent press,' says John Best, who started on the production side of magazines like *Tunnels and Tunnelling* and then got a job at Virgin Records before he set up on his own, 'is that you don't have to have much money to begin with. You need a phone and a good contact book. I now employ about 25 people and earn £40,000 a year. I might not earn as much as I would as part of a major record label – if I was head of press in-house at a major label I'd probably get another £30,000 – but we *care* about who we represent. My staff are paid fairly well, and I'm much happier employing people who love the bands they're working with rather than being in it for the money and the lifestyle.'

Some of the jobs previously held by press officers currently working in the music business are: forklift-truck driver, ballerina, pop star, artist, receptionist and model. There are many roads to this particular palace of wisdom.

GLOSSARY
● **Roster**
The full list of artists currently signed

to one record label. Can range from one (on independent labels) to thirty (not all bands will be active, but they are still signed in case the muse arrives).
● **Fanzine**
Mini-magazine privately produced by ardent music fans who don't mind wasting all their time sticking bits of paper to other bits of paper then photocopying them. Mostly non-profit-making.
● **Press pack**
Collection of recent cuttings about a particular artist, plus glossy picture, new press release, and sometimes video. Sent to journalists who want information on a band they plan to interview, or used to persuade them that the band are ace and will increase their magazine's circulation threefold.
● **Strategy**
The plan to get your band in every single magazine and newspaper, sometimes highlighting their sexy side, or their cheeky side, or their mad rock pig-death side. It's your job to make them appear new and exciting to the press, even if they've made thirty albums which all sound the same.
● **Advance cassette**
Audio cassette which features the new single, before the finished copy is completed and released. Other advance cassettes sent out contain a few tracks from a forthcoming album, or the album itself. Journalists often tape over these (with interviews etc.) before realising they haven't listened to them.
● **Intellectual bits**
Don't worry if, in some articles, you don't understand the intellectual bits.

They are made up by the writer who has been told to portray the band as socially relevant. This doesn't always work.

● **Fanbase**

Loyal fans who keep the band afloat when Radio One won't play them, thus ensuring top-forty placings for singles before the eight-year-olds think it sounds cool. Indie bands survive on 'fanbase' before they get famous, or when their records go crap.

SKILLS YOU'LL NEED

Communication skills, perseverance, enthusiasm, literacy, diplomacy, organisational skills.

TIPS

● If you show enthusiasm and are willing to work long hours, work-experience jobs often turn into real ones. Ring record companies to ask if there is anything you can do in any departments during your allotted work period.

● The more you know about magazines and the more gigs you go to, the better a chance you'll have. An obvious truth, but one to keep in mind.

● When you get your job, don't bribe anyone. It shows lack of professionalism and is also awfully old-fashioned.

USEFUL ADDRESSES

● Bad Moon PR, Unit 6, The Bus Space, Conlon Street, London W10 5AP.

TEL 0181 960 9899. **FAX** 0181 960 9502.

● BMG Records, Bedford House, 69–79 Fulham High Street, London SW6 3JW.

TEL 0171 384 7500 **FAX** 0171 371 9298.

● EMI Records, 43 Brook Green, London W6 7EF.

TEL 0171 605 5000 **FAX** 0171 605 5050.

● Hall Or Nothing, 11 Poplar Mews, Uxbridge Road, London W12 7JS.

TEL 0181 740 6288. **FAX** 0181 749 5982.

● Polydor Records, 1 Sussex Place, London W6 9XT.

TEL 0181 910 4800. **FAX** 0181 910 4901.

● Savage And Best, 79 Parkway, London NW1 7PP.

TEL 0171 482 7166. **FAX** 0171 482 7216.

● Sony Records, 10 Great Marlborough Street, London W1V 2LP.

TEL 0171 911 8200. **FAX** 0171 911 8600.

● Virgin Records, Kensal House, 553–579 Harrow Road, London NW10 4RH.

TEL 0181 964 6000. **FAX** 0181 968 6533.

● Warner Music, 28 Kensington Church Street, London W8 4EP.

TEL 0171 937 8844. **FAX** 0171 938 3901.

RADIO DJ

Broadcasting your favourite records for a couple of hours to a rapt audience, interviewing the stars, reviewing gigs on air and introducing acts on stage is all part of the DJ life. On the whole, it beats coal mining.

Radio DJs are some of the most influential people, in terms of record sales, in the whole of the universe. You can put a new band in a fluffy jumper and call them Free Beer, but if the radio doesn't like their record you'll have a hard time making it a hit. Even television follows the lead of radio in music broadcasting.

The radio producer will work together with the DJ, sorting out a list of records for each show. Most radio stations work on a playlist system: the station chooses a bunch of records to play each week, which you as a DJ can pick and choose from, as well as bunging in your other favourites. This helps the station have some defined identity, as network bosses generally feel that, were DJs to play the diverse records they wanted to, no one would tune into the station because they'd have no idea what to expect.

There is no one set route to radio DJing. Some DJs come through from journalism, others from more officey-type jobs at the BBC; still more work their way up through the role of production assistant. Commercial radio DJs may switch from **local** or national BBC **radio**, and vice versa. Almost everyone has started broadcasting with a passionate love for music and will find satisfaction in being able to talk to swarms of avid listeners.

Steve Lamacq from Radio One's *Evening Session* wrote a piece about the pirate station Q102 a few years ago for *NME*, where he was a writer. They were so impressed he was asked to join and did a show for almost three years. He skipped to XFM – London's indie station – then hopped over to the BBC to present the *Evening Session* with Jo Whiley when Mark Goodier was away doing the roadshow. Eventually he was given the job permanently.

He actually started his career on his local paper in Harlow before joining *NME* as a sub-editor. He loves being a DJ. 'This is a great job,' he enthuses. 'Very rarely are two days the same. I get up about eightish, have two coffees and ten cigarettes, listen to CDs and demos and things, then get in the bath before ten when the phone starts. At 3 p.m. I come into Radio One and look through the post, then at 4.30 p.m. I go and have a pint for Dutch courage – even now! I get back by 5.30 p.m. unless I have a pre-recorded interview with a band. I'm out of the station by 8.30 and can get to Camden for a gig by nine.'

Most people who start broadcasting get help from the producer involved in the show, and also have a production assistant. Clare Sturgess, who now does the afternoon show on XFM, started out as a production assistant. She had originally written to the BBC literally asking 'Can I have a job please?' and managed to get a post filing and photocopying as a clerk in a small department in Broadcasting House. She then saw an advert for production assistant for Radio One, applied, and got the job working for

RADIO DJ

Simon Bates' morning show. Clare did a 'glorified secretary' job there, but it included some on-air and **OB reports** and she even managed to get old Simes to play Nirvana and The Pixies. After a week filling in for Mark Goodier on – yes – the *Evening Session*, she presented the *Rock Show*, which was in the middle of the night. Someone has to do it, after all.

'My doctor told me that, no matter what, your body will never be programmed to work at night and sleep all day,' says Clare. 'But I did get used to it. I had power naps in the afternoon. It's like a little club when you broadcast in the middle of the night because you have a dedicated crew of listeners. Though I must say some were a bit bonkers ...'

Being a radio DJ isn't all about this sort of glamour. You'll have to go through every new record before the show to ensure you haven't missed any brand-new gems. At Radio One, DJs used to have an engineer who would flick all the switches. Now DJs have to deal with the technical side and operate the studio themselves. This isn't a spectacularly brainbox job and you get taught along the way, but it does help if you're not too intimidated by machinery. Practise using a video recorder at home.

'I've stopped a few CDs while on air,' says Lamacq. 'When Jo Whiley and I were doing our trial period, I stopped the CD midway through Nirvana by

mistake – and all the management people were listening in. I turned the **mike** on, and said, "Oh dear, a wire has come out of the back of the machine. What a shame." I got away with it.'

As a radio DJ you have to be reasonably polite so you don't get sued for slander, and it's obviously a career-shortening move to swear like a trouper. Clare Sturgess says she's never sworn on the radio but she's 'sometimes tempted to say, "That was fucking brilliant!" I've cultivated "fantastic" instead, but I think I'm overusing that ...'

A BIT ABOUT COMMERCIAL RADIO

Commercial radio is a different kettle of onions altogether – although you're still not advised to turn the air blue. Commercial radio needs to play music that everyone likes in order to maximise the station's popularity and ratings, because it survives through advertising and sponsorship deals. Commercial radio DJs also get paid a lot more than BBC

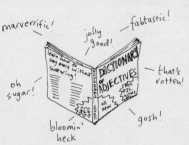

marverrific! jolly good! fabtastic! oh sugar! that's rotten! bloomin' heck gosh!

YOU ARE NOT ALLOWED TO SWEAR.

DJs and are often more 'personality' inclined. Pat 'n' Mick, who worked for Capital Radio – London's mainstream commercial station – even released a string of singles in the late eighties. They got on telly well before the BBC had got round to creating such diversity and cross-media identity. Commercial radio has no shame, which is exactly why it is sometimes ever so good. And why it is sometimes awful.

The not-very-aptly-monickered Dr Fox is probably the best-known commercial DJ in the country due to the Pepsi Chart, which is broadcast on Sundays on every commercial station in the land. He took a business degree, had a go on university radio in Bath, and then got 'a normal job' in Worcester. He landed a job at Radio Wyvern after entering a competition: he didn't win, but he became buddies with a DJ there and started helping him out. He then went to Radio Luxembourg, and moved to Capital two years later. He got the job of presenting the Pepsi Chart in 1993. Like Steve Lamacq, Dr Fox loves his job.

'I love what I do,' he reflects. 'DJs are lucky because we get all the benefits – all the trappings of success without the shit which goes with it. I can walk down the street and get no hassle, but I travel, meet famous people and get free records.'

Neil, as Fox is known to his mother, often invites the stars to play live in his studio, an invitation which has been accepted by Bon Jovi, Sting, Bryan Adams and Noel Gallagher. He's met Madonna and Cindy Crawford. He also does the traditional DJ sidelines: **voice-overs** for adverts ('I did a load of stuff for Cadburys, so I got a load of chocolate.') and he DJs at corporate parties ('Nice functions like dinner dances where I'm the star DJ. That's money in the bank.').

Nobody is exempt from these little earners, even if they are a 'cred' DJ. Steve Lamacq tells a story of John Peel

taking him around to his house, pointing to each of his rare records stacked up alphabetically in a huge extension to the house, and reciting which advert voice-over paid for which.

Lamacq also has other interests – he was one of the people who founded the Indolent record label – home of Sleeper and Elastica – and writes columns for *Melody Maker* and trade magazine *Music Week* as well as DJing at festivals like Reading and Phoenix. He's quite accustomed to being stared at at gigs and asked by people to play their mate's brother's band's cassettes on his radio show.

DJs do not generally have a high cred rating, which is maybe a hangover from the wacky Smashie-and-Nicey fabtastic Radio One days of the seventies and eighties. Expect to be ridiculed for your dress sense, your worthy tones and your 'amusing' accent. However, radio isn't the plummy world of posh that it used to be. Regional accents make the stations seem more with it, nowadays. Oh, and Welsh people take note – yours is the accent that hasn't really filtered through to the mainstream just yet so you'll be in with more of a chance if you're a budding platter-spinner from Pontypridd. Such prejudices may be a bit sad, but it's the way the world works.

Listen to the radio and find out who plays which sort of music, and note the different DJing styles. You'll notice that some DJs hardly ever say 'That was "Doing It With You" by The Springy Mattresses' but rather '[Silence] "Doing It With You" [Pause] Springy Mattresses there', which makes very little grammatical sense but at least serves to keep the DJ awake.

'I listened to radio and I think subconsciously I picked up when to talk and when to shut up,' says Steve Lamacq.

'I think anyone can do the job,' says Clare Sturgess, 'as long as they have confidence.'

GLOSSARY
● **Local radio**
Commercial, pirate or run by the BBC. Always looking for people to help out.
● **OB reports**
'Outside broadcast' reports. The *Radio One Roadshow* is one big OB hell. Good experience.
● **Mike**
I.e. microphone. Essential part of the DJ kit. Headphones, or cans, are a must as well. If you DJ at parties and events, you have to bring your own.
● **Voice-overs**
Providing a soothing, excited, sultry or informative commentary to go along with the visuals in the adverts. Good money.

SKILLS YOU'LL NEED
An ear for a nice tune, being able to talk reasonably coherently, an idea about what people want to listen to, being able to sound chirpy even when you feel glum.

TIPS
● University radio is a good place to start. So is hospital radio.
● Look for adverts from the BBC, in the Monday and Saturday *Guardian* job sections.
● DJ at friends' parties, then you get a good idea of what floor-fillers are

and how to pace a set, man.
● A lot of people start by helping out at a local radio station for free.
● Make your own tapes and listen out for DJ competitions on local radio. If there are no competitions, send them in anyway.
● 'Decide what kind of DJ you're going to be,' says Neil 'Dr' Fox. 'A personality DJ, or a muso DJ where the music is the star.'

USEFUL ADDRESSES
● BBC Radio 1, Yalding House, Great Portland Street, London W1N 4DJ.
TEL 0171 580 4468. **FAX** 0171 927 5869.
● Capital Radio, 29–30 Leicester Square, London WC2H 7LE.
TEL 0171 766 6000. **FAX** 0171 766 6100.
● City Radio, 8–10 Stanley Street, Liverpool, Merseyside L1 6AF.
TEL 0151 227 5100. **FAX** 0151 471 0330.
● GLR, PO Box 94.9, 35C Marylebone High Street, London W1A 4LG.
TEL 0171 224 2424. **FAX** 0171 487 2908.
● GMR, PO Box 90, New Broadcasting House, Oxford Road, Manchester M60 1SJ.
TEL 0161 200 2000. **FAX** 0161 236 5804.
● GWR, PO Box 2000, Bristol BS99 7SN.
TEL 0117 984 3200. **FAX** 0117 984 3202.
● Kiss FM, 80 Holloway Road, London N7 8JG.
TEL 0171 700 6100. **FAX** 0171 700 3752.
● The Radio Authority, Holbrook House, 14 Great Queen Street, London WC2B 5BG.
TEL 0171 430 2724. **FAX** 0171 405 7062.
● XFM, 97 Charlotte Street, London W1P 1LB.
TEL 0171 299 4000. **FAX** 0171 299 4010.

RADIO PRODUCER

MONEY: Can be anything from volunteering to do it for nowt to a good wage of over £30,000. It depends what level you're at. Oh, and independent radio pays more.

HOURS: Few jobs are 10 a.m. to 6 p.m. and there are definitely a lot of late nights here.

HEALTH RISK: 8/10. Similar to radio DJ, except the responsibility for the programme is all yours.

PRESSURE RATING: 8/10. Having to see that a live show is running smoothly is some stress indeed. Mr Pop Star will invariably turn up late if s/he has to be interviewed bang on 7.30 p.m., for instance.

GLAMOUR RATING: 2/10. It's not glamorous. Full stop.

TRAVEL RATING: 7/10. All those roadshows and special broadcasts live from the Reading Festival! Yes, the world of standing in the rain with a tape recorder in your hand trying to get the bassist from Jack to talk about his favourite sort of tent is most likely as good as it gets.

The radio producer is responsible for a specific radio show, dealing with content, style and format of the whole thing. Producers have to be responsible for everything, as it's them wot gets told off if things go wrong.

The world of radio would be precisely nil if it were not for reliable producers slaving away behind the scenes to bring you your daily load of smashing tunes and top interviews. The actual skill of the job is precisely that – if you *noticed* the producer butting in or heard long ominous spells of silence, something would be up and the producer wouldn't be doing his/her job properly.

A radio producer will typically work on a specific time-slot and is involved in every show that goes out within it. The nature of the job depends on the nature of the show, but producers do follow similar ways of working. They will make sure that the station's playlist is adhered to, book guests for interviews and studio sessions, and where appropriate often edit the pre-recorded sections, too. It's a long, time-consuming business and means far longer hours than the dead famous, high-profile DJ has to keep.

You have to be an organised old beggar to do this job, and not mind taking all the responsibility for things. Most producers start with some experience of radio. Local radio is good, as many have programmes in which youngsters can volunteer their services, and learn how to produce and broadcast. The same goes for **hospital radio**.

Emma Lyne is the senior radio producer at Wise Buddah (sic) Music Radio, Mark Goodier's independent production company which makes Goodier's Radio One weekend show,

Pete Tong's, Judge Jules's and Trevor Nelson's programmes, and also created *Collins and Maconie's Hit Parade*. She started at Radio Stoke at the age of sixteen, helping to make a magazine show that was staffed by volunteers. She interviewed and reviewed bands, put stories together, and learnt technical and interviewing skills, while doing A levels at the same time. A couple of years later, she saw an advert for a trainee producer at the BBC, applied for the job, and was offered five weeks of work experience on the Steve Wright show. She asked for more time at the end of it, because she was enjoying herself so much, and got three weeks extra. Emma was convinced that she had found her calling.

'I heard that a production assistant was taking leave for three months, so I rang up my boss and said, "Can I have Lisa's job?" He replied, "That's not how it works, Emma," but half an hour later he rang me back and told me the job was mine.'

A production assistant is a rung down from being a producer. It has a higher secretarial quotient [as noted in the 'Radio DJ' chapter by Ms Clare Sturgess, who had the very same job title]. Emma worked for Jackie Brambles and then Gary Davies's lunchtime show. When she told him that the new Verve single was brilliant, back in the early nineties, he listened to it and then played it on his show – so the position is certainly not without influence.

Emma soon found herself travelling in vans to obscure towns nationwide, finding people in hairdressers who were willing to talk to Gary Davies – no easy task – and setting up pop stars for outside broadcasts: Take That in the underwear department of Marks and Spencer in Warrington, for example.

Virtually all radio producers begin as assistants, performing every lofty and menial task needed to keep the show going. In Emma's case, she had wanted to work for Mark Goodier's *Evening Session* on Radio One for a while, and after much badgering the men in suits gave her a job as his **PA**. When Goodier set up Wise Buddah, he offered Emma a job as producer on *The Hit Parade* – the new releases show presented by ex-*NME* journalists Collins and Maconie. It's the eternal story of a foot in the door and talent leading to that all-important break.

There are several similar

RADIO PRODUCER

production companies in this deregulated age, such as West End, who make *The Essential Mix* and Danny Rampling's show. Many people prefer to work in this smaller, more intimate environment, but in these cases the producers liaise as much with Radio One as they would were they employed purely by the old-style corporation. Independent radio producers have to be a little more ratings-conscious, as the stations need to be as populist as possible, seeing as they have advertisers who want to reach all those consumers who are obviously listening to the radio between shopping.

Producer satisfaction lies in a top-rated programme, which is doing as much with the medium in the slot that it's in as possible. Producers can influence what goes on the playlist, can bring in new voices (often music journalists) for individual sections of their programmes, and overall have a chance to really shape an exciting radio experience. **Feedback** is very swift on radio, as listeners love writing letters, faxing and E-mailing, and being a bit obsessive. It's all a lot more immediate than TV.

There are courses in radio engineering and production at university, and these provide a good grounding, but it's experience that will really get you in. And, as ever, you can get this only by badgering radio stations or production companies to give you work experience – for nothing, or for a pittance.

'The job is really stressful,' says Emma, who's now been at Wise Buddah for three years and has spent some of her working life sleeping under her desk – the days were so long. 'But I really enjoy it. You can go out and see lots of bands, and then the next thing you know you might be putting their record on the radio. I always wanted to work in music, but I never thought it would be radio.'

GLOSSARY
● **Hospital radio**
Large hospitals have their own radio station and it's an excellent place to learn your craft. It doesn't pay well, though, if at all. Many 'names' started by playing Elton John to people in traction.
● **PA**
Personal assistant. Does the filing, answers letters, goes to get a sandwich from the corner shop for the DJ, etc. A step on the ladder.
● **Feedback**
All radio stations use this term. Listeners ringing up to complain about rude jokes is 'feedback'. Has nothing to do with musical feedback, which is about electrics and eighties punk rock.

SKILLS YOU'LL NEED
Good organisational skills, ability to work under pressure with people who are often late (i.e. pop stars), thoroughness, some technical knowledge, knowing a good tune.

TIPS
● Look out for courses in engineering and production. Many local colleges do basic qualification courses.
● Try to spot BBC ads in the Monday and Saturday *Guardian*s. They'll train you if they spot potential.
● If your college/place of learning has a radio station, get your experience there. You don't have to be

a DJ to get involved. If there's no
station, badger them to start one up.
Local and hospital radio is always
looking for people.

● Help any pals who want to be DJs
to put together their own tapes to
send out to local radio – then you
have something to show for yourself.

USEFUL ADDRESSES

● BBC Radio 1, Yalding House, Great
Portland Street, London W1N 4DJ.
TEL 0171 580 4468. **FAX** 0171 927 5869.
● Capital Radio, 29–30 Leicester
Square, London WC2H 7LE.
TEL 0171 766 6000. **FAX** 0171 766 6100.
● City Radio, 8–10 Stanley Street,
Liverpool, Merseyside L1 6AF.
TEL 0151 227 5100. **FAX** 0151 471 0330.
● GLR, PO Box 94.9, 35C Marylebone
High Street, London W1A 4LG.
TEL 0171 224 2424. **FAX** 0171 487 2908.
● GMR, PO Box 90, New Broadcasting
House, Oxford Road, Manchester M60
1SJ.
TEL 0161 200 2000. **FAX** 0161 236 5804.
● GWR, PO Box 2000, Bristol BS99
7SN.
TEL 0117 984 3200. **FAX** 0117 984 3202.
● Kiss FM, 80 Holloway Road,
London N7 8JG.
TEL 0171 700 6100. **FAX** 0171 700 3752.
● XFM, 97 Charlotte Street, London
W1P 1LB.
TEL 0171 299 4000. **FAX** 0171 299 4010.

RADIO/TV PLUGGER

MONEY: The classic routine: begin slogging for buttons, start to earn a bit, then progress to a healthy wedge.

HOURS: Can be 9 a.m. to 10 p.m., including loads of gigs.

HEALTH RISK: 5/10. Keeps you fit because you run around a lot.

EQUIPMENT COSTS: All pluggers have those big, black record bags. From free (promotional item) to £25 for a sturdy one.

PRESSURE RATING: 8/10. It's your job to get records played by broadcasters locally and nationwide. There's a lot of pressure there.

GLAMOUR RATING: 6/10. Meeting radio and TV producers is obviously worthwhile and fulfilling, but it's not something to tell the grandchildren about.

TRAVEL RATING: 5/10 Regional pluggers hop about, but only to Burnley and the like.

Pluggers do the same job as a press officer – trying to get publicity for their given acts – but for broadcast media (radio and television) instead of newspapers and magazines.

Without pluggers you'd get Barry Manilow and Abba on *The O Zone* and Radio One instead of the new sounds of the revolution. Plugging, known to poshos as 'Music PR', gets new music heard by radio and television producers alike, who are always after the latest sounds to put in their respective programmes, as well as new videos and bands to interview on air. There are in-house pluggers in major record labels, and there are independent companies who work for smaller labels and bands that the record company see as fit to have independent plugging.

Pluggers take on a number of bands and try to get them exposure. What is different about plugging, as compared with magazine PR, is that the job involves far more legwork and is based not around mail-outs but on actually hot-footing it out of the office to visit producers and physically hand over their wares.

The record company will pay the pluggers to work on a single, and once they've proved successful they hope to be asked to work on the band's forthcoming stuff. Roland Hill works for independent pluggers Anglo, doing London-based radio such as Virgin, Radio One and Capital. Kiss, Heart and Atlantic are covered by his colleagues. There's a regional department for local radio, and a TV department within the same company that deals with producers and band bookers if it's a programme like *The Big Breakfast*.

'The good thing about the music industry is there's no routine day,' says

Hill. There may be appointments with producers at radio stations, plus dropping records in the **pigeonholes** of other producers. There are record-company meetings, to inform them how things are going, how the **press angle** is looking, etc. You have to get bands in the right place at the right time for **sessions** and interviews, then go with them to make sure they're OK. Then there're gigs in the evening, to check out bands you are contemplating taking on.

Pluggers come from different backgrounds. Roland got a degree in philosophy (probably useful – you need to be philosophical when your great white hope hasn't even made Radio One's C list) and started by phoning up record companies asking for work experience – the stuffing-envelopes game. 'I wanted to do it for nothing!' he exclaims. The marketing department at Island Records let him help them out. 'I survived on no money, I commuted from Oxford, then slept on people's floors until I got a job. That's the way it goes.' Work experience enables you to meet up with important people in the industry or, at least, to know who they are. After three months, Roland sent his **CV** to some companies, including Anglo, and got the job he has now. That was three years ago.

'At the end of the day, the job is PR,' he says. 'I could be doing PR for cornflakes, or PR for computer games, but I happen to do it for records and it's easy to be enthusiastic about something that you love. When I was younger, I always used to hassle friends about records – "Hey! Listen to this!" – and that's basically what I do here.'

The pressure is intense, however. The record companies pay you to get results, and it's no good boasting that you had a tasty sandwich at lunchtime with **Richard Ashcroft** when you didn't get his record on the Capital Radio A list. Radio still holds the upper hand over TV, interestingly enough. Television people are far less likely to go with broadcasting a single if it hasn't cut any sway with

RADIO PLUGGER

their radio colleagues. 'Radio is so instant,' says Roland. 'Millions hear a record that might have only arrived at the station that morning. Television requires a lot of planning and is a slower process.'

At Anglo, the pluggers don't have the final say on whom they represent: the boss does. However, pluggers can all make suggestions and the top man may be won round if there's a good case put forward for a certain band. Honesty is a big factor. PRs have to be honest with record companies about what they think the band's expectations are media-wise, to ensure nobody is expecting Dumpy's Rusty Nuts to go on *Top Of The Pops 2*. Similarly, the PRs can't push a band too much and say they're too wonderful when they're patently not. Honesty is appreciated from the producer's side, too.

'We want people to be blunt and we don't want them to tell us they like a band we work with when they obviously don't,' reflects Hill. 'You have to remember that at the end of the day it's just people who have individual music tastes you're dealing with. You have to take the knockbacks on the chin.'

Pluggers work extremely long hours and are expected to go to all the happening gigs, but the joy of hearing a record that you've successfully worked on the radio is a real bonus. Plus, there are other career opportunities. The current MD of EMI used to be a plugger. So did Ash's manager. Once you're in and know the business you can decide where to go next. Plugging has changed a great deal from the payola-laden days of the fifties to the seventies, when pluggers

would fly radio producers to America or give them various promotional 'incentives' to break their records. Those notorious days are gone: now, the only way to be successful is to be upfront about good music. Indeed.

'I don't think people respond to gimmicks now, and ideally the music speaks for itself,' summarises Hill. 'I don't think that bribing is going to get you far and it isn't how you break bands – the strategy has to be long-term.'

GLOSSARY
● **Pigeonholes**
Wooden boxes where faxes, incoming mail and pluggers' little jiffy bags full of hot CDs are left. No pigeons, all being well.
● **Press angle**
The particular slant, or story, a magazine will use when covering a band. 'My drug hell' or 'When I was a woman' are two such angles.
● **Sessions**
When a band goes into the studio to record some tunes. The BBC sessions with The Beatles in the sixties were repackaged by EMI in 1995 and sold by the million.
● **CV**
Curriculum vitae. A list of your qualifications, jobs, interests, age, address, etc. All neatly typed up to give people a glimpse of who you are. Lots of folk lie on theirs to get into jobs that they might not normally be deemed qualified to do. It works. (But don't try it, right.)
● **Richard Ashcroft**
Lanky 'I am mad' singer with The Verve.

SKILLS YOU'LL NEED

Energy; diplomacy; persistence –
but not so as it becomes annoying;
dedication; awareness of all media
and what other bands are up to.

TIPS

● Get a job somewhere in the
business if you can, and get to know
the plugger types.
● Any PR work experience will give
you an idea of this side of the
industry.
● Practise playing your friends tracks
they think they won't like, and
persuading them that they do.
● If they don't like the records, don't
try and force them to by dipping their
ears in cold water or anything.
● Or putting their elbows in pigeonholes with hungry pigeons in them.

USEFUL ADDRESSES

● Anglo Plugging, 72 Black Lion
Lane, London W6 9BE.
TEL 0181 910 4666. **FAX** 0181 741 1209.
● Beer Davies, 3–4 Little Portland
Street, London W1N 6BD.
TEL 0171 323 3003. **FAX** 0171 323 4768.
● Fiveash & Hill, 2nd Floor, 106 Great
Portland Street, London W1N 5PE.
TEL 0171 636 1553. **FAX** 0171 636 1554.
● Intermedia, Byron House, 112A
Shirland Road, London W9 2EQ.
TEL 0171 266 0777. **FAX** 0171 266 1293.
● Phuture Trax, 312 The
Leathermarket, Weston Street,
London SE1 3ER.
TEL 0171 357 0004. **FAX** 0171 378 7377.
● Power Promotions, Unit 11, Impress
House, Mansell Road, London W3
7QH.
TEL 0181 932 3030. **FAX** 0181 932 3031.

PIGEONS DO NOT SIT
IN A RADIO STATION'S
PIGEONHOLES.

RECORD-COMPANY MANAGING DIRECTOR

💰 MONEY: From very little at a small company to a few hundred thousand at the majors. You may find yourself in those *Sunday Times* 'Very Very Rich People' lists if you're not careful.

⏰ HOURS: From 8.30 or 9 a.m. till late every evening – seeing bands (yes, MDs do) or having top-flight meetings with top-flight people in top-flight restaurants.

✚ HEALTH RISK: 7/10. All those fat-cat exec lunches might lead to obesity and heart problems.

✋ PRESSURE RATING: 10/10. You have to translate *grrreat* talent into *grrreat* big amounts of cash. Even MDs have bosses.

🍸 GLAMOUR RATING: 8/10. You get to go to **award ceremonies**, wear penguin suits, and get photographed with Mariah Carey in *Music Week*.

✈ TRAVEL RATING: 7/10. When all is said and done, managing director is essentially an office job. It's not overly exotic.

The managing director is responsible for every single move his/her record company makes in a given territory. From creative decisions to financial ones, and all the bits in between, the MD is pretty much the boss.

Some record companies divide their artists into three categories: newly signed; established, which are those acts with a gold album under their belt; and superstars, which are people with a few gold and platinum albums who've been around for a while. It's the job of a good MD to turn the former into the latter.

It should be pointed out at this juncture, in case it is not violently obvious, that there is a certain quantum leap between a) deciding a career in the music business is for you and b) becoming a record-company MD. It's all very well to aim for the heights, but it takes bloody ages to become an MD. You have to be very, very good and you have to understand, and excel in, just about every area of the industry (except, possibly, roadie). There is, of course, the short cut of starting up your own Nutso Records label and getting access to a photocopier to do your headed notepaper. That way, you can be MD as soon as you like. But, for real, serious players, there's no substitute for years and years of hard slog, dedication, conviction, and inspiration before you start earning sums of money which even Sting or Elton John will gawp at.

There is one question which springs to mind when pondering the sheer enormity of the job that is managing director. What on earth do they actually *do*, these big be-suited fellows? Do they charge around looking important and frightening the office juniors? Do they sit behind a desk doodling caricatures of Mariah Carey? Do they sit around George Michael's talking about traditional cheeses? No – none of the above (except maybe the first one). They do a demanding job like everyone else. It's just that they're a teensy bit more responsible for everything than anyone else, and the first to tick other people off for doodling those Mariah cartoons.

'I think the main job of the MD is to get an idea of the vision for the label,' says Tony Wadsworth, head honcho for the past three and a half years at Parlophone, whose artists include Blur, Supergrass and Radiohead. 'You coordinate various elements of the label, and ensure everybody is moving in the same direction and understands the same **priorities**. Also, it's keeping everyone motivated, to an extent. When people think things aren't going right, you ensure they are put right without demotivating anyone.'

It's a busy job. Managing directors do actually have bosses – Wadsworth, for example, reports to the president and chief executive officer of EMI Records Group UK, who deals with Parlophone, EMI and Chrysalis (including **back catalogue**, compilations departments, etc.), which are all divisions of the same company. Wadworth's responsibility is to deliver a profit figure for EMI Records Group UK. 'I am,' reflects Wadsworth, 'a bridge between

the corporate part of the business – a necessary evil, if you like – and the actual creative workings of the label.'

The president/chief executive in turn reports to the president of EMI Europe, who answers to the president of EMI Records Music Worldwide. Also up in the stratosphere is the president of EMI Worldwide, who also deals with the publishing side. The top dog is the chairman of EMI Group plc. Essentially, record companies contain the same corporate hierarchy as do multinational firms in every other comparable industry.

The managing director gets together regularly with the heads of all his departments within the record

MD

label, such as A&R, marketing and TV and radio promotion. He also receives 'dotted-line reporting' from the head of business affairs and business support, and the finance section, which also includes lawyers and legal advisers.

A typical week for Tony Wadsworth starts on Monday morning when he examines the new single and album charts announced the night before to decide whether any tactical decisions need to be made vis-à-vis promoting his acts. Monday is also the release day for new singles and albums, to ensure these records get maximum time in the stores before next week's chart is compiled.

Each Monday, Wadsworth has a meeting with all his department heads, as do all major-label MDs. Current projects are discussed, as are individual strategies within press, promotion and marketing. **Sales people** waft figures about. 'It's a forum for me to be able to get an idea of anything that's going horribly wrong and identify the things that need to be changed,' says Mr Parlophone.

The rest of the week is spent meeting already signed artists' managers, if the MD wishes to discuss direction, or if the MD or the artist has a problem. Bands may have serious gripes, or might just be miffed that they've written a song about rodents but received no coverage in *What Shrew Monthly*. On the other hand, the MD may be unimpressed with the artist's habit of constantly demanding free helicopter travel to get to and from the shops. There's a constant stream of meetings – with everyone, ultimately. The MD and marketing.

The MD and promotions. The MD and the creative crew. The MD and acts signed to other companies who want to move. The MD and subsidiary labels. Yep, it's meetings, meetings, meetings at the top!

The A&R department will also try and drag the managing director to gigs if they think they've spotted a really cracking live act. Plus, there are other artists signed to American branches of the company, for instance, who are always coming over to play, and the MD has to put in an appearance. He will invariably be expected to show his face backstage to wish the artists good luck. Yet another part of Tony Wadsworth's routine at Parlophone is the monthly financial-forecast meeting, at which he assesses the company's overall performance and considers recent sales figures and future projections. This may involve adjusting budgets for A&R, marketing, etc.

So how do you ascend to such a rarified position of power? Well, Tony Wadsworth completed an economics degree, spent some time in a band he steadfastly refuses to name, then after they split decided that he liked the music industry enough to pursue a career on the other side of the fence. He 'glossed up' his past in his CV – i.e. went on about his degree and not about spending two years in a transit van – then applied for a job as product manager at a K-Tel-type firm called Warwick Records. His job there was primarily concerned with getting CDs manufactured on time, but he later moved on to RCA before fetching up at EMI.

'I made people aware when I arrived at EMI that I was someone who could do more than just phone up the factory and get ten thousand records made,' he says. 'I sold myself a bit and they created a new job for me and called me the catalogue marketing manager. I got hold of the back catalogue and started re-releasing albums. It worked like a dream – it started with a couple per month and ended with a hundred per year.'

This success story propelled him into marketing. 'I guess they thought: Maybe Tony can deal with people who are living as well,' he says. 'I just made people aware I was there and didn't sit in the corner doing my job like a shrinking violet.'

Wadsworth says the toughest part of being an MD is holding on to your initial vision. 'It's hard to keep a level head in a business which is full of people who shout,' he expands. 'A lot of people have short-term ideas and you're trying to maintain a **long-term plan** and vision. The other thing is that there literally aren't enough hours in the day. I could live in my office and not have any personal life whatsoever. You have to know when to stop working. Working nonstop doesn't make you good at the job, and you lose everything when you lose your job if it's all you've got.'

Some MDs are shouty folk who have a vision and make everyone do what they say; others work on more of a consensus approach, which is what

OPTIONAL.

Tony aims to do. Managing directors may be chummy enough with each other socially but: 'You go back to your office and it's war again,' says Tony, who doesn't wear a suit unless he's going to an awards ceremony or popping out for a pint with Tina Turner.

So what happens when people stop being managing directors? Well, some go on up the corporate ladder and become an MD in another country. Others may move into managing a band or artist. One former MD at Warner Brothers went back to being a writer and press officer. There is, however, a stigma attached to moving back 'down' the ladder in this country – whereas in America it's far more common.

Still, who's to worry, eh? Most managing directors can't be worrying about what's next or they wouldn't have time to do the job in hand. They have to be positive to motivate all the people at the label, and to run their company teeth-gleamingly well.

'I love my job,' summarises Wadsworth. 'It's great. I'm lucky to have the best roster of acts, I'm working with really creative artists, and I'm with people who've worked for me for ten years. What could be better?'

GLOSSARY

● **Award ceremonies**

Awful big parties where pop stars get a trophy for still living in the country and not going off to Sweden for tax purposes.

● **Priorities**

In all companies, some artists are prioritised. It generally means more money is spent recording and promoting them.

● **Back catalogue**

The old records that have been released through the years on the record label. Companies make a bit of cash re-releasing them on CD when they think the market is ripe for a particular artist.

● **Sales people**

They work for all labels within the record-company umbrella. They sell records to multiple retailers, like Our Price and Woolworths, and speak to distributors about physically getting the product into the shops.

● **Long-term plan**

While everyone else is talking about the flavour of the month, the MD must concentrate on the next few years' output on the label.

SKILLS YOU'LL NEED

Numeracy, literacy, vision, communication skills, boundless confidence.

TIPS

● Tony Wadsworth: 'As The Clash said, you turn rebellion into money. I think one of the skills of a good MD is being able to have a good conversation with an eighteen-year-old kid in a band you're about to sign as well as being able to connect with the finance director. You go from one extreme to another.'

● A lot of MDs are promoted through the legal and business affairs department. A good knowledge of this side of the business is worthwhile. Train as a lawyer!

● Any degree will stand you in good stead. Serious stuff like politics, sociology or economics helps.

● A wide experience of the music industry is required. Be prepared to work for different departments within the record company.

RECORD PRODUCER

MONEY: You get paid per job, which can be up to £75,000 for an album, up front.

HOURS: You can work twelve- to sixteen-hour days if you're the intensive type. Sensible sorts go for an 11 a.m. to 10.30 p.m. day. Which is still quite a lot.

HEALTH RISK: 9/10. Sitting down in a smoky studio all hours of the day with only tapping toes for exercise.

PRESSURE RATING: 9/10. You've got to come up with the goods, for the band, management, and bloomin' record company.

GLAMOUR RATING: 8/10. You get to sit in a room with the stars for hours and hours, and they think you're tops if their tunes sound great. It's still sitting in a room, though, when all is said and done.

TRAVEL RATING: 7/10. You can get to go all over the shop when you're a famous producer. But you'll end up in a studio with no windows, wherever you go.

You work in the recording studio producing recorded sound with the band or artist that you've been asked to create with. Singles, albums, spook tracks for bizarre compilation LPs – you have to turn your wizard hand to all sorts of sounds.

Record producers sell millions of records and their artistry is heard by hordes of folk across the land: on the radio, telly, adverts, and in the background on *EastEnders*. Yet they never get on *Top Of The Pops* and are rarely noticed when walking down the street or buying pants in Marks and Spencer. Being a producer is just as creative and satisfying as being a musician, but you don't get the aggro and you do get to talk about plectrums with the stars. It's not at all bad, really, but it's a lot of hard work.

What producers do can vary from bod to bod, but there is a general job pattern. Generally, producers are commissioned by a record-company A&R department to go into the studio with a band or artist to record a single or album tracks. This can vary from one day in the studio to several months, depending on the project. Most established producers have an agent or manager who maintains their client's diaries and will negotiate a fee. Fees can vary: if the producer really likes a band but they have no money, then he might waive his usual charge and go for something they can afford; with a major-label deal, the A&R department will have already set a budget that the band cannot go over.

The producer hears demos by the band, usually many more tracks than will land on the album, and decides whether he likes the stuff. S/he then cites which studio is preferable, and decides which engineer to work with – often the two will see themselves as a team. These details are sorted out by the A&R coordinator of the record company, who also checks whether supercool backing singers or any accordian soloists will have to be booked, and makes sure their fee is included in the A&R budget as well.

Most albums with a bit of major-label finance behind them will go through pre-production. This is rehearsals with producer and engineer, working out the ace guitar licks and swirlaway drum solos that might be appearing in the track. If any choruses need changing, **keys** altered, or **intro**s fiddled about with, this is the time to do it. Not all songs are quite 'there' when a band goes into the studio. Some of them are over in a corner and need to be coaxed out. The producer gets a feel of the tunes, decides an order in which they should be done, and is able to have a coffee and a Hobnob with the people he'll be trapped in a room with for weeks.

Then the production starts. The band, if we're talking a basic guitar-band set-up, files into the studio every day. Each member does their individual bits and the track is built up from there. The band playing together and performing a song straight through doesn't happen much any more. Instead, a microphone is set up each time an instrument is plugged in, and all those buttons on the mixing desk tweaked to get it going through a channel.

Desks can have between eight and 48 tracks, although 24 is the average in a reasonable studio. Each track is given a channel, between one and 24, f'rinstance. Those desk buttons can boost the lower frequencies and higher frequencies and are known as the EQ (equaliser). Bass gets a lower boost;

sometimes guitars get a higher frequency treat. It all depends. The producer just tries to get the sound he and the band like the best, that they think will fit the track.

The producer and band then go through all the tracks, choosing when the best time to do them is, according to how they're feeling and whatnot. It's obviously no use trying to sing a song about children dying when the singer's just had a lovely slice of cake, and hopeless trying to persuade the guitarist to play the 'poppy number' when he's just found out the Cup footie has been cancelled. Producers aren't just there to twiddle knobs; they're there to get on with the artists and draw the beast inside right out of them.

'A producer is like a director of a film,' says Stephen Street, who's produced the likes of The Smiths, Morrissey, The Cranberries and Blur. 'You're working very closely with an artist and you've got to make sure that they're in the right frame of mind. You make decisions which aren't purely technical decisions. There are some songs you don't touch, but that's a skill: if it ain't broken, don't try to fix it.'

Stephen Street started off as a musician, playing with different groups who weren't very successful. He didn't reckon he was much cop at the guitar or bass, his chosen instruments, but he liked being in the studio. He decided to write to lots of studios and get a job as an assistant engineer, learn how to use the desk, and progress up the proverbial ladder. He didn't get many replies, but a friend told him the Island Records studio, situated in the basement under

RECORD PRODUCER

their offices in London, was looking for someone. He went and saw them that same day, made out that another studio were interested in employing him, and got the job.

Stephen was the only assistant there for a time – a lot of studios have more than one – so he worked on almost every session. Often 'assistant' is just another term for 'tea boy' and you are allowed to do precisely zero good stuff but, because Mr Street had been in a studio before with his band chums, the engineers there let him be a little more 'hands on' (i.e. touch things), and within a couple of years he was a house engineer working with whoever came into the studio.

'Then,' he says, 'you've just got to wait for that lucky break. When something comes along and you do a good job, you may hopefully hang on the coat-tails of their success.' Stephen's big break was The Smiths in 1984. The studio manager told him they were coming in and asked him if

he wanted to do the session. He jumped at the chance as he'd heard their first single and loved it. They came in to record the single 'Heaven Knows I'm Miserable Now', produced by John Porter.

'I think my natural enthusiasm pleased them,' he says. 'Morrissey and Marr took my number. Then they did the next single without me and I thought: Oh, they've forgotten about me! Then I got a phone call from their manager saying that they wanted to record and produce the *Meat Is Murder* album themselves, but would I be prepared to go along and engineer it? That was my first step into something that was beginning to take off.'

When you're an engineer, says Street, it's inevitable that sooner or later you begin to make production decisions. The more knowledge you have gained, the more input you have. The trick is making sure you're recording everything in the best way possible. Ultimately, you have to please the record company, as they have employed you, although most producers would rather go with what they and the artist are happy with.

Once the recording has been done, the record is mixed: this is the stage which always seems a whole lot of hassle. The volume levels have to be adjusted on every single channel, i.e. instrument. Some volumes will change as the song progresses. Most guitarists want their fingerwork nice and loud, and most singers will insist that you can't hear them and demand that you turn them up. Get the mix wrong, and the track won't sound right. It's like when you hear so-called 'critics' saying a track has been 'over-produced', because all the squelchy 'I am an alien' extra noises have been turned up too high and no one can hear the tune. Thus producers are always listening to the songs they've produced and wondering whether the drums should have kicked in earlier, or the bleeps sound too New Romantic. 'Yes, I have been known to say, "Those hi-hats are a bit toppy." I can't bear to listen to my own stuff at home. I'm never completely happy,' admits Stephen.

Record companies can be a nightmare to work with, especially if the A&R man wants to have his or her say about what the album should sound like. Then you've got the artists who might think they're the latest hot cheese and storm about the studio trying to look powerful and not switching off their mobile phone when the poor keyboard player is trying to find **middle C**. A producer's life is not always a happy one.

'Sometimes the most intense people who have a natural-genius ability can be frustrating,' says Street. 'You can't expect everyone to be easy-going. If they're not entirely happy about the conditions they're in at the time, they can make the day really feel quite awkward. Look at the way George Martin worked with The Beatles. If they wanted to be they could be bouncing off the walls, and Martin was always there as the sober straight one, keeping the lid on the pot as it were. I don't believe in getting out of my brains while I'm in the studio, 'cos I don't think anything works that way, to be honest.' Street refuses to work deep into the night, as many producers do, because he says you lose the ability to make the right decisions and make them quickly. He says some singers do like to have a snifter before they sing because they get nervous, but he's personally content with a beer after the session.

Street has worked with Blur since the beginning, but still finds it a wheeze. 'Last year I worked on Blur's fifth album,' he says. 'People think that by the time a band are

HI HATS (CAN BE A BIT TOPPY).

working on their fifth album it's going to be business as usual, but I was just as het up about making that album as any of the others. I enjoyed the challenges. We went to Iceland for a couple of weeks to work out there.' Yes, if you have the **budget**, recording one album in a few places keeps the excitement up.

Street likes to work with a lot of new bands, so he's constantly doing different things and at different levels. 'I've had the pleasure of working with Morrissey and Damon Albarn, but I look forward to working with a new band who hopefully will be signed next year. If I went into the studio with David Bowie I'd be so in awe I'd end up a quivering wreck in the corner.'

Street reckons there's not much time for egos in the business, although there are producers who are notoriously picky. When you hear the album you produced is number one, you're often in the studio with someone else, laying down a meaty saxophone solo. Hearing your tunes on the radio, he says, is the 'best buzz'. It might as well be, because you don't get many perks in this job. You have to pay for gold discs now, you know: they don't just get doled out to all and sundry.

Producers can lose their edge – you can burn yourself out, or sometimes become unfashionable if you're seen as being allied particularly to one movement that's had its day. You can also get bored. Producers can come and go. They might end up doing jingles, or soundtracks for telly and film.

Would Stephen advise anyone to do the job?

'No, there's enough competition out there as it is!' he jokes. 'It's all about lucky breaks and being in the right place at the right time. I still do it because I still enjoy it. Perhaps you might just be a great engineer and that's your thing. It's up to you to know your limits.'

A BIT ABOUT ENGINEERS

Engineers help the producer on the more technical side of production, learning their trade as they go on. They're responsible for setting up the equipment for the day: checking the tape that the band record on to, labelling tape boxes, loading samples, anything that needs to be done in preparation. Engineers can earn from around £8,000 a year to £20,000 and over. They have to make sure the band don't walk away with any equipment – which they are prone to do. Says Street, of his engineering past:

'Often you're determining what the drums sound like, what reverb you need – you are making some production decisions. Whether you as a person have the wherewithal to carry on and develop that and turn into a producer is another thing, but there's sometimes no clear division between engineer and producer.'

GLOSSARY
● **Key**
The range of notes the song is written in. The key of C, for instance, has no sharp or flat notes. The key of B, conversely, is a bugger with semi-tones all over the shop.
● **Intro**
Start of the tune. 'Wooooooosh!' it often goes, or 'Brrrrrrr!', to give the song momentum.

● **Middle C**
The C note in the middle of the keyboard.

● **Budget**
Set by the A&R department of the record company and governed by how many records they think they'll sell. Some albums are recorded in space-age technology studios in Jamaica (Happy Mondays) and others are made in bedroom studios in Wolverhampton (lots of dance bods).

SKILLS YOU'LL NEED

Diplomacy; a bit of technical knowledge; ability to bone up on all new music – and old music; being nice to people; letting your ears, not your brain, do the thinking; reliability; creativity.

TIPS

● Ring up studios and see if they need anyone to help out doing anything at all.

● A few colleges do sound-engineering courses which will give a basic know-how. Check with your local authority.

● Listen to records and see what extra bits are added that are not part of the main 'tune' – riffs, twinkly sounds, cymbal hits. This is how producers listen to music.

● If you have friends with equipment, offer to help them out and learn your way around. More and more people have home studios, and experience really is invaluable.

USEFUL ADDRESSES

● Abbey Road Studios, 3 Abbey Road, London NW8 9AY.
TEL 0171 266 7000. **FAX** 0171 266 7250.
● Air Studios, Lyndhurst Hall, Lyndhurst Road, Hampstead, London NW3 5NG.
TEL 0171 794 0660. **FAX** 0171 794 8518.
● Nomis Studios, 45–53 Sinclair Road, London W14 ONS.
TEL 0171 602 6351. **FAX** 0171 603 5941.
● Rockfield Studios, Amberley Court, Rockfield Road, Monmouth, Gwent.
TEL 01600 712449. **FAX** 01600 714421.
● Sarm West, 8–10 Basing Street, London W11 1ET.
TEL 0171 229 1229. **FAX** 0171 221 9247.
● Swanyard Studio, 12–27 Swan Yard, London N1 1SD.
TEL 0171 354 3737. **FAX** 0171 226 2581.
● The Town House, 150 Goldhawk Road, London W12 8HH.
TEL 0181 932 3200. **FAX** 0181 932 3207.

ROADIE

> **MONEY:** From around £50-£100 per day, to £1,000 per week and over for the U2 roadies of this world.
>
> **HOURS:** Eighteen or more every day when you're on the road.
>
> **HEALTH RISK:** 7/10. Lots of running around, but lots of fags 'n' booze late nights as well.
>
> **PRESSURE RATING:** 7/10. If you barge into Noel and knock him over as you hand him his best Rickenbacker on stage, he won't be best pleased.
>
> **GLAMOUR RATING:** 5/10. Scrabbling around at the feet of the stars and trying to fix their effects pedals. Hm.
>
> **TRAVEL RATING:** 10/10. Your very job is on the road … So, yes.

The roadie is responsible for the practical smooth running of the tour – from loading equipment to stopping the audience being sick on the artist's shoes.

'**G**oing on the road' is a phrase that roadies say a lot. The Road is the magic land of tour buses, defective leads, and cans of beer. It is a Camelot, a mysterious place that doesn't exist to anyone but those who are in it. A bit like being drunk. Which people on the road normally are.

'Roadie' is a very un-nineties term. 'Backline technician' is the 'now' phrase. When a group goes on tour, they employ backline technician people to carry and polish their guitars. These people are jolly sorts who enjoy the road lifestyle that bands lead – the moving about, the interesting people, the booze, and the pies at service stations. You get all the good bits of being in a band, but without having to ever utter the phrase 'Good evening, Leicester!'.

Digby Cleaver wanted to be a roadie (we're allowed to call him that: he's old-school and doesn't mind) since he first found out what one was as a teenager. 'I tried to play guitar, but I was appalling at making chord shapes. Then I suddenly realised there were things called roadies. I thought: What a brilliant job! From then on I was intent on doing it. So I am actually a career roadie.'

Cleaver was serving in a record shop and working three nights a week in a pub to earn extra money. The drummer of a rock band (UFO, old rock fans) used to drink in the pub, and that's where Digby got his break. Old drummer bloke happened to share a flat with **Hawkwind**'s head roadie and knew he needed someone.

'This roadie chap immediately took me under his wing,' says Digby. 'He showed me which end of the plug went into the wall and which one to the back of the amp.' A couple of months later, Digby was in Sweden, crawling around with leads and things.

A roadie is employed for a tour either by an artist's management or by a tour manager already commissioned to do the job. His employment starts with pre-tour rehearsals, checking the equipment which is going on the road.

You have to make sure the leads are good, find out which guitar strings are used, and order picks and enough parts to get you through the tour. You may find you're asked to go to the launderette for a bassist who's forgotten to wash his smalls and is too busy trading football cards with the keyboard player. When the band are having an argument about how the song ends at the end of the rehearsal, you have to get them out, turn everything off, clean up, and perhaps drive half of them home. Then next day you're on the motorway again in search of the next Ginster's pie. Digby calls the whole process 'submarine living': living on a big tour bus until 'once a day you up periscope at a gig'.

Between 8 and 9 a.m. the first truck rolls into the loading bay at the chosen venue, but you may begin earlier if there's lots to sort out. The trucks full of equipment and crew (caterers, sound and lighting, backline technicians) will have been travelling all night to get to the venue, if it's a long way from the previous night's gig. (If it's less than twenty miles away, the crew might hotel it for the night.)

There will be a local stage crew, employed by the promoter, who unload the first truck with the lighting equipment on it. They hang all the lights up in a dandy fashion on the rig that eventually towers over the stage. Then the sound truck arrives and the sound boxes are unloaded, the **PA** built and the **monitors** for the band to hear set up. Then the band's equipment lumbers on stage. Digby will be making sure nothing is dropped or thrown around. He'll devote attention to the guitars: putting them on their stands, cleaning them, and checking the strings are all in place. The lights are positioned on the **rig** and the crew members who are milling around scoff breakfast courtesy of the caterers: the catering equipment is always the first gear off the trucks and the last back on.

The band or artist arrives in the early afternoon and does their soundcheck. Some hate this ritual and go through one or two songs while snarling or chewing gum – American thrash/grunge band Babes In Toyland were known to soundcheck for a mere three minutes. Others love them and jam for hours – indie perennials The Wedding Present have played soundchecks which were

↑ pop star

↖ important bit of live equipment

ROADIE

longer than their actual gigs. Primal Scream like to 'jam', ie play none of their songs but old blues nonsense. Any technical problems are cleared up at this point, using the roadies' expansive knowledge, and then grub's up for everyone. And so the show begins.

We've all seen a bloke with his bottom hanging out of his trousers fiddling around at the ankles of some surly guitarist during a gig. That is a guitar roadie trying to fix an electrical problem. Backline technicians have to be alert all through the gig, ready to pounce upon a problem as soon as it occurs. Although, as Mark Radcliffe once famously asked on Radio One, 'Why do roadies always bend double when they come running on stage during a show? Do they think it makes them invisible and if they stood upright we'd all see them?'

After the show, the procedure is repeated in reverse as the roadies reload all the equipment on to the trucks as quickly as possible while the band and all their hangers-on are swanning around backstage drinking Cognac and smoking unfiltered cigarettes. The crew eventually climb into their own vehicle and put the video recorder on, play some hot tunes, drink lager, play cards, and whatever else.

'No one tells anyone to go to bed,' says Digby. 'But you have to be self-disciplined, because no one will come along and say "You're not doing that very well" – they'll just sack you. You have to do the job because you're proud of what you do.' You won't last if you're a slug-a-bed surly bloke who likes kissing strange women. No, you have to be keen on the job.

It must be said at this stage that there aren't very many female roadies. Women minded towards the on-the-road technical side of the music business are far more likely to become lighting or sound engineers. Roadieing unfortunately remains very much a laddish, all-blokes-together calling and, although this situation may change, it's going to take time.

Roadieing is not without its in-built travails. Vehicle breakdowns can throw a tour into turmoil, as can equipment breaking when you don't have the budget to fix it, and truck drivers getting busted at borders for drugs. You have to be as diplomatic as the tour manager in order to be part of the team. You can't just go off and sulk because the drummer beat you at cards the night before. You have to be friendly: you're living with twenty strangers in confined conditions for weeks on end.

YOU TEND TO GET YOUR GRUB FROM SERVICE STATIONS.

Digby philosophises about his job. 'You have to be incredibly diplomatic and very courteous, to know when to joke and when to be sympathetic. Half of the job is handling people, whether it's musicians or the idiot jobsworth in the village hall who's hired four children as the stage crew. And, to be successful, you have to really want to do it. No one says, "Thank you very much, you've done a good job." You know you *have* when you haven't been sacked.'

Roadies spend a lot of time polishing Rickenbackers and Les Pauls (a guitar, not a bloke) – bands love to have their guitars shining in the glare of the spotlights. You will also need a good knowledge of basic electrics – how much electricity comes out of the wall and the difference between alternate or direct current.

'Being a roadie is harder to get into than you might think,' continues Digby. 'The level of professionalism is higher than it used to be. Fewer bands will take a chance on a nineteen-year-old who's dead keen on working for them.' Like any business, roadieing is quite insular: friends of friends get jobs, or else people who have mates in groups. Bands will recommend their favourite roadies to each other, as will tour managers. It's all about reputation. Digby has worked with bands such as Madness, The Clash, The Only Ones and The Wonder Stuff.

When is he happiest?

'The day the cheque clears, to be brutally honest,' he says. 'But also, you'll never feel anything else in your life like the buzz of 80,000 people screaming as your band come running on to the stage. I experienced that with The Clash at Shea Stadium, and most of the audience hadn't come to see them – they were supporting The Who! On the other hand, there are days when I wish I was a chartered accountant with a pension and a secure future. But there are plenty of guys who are envious of me and say "You don't know how lucky you are!", and I always answer, "Yes, I do."'

GLOSSARY
● **Hawkwind**
Dodgy seventies rock band which once used to contain Lemmy.
● **PA**
Literally, public address system. The big speakers which stand on the stage and pipe out the music to the fans and headbangers out front.
● **Monitors**
Those boxes on stage that you see by everyone's feet. They play back the sound the band are making so that they can hear the music themselves.
● **Rig**
The bar over the stage which the lights are hung from. It has to be raised above the stage before each and every show.

SKILLS YOU'LL NEED
Diplomacy, knowledge of basic electrics, being handy with a screwdriver, enthusiasm, being willing to get up early in the morning even if you've had a late night, being nice to fans who are frequently profoundly annoying.

TIPS
● Help out local bands for free and see if you like it.
● Many colleges have technical drama courses where you can learn about lighting and sound for plays: the principle for gigs is basically the same.
● Local venues often hire local crew: you can start there, loading and unloading equipment.
● Ask a roadie at a gig for a few hints – if you're lucky, they'll feel flattered you're taking an interest, as they're normally the unsung heroes of the show.
● Practise carrying your hi-fi speakers up and down the stairs and around your house. But only if you're *really* bored.

ROCK HOTELIER

MONEY: From peanuts to millions. Depends whether it's Margate or the Strand.

HOURS: Eighteen hours a day, in some cases. Hotels never close. Therefore they never stop having problems.

HEALTH RISK: 8/10. You may get flattened in your car park by a television thrown from the penthouse suite by a rock star.

PRESSURE RATING: 9/10. Keeping everything running smoothly and being able to make a profit in today's competitive market ain't easy.

GLAMOUR RATING: 3/10. You work for people you may never see again. They come and go and nick your towels.

TRAVEL RATING: 2/10. Perhaps down the road to go to a conference centre for the Dealing With Tricky Guests hotel summit.

The rock hotelier deals with Tricky guests. And Portishead and Massive Attack, ho ho.

The Columbia Hotel in Bayswater, central London, is known in some circles as *the* rock hotel. Bands flock to it. Partly, perhaps, because it's known as *the* rock hotel and they want to keep within the fine tradition of being a bit rock and not staying with their auntie.

If you own such a place, you've got to put up with a lot. Musicians keep different hours from normal people and they also like to drink during these different hours and perhaps invite a friend or two to join them. They like to get up and check out late. They used to like throwing televisions out of windows, and sometimes enjoy 'accidentally' smashing into mirrors. They are the bane of the sane hotelier's life, but they bring in business.

The Columbia is relatively cheap at £69 per night (early '98 prices) and has rooms that sleep three or four so that bands can bed down even more cheaply. 'About 15% of our clientele are people in the music industry at any given time,' says hotelier Michael Rose. 'There is nothing to suggest that they upset the other 85%. 90% of the pop groups are polite and reasonably turned out. They stay and they go. Only a minute proportion produce incidents, and no one tries chucking televisions out of windows any more. Teenagers from Europe actually cause us more problems.'

Rose is very dismissive of people who come in hoping to see pop stars whooping it up all over the shop. 'If they get up late and keep different hours the other guests will have gone out anyway so they won't disturb them.' However, he does say, 'Pop groups are popular with the staff and the front desk enjoy having pop stars here.'

Some pop stars are awful. They get back from a gig and want to drink all night with several thousand 'close friends', some of whom may be ladies of dubious morality. Allegedly. They're sick in bins and order **room service** for ten people at 5 a.m. and then deny it when the night porter knocks on the door. They cram in seventeen to a room when all their 'friends' realise they can't get home and need somewhere to kip for the night. Or they play parlour games in the lobby until 6 a.m.

However, Rose is giving nothing away. Part of the skill of hotel business is to be discreet. 'We don't have an all-night bar, despite what some people have said,' says Rose. 'A group might bring one or two friends back, which they are entitled to do, but if it turns into a private party no more liquor is served. The problems that arise are very, very rare. We treat all pop stars who stay here in exactly the same way as other customers. We offer them the same services and facilities.'

If you're a hotelier, you can always chuck the offenders out and bar them for good. Or you can charge them lots of money for the

wrecked hotel room, the ketchup on the walls, and the broken mirrors. (Shampoo used to have to pay for all of these things – good job they made lots of money in Japan, eh?) You really are on top. The bands that you like will come back when you're tolerant, and develop into loyal customers. Some hotels, it is true, don't like having pop stars staying, but most adore it. It gives them something to talk about, for one thing. The only thing you must ensure is that the **less discreet members of staff** don't leak secrets to the press. There is no surer way of losing celebrities' custom – and your hard-earned credibility.

GLOSSARY
● Room service
Pop stars are particularly fond of ordering room service, particularly in liquid form. However, hotels prefer them to use the mini-bar: it earns the

warble!

CRASH!

HOTELIER

MR. HOTEL MANAGER

hotel more money and means the staff aren't so harassed.

● **Less discreet members of staff**
Newspapers will always try to speak to hotel staff where bands/artists are staying. A place like the Hyde Park Hotel in London, where Madonna frequently stays, will be beseiged with calls and the press will book rooms and stand outside all day. You have to ensure your staff aren't going to the *Sun* to reveal all about Maddie's 5am mooning in the bar.

SKILLS YOU'LL NEED
Discretion, organisational skills, single-mindedness, tolerance.

TIPS
● Take a hotel-management course.
● Learn to cope with irresponsible, immature people. Some time spent in charge of a crèche may prove invaluable.
● Or maybe as a warder in a young offenders' centre.
● The only thing to suggest would be to let your friends stay in your room overnight, and charge them if they break any furniture.

SECURITY PERSON

MONEY: Around £4.50 an hour up to £40,000 and over per year for management positions after years of work. Masses if you own your own company.

HOURS: Any time from very early in the morning to very late at night.

HEALTH RISK: 8/10. You have to avoid getting brained by overexcited fans.

PRESSURE RATING: 8/10. You have to protect the star and the fans. This can mean ensuring the safety of a crowd at Wembley stadium. Without losing your temper.

GLAMOUR RATING: 3/10. Showing people to their seat or making sure that no kiddies fall into the road at a record signing is not the most chintzy thing to do on a Saturday night.

TRAVEL RATING: 9/10. It's one of those jobs – if you get in with a nice, rich artist you can travel the globe helping them to walk through airports.

Safety is the mantra and gospel of security workers. From top-notch star to wide-eyed schoolchild fan, the security person has to make sure that no one is getting pulled about, roughed up, or is fainting or jumping from a great height. This includes the pop star. Oh, and shiny jackets are optional.

Increasing numbers of people are attracted to rock security work. The trade is fast losing its previous, exceedingly dodgy, reputation. In the past, too many venues and promoters would pick up their **bouncers** dirt-cheap and not bother to check their CVs and career histories. People with criminal records and GBH convictions were manning doors, and **dodgy dealers** used to abound. In old Dickensian times, security people at Ma Purseshifty's Olde Coffee House would duff you up before you came in the door, set fire to your eyelashes and nick your hat. Now it's a respectable job.

All kinds of different people now get into the security line. One of the biggest event-safety companies in England, ShowSec, carefully vets all its prospective employees in case they just want the chance to shout at and bully people. They have their own training and safety department to put recruits through their paces.

'With gigs, we deal direct with promoters or record companies,' says JC, who runs the ShowSec training centre. 'If it's a band we know, then we'll quote them the standard arrangement. With boy bands like Boyzone you're assured a young female audience, so you make sure plenty of first aid is available and bring a trained team who can look for the first signs of distress and hysteria. You can have thousands of young girls, so you need barriers outside. You have to keep people from getting knocked over.'

There are also security people backstage. If the venue doesn't have its own staff to collect tickets, ShowSec will also perform this duty. It's hard work. Around 400 security staff are generally required to man an arena show of 20,000 people. They need a multitude of skills, from being able to be calm when someone's being rude to them to knowing the exact whereabouts of the telephones in every venue they work at.

'When the seats collapsed at the Pink Floyd show at Earl's Court,' recalls JC, '1,100 people suddenly had a flying lesson. It was down to us to help the people who were trapped and you need a calm temperament in a crisis. A lot of people think the job's all about violence and martial arts but we don't carry guns; we carry first-aid kits.'

And it's all right, you shorties! You only need to be burly if you are at the front of the stage lifting fainting girls over a barrier. Otherwise, you can actually be quite tiny – *and* you get to wear the nice shiny jacket so that people can see you.

Personal security guards are not needed as much as you might think, but they do need to be hyper-professional and very well trained – it's not all free albums and luxury-liner travel. If an artist is touring there'll be a team of people around them who are **crowd-management** specialists. In Japan, Italy and many other countries, security teams will liaise with the local

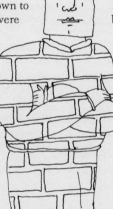

SECURITY

police to discuss how big the crowds will be. The job involves far more than just being an intimidating man-mountain walking around next to Liam Gallagher.

However, some misguided people try to get into rock security purely because they think it's a short cut to meeting the stars. 'They think they can get their photo taken with George Michael,' continues JC. 'But George doesn't want that; he wants efficient people who can help him. He gets that other rubbish all the time. And don't think you'll always be backstage or can get anybody you want backstage. A lot of girls – especially at boy-band gigs – will come up and say, "I've written a card – can I take it into the dressing room? It'll be OK, four years ago they said hello to my sister!" You have to be polite but firmly insist that no one comes backstage. The artist doesn't want to be seen in the dressing room putting his feet up, without his wig, by *anyone*. Keeping them out can involve huge amounts of diplomacy.'

JC is realistic about promotion prospects within the security world. 'I'd be reluctant to say you can make a career out of security,' says JC. 'In our company there are only eight people who earn really good money and tour round the world. It can take years before a band will put their trust in you. But there *are* prospects for progression, and if you're smart,

efficient and polite you can be made into a supervisor.'

On the whole, JC enjoys the life of a rock security person. 'To me, it's the best job in the world,' he enthuses. 'You meet so many different people, and there's a great feeling of satisfaction when people leave a show, shake hands and say, "Thanks, we had a great time."'

GLOSSARY
● **Bouncers**
Slang for security people, because they 'bounce' people out of a building.
● **Dodgy dealers**
People who get involved in schemes and scams which are illegal and would have them banged up in chokey were they to be found out.
● **Crowd management**
What security people are skilled at. They like to use this kind of term.

SKILLS YOU'LL NEED
Being calm – especially under pressure; being patient; liking those shiny jackets; efficiency; politeness; looking a bit scary sometimes.

TIPS
● There are some dodgy companies out there. Before joining any company, ask these questions: Do they have a health and safety policy? A training policy? Are they registered in the UK? Do they have insurance for their staff? (If you get smacked around the bonce by some deranged Metallica fan, you will quite fancy the idea of receiving some compensation.) And, remember, be careful: *anyone* can set up a security firm.

SINGING TEACHER

MONEY: From £20 an hour to £60 for forty minutes, but always on a freelance hourly rate: you'll invariably be working for yourself.

HOURS: As many or as few as you please.

HEALTH RISK: 3/10. Strained tonsil, maybe?

EQUIPMENT COSTS: You need a piano, a keyboard, or something else to strike a note on.

PRESSURE RATING: 5/10. It's not your fault if they can't parple properly, is it?

GLAMOUR RATING: 7/10. You'll meet rising stars and if you're lucky they may bring you nice chocolates.

TRAVEL RATING: 3/10. You tend to sit in your house waiting for budding pop stars to tread grit into your carpet. You might possibly get to the recording studio once in a while.

Singing teachers help the stars to sing out those lovely notes and bring out all the richness and timbre in their voices: notes they never knew they had, vibratos which have been locked inside from childhood. Or to at least hold a tune so that no one can tell they're teetering on a vocal precipice.

Singing teachers are essential to the music business. They are the pinch of salt to the baked potato, the spice to the lentil, the ketchup to the chip. They're there to bring out the potential in all the top crooners, and some of the not-so-top ones. Almost every pop star goes to a singing teacher, although most of them don't like to admit it, and some only go because they're made to. Singing teachers love to teach the famous and not-quite-so-famous-yet to get up to the top C and right down below middle C and what-about-a-bit-of-arpeggio-while-we're-at-it? They are cool and collected, because they live in a world of skylarks and melodies, unravaged by a cut-throat industry that is nasty to bands and eats kittens for breakfast. Going to a singing teacher, if you're a nice pop star, is something like chancing upon a dappled glade in a country field when you've just come out of Dingwalls and someone has spilt bitter on your **Alexander McQueen** knee-pads. No, really ...

Singing teachers teach by the hour, and give weekly, fortnightly or 'once in a while' lessons, depending on the pupil and what's coming up. A lot of singers will go to a teacher before a tour, so they know how to cope with singing every night (v. difficult). Some go before recording an album and others go reluctantly because their manager tells them to.

Tona de Brett is world famous for training the tonsils of the stars. She's been doing so for over forty years, although not always teaching pop singers. After a classical training, she started teaching singing and was working at the City Lit in London full time when she met Malcolm McClaren. He asked her if she could teach his young protégé to sing – Johnny Rotten. Tona was, appropriately, teaching musical-comedy singing at the time.

'I thought: Well, a voice is a voice. And that's where my career teaching pop singers started. I taught Johnny, then Malcolm told everyone about me. One fine day before his film *The Great Rock 'n' Roll Swindle* came out, he rang up and asked if I could tell him how I taught Johnny Rotten. A camera crew came along for a couple of hours – it was all quite a laugh – and at the end they said they'd like to pay me £25. I thought this was rather good and I wasn't earning much in those days so I signed a receipt. Then, the next thing I knew, there was the film in the West End, with me in it! Still, at least it began to spread my name around ...'

Tona's son advised her to make a tape of her vocal exercises. The cassette cost a thousand pounds to make and has been selling ever since. She thinks it's important that 'any singer who's going to make a living out of singing should know how their voice works' and so gives people a basic grounding in voice production and tries to help them change any bad habits. She doesn't follow any one particular method or try to force people to change. And you have to be careful with singers.

'There's nothing so fragile as a singer's ego,' she says. 'It needs all the boosting it can get. Even in the most dire cases you can find something to say that is positive.' Singers who are good to teach, according to de Brett,

are the people who 'want to make a lasting career of it. Most people who come to me are basically nice. I've not met any "I'm the big rock star" types.'

There *are* a fair few charlatans in the business because you can start teaching singing whether you've had any experience or not. And, if you're a good teacher, you will get a lot of people coming to you who have already been taught to sing, but badly. A lot of the job involves correcting other people's mistakes. One pupil of Tona's admitted her last teacher had made her sing to the wall. One day she turned round before she'd finished and saw her teacher deep in a novel!

'The teacher jumped up and said, "I've been teaching for years! I can teach and read a book at the same time!"' says Tona. 'Another singer brought his teacher to the recording studio and the teacher couldn't sing himself – he was a failed dancer who thought he'd teach singing.' A few ex-pop-stars teach, including Sarah-Jane Morris, formerly of The Communards, and many drama teachers double up as singing coaches.

Tona has all the relevant qualifications and is an Associate of the Royal College of Music. She works for three and a half hours per day, five days per week, and charges £40 per hour. 'I'm not making a vast packet,' she insists. She would most certainly never have wanted to be a pop star ('No fear, mate! It's a hell of a job!') and much prefers teaching. She reckons that singing teachers don't even need a particularly good voice, just be able to sing in tune, play the piano and read music.

'You can't be nasty to people. Johnny Rotten came along for a consultation but hardly sang at all,' she says. 'Some are too shy to sing first time round. Others might come in a little drunk. It can be a soul-destroying job if you're not the sort of person who really wants to help others. You must like people, and be willing to learn as you go along.'

De Brett finds it frustrating to listen to singers on records who she doesn't think make the most of their voices. 'People have wonderful gifts and they don't use them!' she complains. 'Brett Anderson from Suede has a fabulous baritone but doesn't use it – he uses his "pop voice". Skin from Skunk Anansie has a glorious voice but only uses it in bits. And I don't approve of that Jimmy Nail "Crocodile Shoes" style ...'

Essentially, though, Tona de Brett loves being a singing consultant to the stars. 'Yes, because you never know who's going to come through the door. Every individual has their own approach and way of doing things. Sometimes they can't string two notes together and it takes enormous patience on both parts. But it's an exciting and worthwhile job and I have no plans to stop.'

GLOSSARY
● **Alexander McQueen**
Snoot designer deeply beloved by pop stars. They'll wear anything if it's been designed by someone more famous than they are.

SKILLS YOU'LL NEED
To be able to hold a note, patience, understanding of the way the industry and its stars work, a degree of personal experience helps.

TIPS
● Get a qualification – a reasonably high music grade or singing qualification – to prove you're worth your salt.
● Studying drama and movement as well as singing helps.
● Once you have the requisite qualifications, send your details, address, etc. to A&R managers at major record labels

SLEEVE DESIGNER

MONEY: From £20 an hour if you work freelance. In-house designers get a standard wage from £12,000 to £30,000 and over.

HOURS: From 10 a.m. till sometimes very late, because the deadline demands it.

HEALTH RISK: 6/10. You might accidentally whip off a finger with a scalpel knife.

PRESSURE RATING: 8/10. The turnaround time for sleeves is very short, so you might be working against the clock. And you might have to change things quickly because the guitarist 'isn't happy with red'.

GLAMOUR RATING: 4/10. You might get to drink with someone who wants a horse on their cover, but you have to be really in with your stars to stay on their ranches.

TRAVEL RATING: 3/10. Via the Internet, perhaps. Otherwise, you have to be really, *really* in with the stars to even get to Bournemouth.

The sleeve designer is commissioned to design the covers for record releases in all formats by specific acts. They either work for an independent company or in-house for a record company.

Sleeve design can define a decade. Think of that *With The Beatles* cover which has the four moptops, in black and white, peering down a stairwell. Seminal. The Velvet Underground album with the banana on it. Epoch making. Bruce Springsteen's *Born In The USA* with his bottom representing the death of the American Dream. The Rolling Stones' *Sticky Fingers* album with, er, a crotch representing the sexual decadence of

SOME BANDS HAVE A PROBLEM
WITH CERTAIN COLOURS.

the seventies. The Smith's archive sepia snaps of long-dead stars. Björk's futuristic computerisations. Pulp's tacky seventies pastiches. Design a good sleeve and it will help zoom records into higher chart placings as part of the overall marketing package – and you'll receive both artistic and professional satisfaction. And you get to use computers and jiggle things around, which is far better than the felt-tip pens which were the height of design innovation many moons ago.

Most designers start with an interest in art, graphic design or illustration, and do a foundation art course at college. They then specialise for their degree. Some sleeve designers come from a fashion background and some from illustration or graphic design. Junior jobs at design companies and for in-house designers at record companies are regularly advertised.

Brian Cannon, who has designed all of Oasis's and The Verve's sleeves to date, did a degree in graphic design at Leeds Polytechnic, but went about things his own way. 'I was a fan of the **electro and hip-hop scene** in the mid-eighties,' says Brian. 'I wasn't musical and I couldn't breakdance, but one night I drew this big graffiti mural in Wigan, where I'm from. A Manchester band – Kermit from Black Grape's old band, The Ruthless Rap Assassins – noticed this and nearly crashed their car!

'I heard word on the grapevine about this, met them, and did their artwork from then on. Then I was at a party in Wigan in 1989 and a spotty student wearing funny clothes started chatting to me. It turned out to be **Richard Ashcroft** and he promised me I'd do his artwork when his band got famous. I bumped into him at a petrol station in Wigan, and he'd just signed to Hut Records. It started from there.'

Brian never wanted to work for anyone else or be answerable to anybody, so he got office space in Manchester, where he bumped into a bushy-eyebrowed bloke who was working with Inspiral Carpets in the same building. They talked about his obscure Adidas trainers and the guy said, 'When my band get signed you can do my artwork.' It was Noel Gallagher and he proved true to his word. Brian's company, Microdot, is now based in London, and he has diversified into directing videos.

Sleeve designers will generally begin by listening to the songs they are working with and seeing what ideas spring to mind. 'If you look at my previous work you can see the stuff I'm not into,' confesses Cannon. 'I designed Inspiral Carpets' stuff because I was skint, and on Noel's recommendation.' The designer and the band will then come up with an initial idea, and plot it out: commissioning a photographer, choosing graphics, providing a logo if the band don't already have one. The Verve's cover for *Urban Hymns* was taken before the shoot had even been set up, but it had that natural feel, man, and so the band preferred it to the other, more formal shots.

Brian also likes to go overboard on Oasis's covers and make them a spectacular roller-coaster ride of allusions to old Beatles records, Noel's pub gags, friends of the band, and a million other things. They certainly go to town. The famous cover of *Be Here Now* cost £20,000 to shoot. Cannon hired a swimming pool and bought a knackered Rolls Royce for £1,500. The shoot took three months to sort out – from start to finished product. This, however, is classic old-school decadence. Most bands don't have that sort of money. By the same token, you can only make a lot of money as a designer if you have your own company or are at the top of an in-house team.

'I always tell people,' says Brian, 'forget going to a record company, because they're not interested in sleeve design. They don't know what the fuck they're talking about. Why on earth would they give a kid who's **wet behind the ears** the new Oasis sleeve? Get well in with bands when they're unsigned and do stuff for nothing. Noel and Richard are personal friends of mine and that's the best way – I wouldn't bother with people I don't like.'

Sleeve designers have to produce computer-processed artwork, on the whole. It has to be clear, eye-catching, and work well within the whole context of the band. They have to know where the music is coming from, and what imagery is suitable. Sometimes the stars are too busy to say what they want or give you any clues, though, so you have to be sharp. It's no use putting a photo of a parsnip on the new Paul Weller album when he wants some mod-inspired nonsense on it.

Likewise, George Michael won't want some hand-drawn cartoon of a monkey; he'll want something swish and glossy. Stereolab are best left painting singles sleeves in their bedroom, which they do because of their individualistic nature. (Whether design is anti-individualistic per se is another matter entirely, and not one to be pursued here.)

In-house designers are given projects by the company they work for, rather then being able to choose them, so sometimes the job is rather more stifling. However, in this role you will work on a broader selection of music and related design, which means more variety for the easily bored. In-house designers have the advantage of being able to hear some releases a long time before they come out, and can build up exciting visual treats in their head before they go down on paper. All in-housers agree the most boring thing is thinking up covers for anonymous compilation albums. This task can be inspiration-free, but at least the money is regular; whereas designers working for independent companies are paid by the hour and fill in timesheets for every job they do.

Vaughan Oliver has worked for

← record sleeve

SLEEVE DESIGNER

4AD Records for seventeen years, first on a part-time basis then as in-house designer. He studied graphics at Newcastle University and decided he didn't fancy that, but still had a longing to do sleeve design. He began freelancing for Ivo Watts-Russell, who was then engaged in setting up 4AD, in 1980. Together they created a continuity within the label's design which is now world-famous and has been exhibited all over the place. The Victoria and Albert Museum even bought a **limited-edition sleeve** a few years back (*Lonely Is An Eyesore* by This Mortal Coil). Oliver's sleeves, often looking like nothing you'd ever recognise – mainly out-of-focus swirlings, helping bring back the word 'ethereal' into modern pop parlance – are a good example of sleeve design which suggests more than dictates a mood.

'I like to put a bit of mystery in,' says Vaughan. 'The sleeve has to be instantly seductive or attractive. It may not be an idea you get immediately but something more open-ended. A lot of sleeve design is trend-orientated, and I never wanted that. I don't enjoy stuff that joins in. You look around now and you can't tell the difference between Echobelly and Echo And The Bunnymen.'

Oliver now finds that the budgets for sleeve design have shrunk in recent years. The money tends to be allocated to videos and remixes. 'In record companies there are no art directors now and nobody who comes in with an art aesthetic,' he says. 'Apple Mac computers (used widely by designers in the industry) give a certain level of surface finish all round, but there are no "ideas" buttons

on those machines. Maybe it's old-fashioned but I don't think people dealing with design appreciate the difference between traditional and computer-based design.'

Now Oliver has once again gone freelance, he still gets first choice on 4AD work but also works on corporate identities, logos, brochures and posters – including the graphics for the Young Vic's performance of *Hamlet*. Vaughan is famously pro-aesthetic and likes to spend as much time as possible on sleeves because he thinks they're so important. He's built his career on purist grounds, while Brian Cannon is another type entirely. But both can exist in the art-pop world, you know.

Cannon says he believes arrogance does help you to get in with the stars and get work. But he doesn't consider he has a glamorous existence. At least, not all the time: 'At the minute I'm in a dingy basement with two sweaty Northerners – the sort of thing I find myself doing far too much. But I get to travel all over the world and I'm paid a lot of money, which I guess you can call glamorous. It's better than working in a bank.'

Designers, like all music-business people, also have to work around the fragile egos of pop stars – whether they are your pals down the pub or not. 'I love both Oasis and The Verve, but I am scared of them, fucking right!' Cannon admits, ruefully. 'I've had severe fucking dressing-downs from both of them.'

GLOSSARY

● **Electro and hip-hop scene**
American-led stuff that inspired DJs over here who liked spinning on their head mid-set.

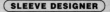

● **Richard Ashcroft**
Lanky 'I am mad' singer with The Verve.

● **Wet behind the ears**
Term for 'not being very experienced'. Not exclusive to the music industry but well-used within it. It can have a positive or a negative sense: fresh naivety brought to a tired situation, or some godawful mistake by someone who should still be in school. People 'in power' use the phrase.

● **Limited-edition sleeve**
Like some records are limited edition. 4AD used to put out a luxury, fold-it-out, open-it-up sleeve once in a while, only making around a thousand, for instance. The sleeve in question here was made out of wood. A beauty.

SKILLS YOU'LL NEED

Artistic abilities ('I can't really draw,' says Brian Cannon, 'but I'm a good draughtsman.'); some knowledge of computers; ability to work well under pressure; some degree of neatness – all those important papers on your desk might get something spilt on them, you know.

TIPS

● Get an art degree. The London College of Printing is good for graphics.

● Try to get to know some bands if you want to be a Brian Cannon type and call them your mates.

● Apply to record companies.

● Assemble a portfolio to show record companies and managers. Include work that might suit sleeve design. They are always keen to see new ideas.

STUDIO MANAGER

MONEY: From £18,000 to £30,000, depending on your experience.

HOURS: From 10 a.m. to 11 p.m., if you've got some obsessive tykes who can't leave that snare sound alone.

HEALTH RISK: 6/10. Unless you pretend to be a pop star and get drunk all the time and develop related illnesses.

PRESSURE RATING: 8/10. Digital and analogue equipment is always breaking down.

GLAMOUR RATING: 4/10. You might end up playing 'gin' rummy with the bassist of Gene when he's not got anything to do. Or snap with Snap.

TRAVEL RATING: 3/10. To and from the shops to get said bassist more plectrums and gin.

The studio manager looks after the recording studio, taking bookings and ensuring the day-to-day running of the studio goes smoothly. As smoothly as possible, that is.

It's all very well musicians creating hot licks and putting them down on to tape while the producer looks on, nodding in time with the axemanship and smirking at the tape operator in an acknowledgement of universal musical healing. It's all very well, but who's there to order the producer a cab when they want to go home? Who has to try to find a bit of pluggy lead when the engineer's gone sick? And who's going to step in when some mate of the band in the studio is trying to nick off with the sampler?

The answer is the studio manager – which is a far more exciting job than it sounds. The good studio manager is a wily beast who looks after the artists, producers, engineers, technical people, and anyone else coming and going around the recording process. Their job is a hectic one, rather akin to being a headmaster at a school for rock 'n' rollers. Studio managers must govern their domain, make the rules, slap wrists, hire and fire, and still get on with the record companies. They have to 'sell' their studio and make sure everyone knows it's good, fine and happening to be in. They take out the swanks of the A&R departments to lunch, laugh at really bad jokes by engineers, look interested when someone's talking about the **EQ**, and try not to shout at people who are complaining about **effects pedals**.

Studio managers arrive from all walks of life, many following the simple route of working on studio receptions then being promoted. Many are ex-managers, ex-engineers and the like. It's rarely a job people plan to do. Julie Vines is American, very friendly, and the studio manager at Nomis in London. She applied for a post as head receptionist at Nomis and was promoted to manager after only seven months, when the studios were taken over by a public company. Nomis is unusual in that it has two studios plus five rehearsal rooms, for which Vines takes all the bookings.

Like all studio managers, Vines also liaises with A&R coordinators to negotiate studio prices and supplementary expenses such as cab costs and hiring equipment. Bands never arrive with all the gear they need: they're always deciding to add a fancy kazoo solo to a b-side then finding they don't have the Fender Rhodes electric piano to go with it. Hiring equipment is never-ending. That is, until the budget your record company has set has been exhausted. And it's the studio manager's job to track down the gear *and* stay within budget.

Julie Vines will check what time every session needs to start and exactly what sort of budget the artists have at their disposal. She is basically the link between every area of practical recording, and therefore has to be nice to everybody. (Interestingly, most studio managers are women.) Sometimes this can be difficult, as everyone gets demanding at times. However, Ms Vines has discovered that producers are often the pickiest of the bunch.

'It's ultimately the responsibility of the producer to ensure the success of the session,' she says. 'Often this pressure results in temperamental behaviour. If they can't suss out a desk they say the desk is broken or they get a bee in their bonnet because things aren't going to plan. After a breather and rethink, eventually they tend to apologise.'

Nomis has had a video recorder 'borrowed' by one visiting band (but their management company was invoiced accordingly). If a studio has a fish tank, music-biz legend says: Don't count on a complete set of guppies after a band has been in. You are essentially playing host to a bunch of stoned, mindless, fun-loving eternal students.

The studio manager has to ensure the studio is as profitable as possible. Studios these days aren't as well off as they used to be, as technology changes with frightening regularity and it's imperative for studio managers to update equipment and monitors or producers will go somewhere else. It's the producers, more than the bands, who call the shots: they (and engineers) will have favourite studios and can influence record-company choice by passing on their opinions. To choose the top ten studios in London, therefore, is a fairly arbitrary process.

'It depends on which producers have worked there and what equipment they have, location, parking – parking is so important, because most of them have cars, and, like everybody, want to get home at a reasonable time. Record companies base their choices on which place to book from the feedback they get from producers.'

Typically for a modern studio, Nomis spends between £75,000 and £100,000 per year on coloured leads and black boxes with buttons on them. All the studios, recording and rehearsal spaces need to be booked up pretty much nonstop in order for the place to have the means to buy these extra goodies. Julie's main job is to persuade record companies, via producers, to book into Nomis. She has a minimum fee that she can go down to in order to break even if the record company is really tight, although,

STUDIO MANAGER

unsurprisingly, she won't divulge what the figure is. However, studios generally charge by the day (twelve to fifteen hours) and then into overtime, where you really make your cash.

At Nomis there is also a rehearsals coordinator, a technical director, technical manager, in-house engineer, assistant engineer, plus restaurant staff. Studio managers don't always know how the **mixing desk**s work, but it's much better if they do. However, you don't particularly need to read any of those nerdy magazines about different plug sizes for half-rack sound modules and the effect on EQ – that's up to the technical boffins. The studio manager and technical director are the folk who decide what new equipment they'd like. The rehearsal rooms also need in-house, live studio

engineers, but most recording studios contain just a couple of **mixing rooms** and **live room**s.

Bearing in mind that the best studios cost between £800–1,200 a day, it's easy to see why very successful pop bands prefer to build their own. This eventually turns out to be cheaper – eventually, because a top-flight mixing desk can easily cost £250,000. Studios will do a deal if a band are recording an album, and can often make more money on shorter bookings for things like bands recording singles.

When studio managers leave the job they often move on to managing producers or artists, A&R, or 'something completely different such as massage or meditation', says Vines. But she finds her hectic and complex job consistently stimulating. 'I absolutely love it, because it's so diverse,' she sums up. 'It's all over the place and you have to keep it together sometimes by the skin of your teeth. It's so much fun.'

A BIT ABOUT STUDIOS

Studios are bizarre places which are just full of wires and twiddly knobs and never have posters or windows or anything remotely reminding you that you are in the outside world. They also look completely inconspicuous on the outside, so that robbers are put off nicking the pricey equipment inside. There are no worldly distractions: studios are very boring places, which ensures that nobody gets too excited about anything but the music. Man.

The building will contain a lounge and a pool table. There is *always* a pool table. You have to like pool or video games if you are in a band, because there's always a great deal of time when you won't be doing anything at all but waiting for the tambourine player to **lay down the middle eight**.

There are residential studios like Mono Valley in Wales, for people recording albums. The advantage of recording away is that you can get drunk in the countryside and have someone make your meals for you. However, artists can get distracted there: The Stone Roses famously went into the studio to record their second LP in 1990 and didn't emerge for four years. Essentially, though, being in a studio is a laborious and tedious process. Anyone who's visited a studio and said that it was 'Great!! Really, really interesting and wiiiiild!!!, man!' is lying.

GLOSSARY

● **EQ**

Equaliser. Something to do with making the bass less toppy, the high sound less piercing. Linked with a frightening word called 'compression', which is similar, and often linked with vocals. So they don't sound as if they've been recorded in a bin.

● **Effects pedals**

Put them on your guitar and hey! It sounds like a squirrel is gnawing the wires!!

● **Mixing desk**

The big table with all the knobs on. Controls the sound coming in from live recording, like vocals, and from digital sound generators, i.e. those machines that make techno beeps. Used for volume and frequency effects, i.e. making the bass less 'toppy'.

● **Mixing room**

Where the desk is: where the producer and engineer sit and ponder the best way to compress the vocals.

● **Live room**

Where the drummer and the guitarist go to record their stuff. The live and mixing rooms are separated to get a nice sound in the live room. There should be a big pane of glass so the engineer can make comedy gestures at the singer to put him/her off.

● **Lay down the middle eight**

Nothing to do with taking a quick forty winks; it means putting down on to tape (i.e. recording) the middle section (often eight bars) of a song.

SKILLS YOU'LL NEED

Ability to get on with people, being a good salesperson, ability to cope under pressure, persuasive skills, general chirpy manner; not yawning when someone mentions patch leads.

TIPS

● Apply for jobs answering the phones at studios. Secretarial skills might be useful.

● Apply for jobs at equipment and instrument hire places so you can get to know the studios.

● Tea boy/girl jobs at a studio can show you the ropes. You can work your way up to sound engineer or studio manager.

● Sound-engineering courses will show you how to use a mixing desk and all the other equipment. Useful training.

● Practise charging your friends for using your stereo and see how far you get.

USEFUL ADDRESSES

● Abbey Road Studios, 3 Abbey Road, London NW8 9AY.
TEL 0171 266 7000. **FAX** 0171 266 7250.

● Air Studios, Lyndhurst Hall, Lyndhurst Road, Hampstead, London NW3 5NG.
TEL 0171 794 0660. **FAX** 0171 794 8518.

● Nomis Studios, 45–53 Sinclair Road, London W14 ONS.
TEL 0171 602 6351. **FAX** 0171 603 5941.

● Rockfield Studios, Amberley Court, Rockfield Road, Monmouth, Gwent.
TEL 01600 712449. **FAX** 01600 714421.

● Sarm West, 8–10 Basing Street, London W11 1ET.
TEL 0171 229 1229. **FAX** 0171 221 9247.

● Swanyard Studio, 12–27 Swan Yard, London N1 1SD.
TEL 0171 354 3737. **FAX** 0171 226 2581.

● The Town House, 150 Goldhawk Road, London W12 8HH.
TEL 0181 932 3200. **FAX** 0181 932 3207.

STYLIST

MONEY: From 'helping out a friend' for nothing, to hundreds of pounds per day just to bring along a pair of gloves. The average wage is around £250 per day if you're established, and can be as high as £600 and beyond if you're a bit of a name on the **scene**.

HOURS: Can be any amount of time, as you'll be a freelancer and thus expected to turn up as and when you're needed – for photo shoots, video shoots, TV shows, etc.

HEALTH RISK: 7/10. You may become so trendy you die.

PRESSURE RATING: 8/10. If the backing singer is shouting at you because you didn't get the purple feather boa, quite high. If you lose all the stuff the shop's lent you, very high.

GLAMOUR RATING: 5/10. You might be shopping with the stars one minute, then having to pin plastic fish on to hemlines the next.

TRAVEL RATING: 7/10. Good. If you get in with a successful band and they like you and can afford to take you on the road to the US. Otherwise, it may be another trip to Top Shop or Camden Market.

The stylist is in charge of getting the right sort of shirt to dress pop stars in – so that they are vaguely presentable for photo and video shoots.

About fifteen years ago, stylists didn't exist in the music business. Bands wore clothes they'd just bought down the market and quite frequently looked absolutely rubbish. Then everything changed in the eighties. Once the first poncey picture was taken by a style magazine – *The Face*, who were at the forefront of the early part of the decade's **wafty blouson** movement – record companies realised that the kids wanted bands to look stylish. Something had to be done. The first stylists appeared when promo videos started. They put tea towels on people's heads and the New Romantic movement was born.

YOU FIND YOURSELF GETTING POP STARS TO WEAR TEA TOWELS ON THEIR HEADS.

At this time, the bands getting styled all pretended it wasn't really happening, because they were ashamed of the whole business. It also went against the grain of 'raw', 'street', punk authenticity. Artists wanted fans to regard them as bleeding soul and honesty from their veins, not clotheshorses or manipulated puppets. Even now, when Blur came out dressed in shellsuits during the *Parklife* era, the music press sneered copiously: they had a *stylist*! who went to Cobra Sports for them! How dare they! Now, cynics claim that you hardly need a tune to cut a swathe in music these days, just a nice pair of Wellingtons or the one-trouser-leg-up, one-trouser-leg-down rap style.

Most stylists start out through a friend of a friend because someone needs a favour, or they meet someone influential by accident. It's a difficult thing to get into and also very competitive. You don't earn much cash at first – you spend your time doing favours and assisting other stylists on shoots for precisely nought pence. Try to view it as a learning process and that all-important first break.

Stylists are invariably required for photo sessions, whether for promotional photos, record sleeves or magazine shoots. They are hired by record companies. The stylist is either given a budget to trail around the shops for puffy jackets and silver boob tubes, or else borrows clothes from designers, which you obviously have to give back later. You're best advised to keep a record of every single item, as you'll be asked to fork out for the clothes you lose, especially if Jenny Pop Star decides to nick off with a couple of tops.

It's a myth that you'll be given free trainers for every day of the week, and you can often only borrow stuff if it's credited in a magazine: this works at *The Face* but not at *Smash Hits*, who don't give credits. Some stylists like to boast that they go to charity shops and jumbles for their 'funky' gear as such anti-elitism has a certain hip cachet.

Stephanie Kaye, who lives in New York, became a stylist by accident. 'It wasn't until I was actually in the midst of this big job earning big bucks that I even realised I was a stylist,' she marvels. 'I'd never even heard of the job before. I went to stage school in order to be an actress.'

Stephanie did many things before she found herself dressing the stars. She invented a model agency 'for weird faces' that saw her dressing as an elf for Petland Discount. She was in a band which was 'more about changing our costumes for every song then music' and had fancy bohemian musician friends. Then she became friends with acoustic singer-songwriter Suzanne Vega.

'We didn't think she'd be big, because she was one of our friends and none of us ever did anything!' admits Kaye. 'I would always shop with her, and by the way she tipped her beret I knew there was this fashion beast waiting to come out, even though all she ever wore were cords.'

Vega's record company were ready to release the single 'Luka' and put a bit of cash behind it because they thought it would be a hit. 'They said, "We'll give you oodles of money to do a stupid video!"' giggles Stephanie. 'Suzanne asked me, "Will you be my stylist? They told me they want one, will you do it?" And I replied, "Of course!" We had a virtually unlimited budget, so we went to a department store and bought some expensive clothes. I thought: Well, this is *great!*'

At the end of the shoot, someone stuck a **time sheet** under her nose and the baffled Kaye wrote 'fashion stylist' in the space left for job description.

There was a blank space for her to fill in her fee. 'I thought: Well, I didn't do anything – I just sat and drank a lot of coffee! So I wrote down $125. The video producer came over to me with the form later and asked, "Is this a joke? It should be around $650 shouldn't it?" So I said, "Er, yeah."'

Stephanie was given more work, essentially because the producer liked her and her fancy way with stripey tops. She was next given the task of styling a **Debbie Gibson** video. 'It was no easy job,' she recalls. 'I had to begin by trying to get the palm tree out of her hair. Had I known what I was getting into, I may well have thought twice.'

However, once you are at least slightly established, you may find yourself on a roll. People know your name and pop stars learn to like your tricks with leggings, and you should get regular work. However, there are a few things to understand: primarily that the job isn't just shopping for a living.

'It's weird, but stylists have to virtually be psychologists,' says Kaye. 'With pop stars you have to hang out and be friends and find out what their biggest fears are about how they look – *that's* what stylists get paid for. With **Edie Brickell** she'd never worn anything but a pair of jeans and it was my mission to get her into leggings and a jacket.'

It can be tricky stuff. However, nice elements about styling include being given a small budget for extras, and going to markets and haberdashers to buy feathers and ribbons and pieces of old curtain to dress them up in. On the other side of the sartorial coin, it can be a chore to find out exactly what size everyone is and exactly how many extras there will be on the set.

One of the trickiest tasks is styling bands who have an identity already but need a bit of tweaking. Ms Kaye has had to help out Heavy Metal 'big-hair bands' like Motley Crue: 'Obviously, my idea of what they looked good in wasn't their idea of what they looked good in. You have to know when to step back. It's not your creation – it ultimately comes from the artist.'

You also have to look reasonable yourself. This doesn't have to cost much money, as we live in a world where jumble sales and charity shops virtually litter the pavements with cheap tat which can sometimes look fairly stylish. Some stylists are relatively poncey (remember, they are, when all is said, a similar breed to the hair and make-up personages) and they like their rucksacks to be Prada, but it's not necessary. There's no real need to swank about – you especially shouldn't do it in front of your artists, or they'll get the hump that you're better dressed than they are.

Maria is a stylist who works in London. She originally studied illustration, then got a job with model agency Storm and helped them put together their *New Faces* magazine – a tome full of young models which is sent out to clients. She got in via her best friend, who worked for another model agency. The owner of Storm suggested Maria should do styling because she was 'good at borrowing clothes from top names'. However, Maria hates carrying bags of clothes around and thinks the greatest crime of styling is 'over-accessorising'.

You will easily notice when a band

has been over-styled – they will look like they have been dressed by a short-sighted kipper after a few too many sherries. Kris Kross, child rap stars from Los Angeles, made the grave mistake of trusting their stylist, who told them to wear their dads' dungarees backwards, the crotches of which billowed by their ankles. They were not to worry the charts again after their first hit, 'Jump'. A coincidence? Who can say?

Many stylists will actually move on from dressing pop stars for photo shoots and videos to advertising work, which is on the whole better paid but may involve the soul-destroying element of promoting a product you have utter contempt for.

Stephanie Kaye is honest about what you can do after you've styled the stars. 'I believe in music and that's why I love the job,' she says. 'On the other hand, it's hard to believe in yet another deodorant. That rubs me up the wrong way. Styling work can be surprisingly tiring, though, and now the field is so saturated. You have to work for free if you want to be a stylist's assistant. Everybody wants to be a stylist these days because people perceive it to be an easy job – but it isn't.'

Alice is a full-time stylist for MTV in London. She got a job as assistant fashion editor on *Brides* magazine, of all things, did a spot of freelance assistant styling, then heard there was

STYLIST

a job going at MTV. She had built up a portfolio through assisting and this helped land her the job.

TV styling is different from magazine styling. For a start, Alice works full time and not on a freelance basis. She styles nine of the VJs – they each get a budget and she takes them out shopping twice a month. Bizarrely, she can't buy them anything blue, or that's got a bit of blue in it, in case they have to stand in front of one of those **chroma key** screens, in which case their clothing would merge into the wildly swirling graphics superimposed behind them. Small stripes and checks are also out, because on screen they make your eyes go funny. Because television doesn't 'credit' the clothes, designers are loath to lend out fancy threads. The lovely VJs (all of whom are picked for not only being chirpy but also looking like supermodels) might sometimes mention what they're wearing, but it's fairly unlikely.

Alice agrees that the job is mainly psychological. 'Someone's not going to look happy if they're not *feeling* happy, and everyone has their bad days. Presenters have got to go on screen and convince people they look good and feel good, which is quite demanding sometimes.'

Alice doesn't dress too many pop stars because when they come in they've generally already had their styling persons fluttering around them. 'But stars can ask for advice – some celebrity came in the other day and didn't know what shoes to wear.' And what happens if Coolio comes in and his trousers are falling apart? One crucial point you should never neglect if styling is your calling – stylists *always* carry a lot of safety pins. Remember that, and you won't go too wrong.

GLOSSARY

● **Scene**
All stylists want to be part of this. It is a make-believe group of trendy people and places, and is a load of rubbish.

● **Wafty blouson**
As worn by Morrissey of The Smiths and Robert Smith of The Cure. Even Tom Thingy from The Thomson Twins wafted a bit. Very eighties.

● **Time sheet**
Freelancers have to fill in one of these to show how many hours they spent on a project and what they are owed.

● **Debbie Gibson**
Tousle-haired singer of the late eighties who shot to fame with 'Only In My Dreams'. Starred in the stage version of the musical *Grease*. Goody-goody image.

● **Edie Brickell**
American hippy dippy singer of the late eighties.

● **Chroma key**
TV device that can superimpose an object on to a different background, i.e. a TV presenter looks like she's standing by a waterfall. Looks naff now, in comparison with newer computer graphics.

SKILLS YOU'LL NEED
An interest in clothes, knowledge of what doesn't make people's tums and bums look too big (pop stars are very vain), persuasiveness, organisational and communication skills.

TIPS
● Do whatever work you can, when you start out. You don't know what it might lead to.
● Fashion or styling courses at college may be a way in.
● Moonboots don't look good on everyone.

SUCCESSFUL EX-POP-STAR

 MONEY: From zero, apart from a few royalty cheques coming in, to a hefty wedge if you suddenly become a top businessperson, like Adam Faith.

HOURS: Can be a full-time occupation.

HEALTH RISK: 10/10. You could get depressed and start taking 'to the bottle' and all sorts of other things. Beware.

PRESSURE RATING: 10/10. Living up to expectations once you've left a group or lost a record contract is extremely stressful.

GLAMOUR RATING: 1/10. Well, obviously.

TRAVEL RATING: 5/10. Your band might re-form and then you can play Leicester's Princess Charlotte for years and years. No, come back, you really can!

Send in the clowns, for the ex-pop-star is the modern phenomenon that fascinates everyone. They used to hog the limelight; now they can't even get a light for a solitary cigarette down a dark street. Unless they get themselves together and find a proper job – hooray!

It's difficult being a pop star. Everyone thinks you're great for ten minutes and then they suddenly get into computer games and you're left wondering what happened. Well, this isn't the case for U2 or George Michael, but how many people get into the charts and then swiftly fly straight out of them? It is the pop star's greatest fear – the end. But it's like worrying about when it stops raining, because it will eventually stop raining, and then life will still go on. Anyway, pop stardom is not what it's cracked up to be and is mostly quite useless and damaging to one's sense of self and social life.

Ex-pop-stars are an odd breed but they do share certain traits. Either they are teetotal, no drugs, organic-carrots-type people, newly converted to the idea of 'normality' and thus getting the wrong end of the stick completely, or they remain wild, abandoned ultra-heroes of rock who still don't know when to go to bed or

EX-POP-STARS TAKE UP HOBBIES.

SOME WANT TO PRETEND THEY
WERE NEVER IN A BAND.

the band? To have a solo career?" And, in fact, that was the furthest thing from my mind. I wanted to have a boyfriend, I wanted to have my girl pals back, and I wanted to go out on Saturday night.'

These are the things that are denied to the pop star – any sense of *having a life*. Pop stars work so very hard that they never stop being their perky/smiling/surly/grimacing selves, 24 hours a day. Then, when they decide they want a real life, they get offered another stab at doing the same old thing on their own, and end up deciding that it would seem a bit stupid to turn down such a courteous offer. Holly Johnson from Frankie Goes To Hollywood, all of Take That, Matt Goss from Bros, even Andrew Ridgeley, who was never the wholly musical one in Wham!, released their own solo records.

After a while, however, sensible ex-pop-star types realise this is not the way forward, if it's going badly, and settle for something slightly different. Boy George became a top DJ, remixer, label boss (More Protein), as well as making his own club records under the name Jesus Loves You. Craig Logan left Bros and became a successful record producer. Roy Boulter, from everyone's favourite 'baggy' band The Farm, became a scriptwriter for *Brookside*. For many former pop stars the choice seems to come down to acting or TV presenting – and that's where we find Clare Grogan.

She released a solo single and recorded an album for London Records but it was never released. 'I guess that put me off considerably,' she says. 'I felt maybe someone was trying to tell me something, and because through

get a 'proper' job or anything. Ultimately, these are two sides of the same coin. Some do settle down and pretend to be like everyone else, but it can be hard, especially if you had such a wonderful time and were in a band that enjoyed the fruits of pop success.

Clare Grogan was the lead singer of Scots pop band Altered Images for five years in the early eighties. She was on the cover of glossy magazines, on *Top Of The Pops*, toured the world, and did the whole much coveted pop-star routine. She then left the band and embarked upon a solo career which was 'a kind of half-hearted attempt'.

'I've only myself to blame for it being totally ineffective,' she says. 'I don't really think it was what I wanted to do. People said, "Why did you leave other circumstances I was pulled in other directions – acting and presenting – it didn't become such a big deal that the record wasn't being released. It got further and further down my list of priorities.'

Before joining Altered Images, Clare had appeared in Bill Forsyth's film *Gregory's Girl*, and after they split she was in the same director's *Comfort And Joy*. She was also approached for both presenting and acting roles after she left Altered Images, and was even offered an American sitcom which she refused to do because it meant going away for six months. She puts this refusal down to 'naivety rather than arrogance'.

'I started at the top, so none of it was a struggle,' she says. 'But that gives you a false expectation of what the future will be like. I really did believe that my whole life would continue in that trend – I'd be literally bumping into people who just happened to be film directors. When I left the band, for the first time I had to go out and sell myself, which in the long term has done me absolutely no harm, but it was quite terrifying. I had got comfortable with people handing things to me on a plate.'

Grogan is still acting, and she also presents a music show on VH-1, **MTV**'s more 'mature' counterpart – lots of George Michael, Whitney Houston and Mike And The Mechanics. She spends one day every week writing her scripts, then a day filming four programmes for the next week, and often gets to go to Memphis, or other suitably historical rock cities. She's acted in *Blott On The Landscape*, *EastEnders*, *The Monocled Mutineer*, and in *Father Ted* ... as a rock star.

SOME WANT TO PRETEND
THEY'RE STILL IN A BAND.

'To be honest, it was obvious to me that when I left Altered Images I would be asked to play rock stars, which I said I'd never do. But I loved *Father Ted* to bits, so I thought it would be really great to play an obnoxious rock star. It was a very affectionate thing – it was meant to be a bit Sinead [O'Connor], a bit Dolores [from The Cranberries] – basically a 'bonkers chick in rock', which I'm more than happy to label myself as.

'I think it's too easy to view life after pop stardom as a bit sad,' continues Grogan. 'I know from my point of view that I have no desire to get caught up in that pop-star lifestyle again, but I can't go to see a group I like without wishing I could storm the stage and grab the microphone. Once you've had a taste of that, you never get over it. I never will. It's the biggest buzz ever.'

Clare's old Altered Images compadre, Johnny, is now in **Texas**. The rest of the band have settled down to domesticity. Clare is quite happy with what she's doing and, although she never has a plan, 'if I happen to win an Oscar then I'll be delighted!'. 'I don't regret that my life has moved on,' she reflects. 'I don't mind being in my thirties and doing what I do at all. But I think there is a snobbery in this business to an extent – when you've been a pop star people aren't always convinced that you can be anything else but that. I truly believe that, no matter how much people around you try to put you off, if in the face of all this you think *I'm going to do this*, you've every chance of succeeding.'

GLOSSARY
● **MTV**
Music-only satellite and cable channel. Very popular in Europe. Especially Germany.
● **Texas**
Not the state in North America, but the resuscitated rawk band with a woman singer wot everyone fancies.

SKILLS YOU'LL NEED
To have been a pop star and managed not to become a bitter, twisted individual.

TIPS
● Don't cry; think of what you *can* do instead.
● Look at Edwyn Collins! He kept going and then had more hits.
● Look at Texas, come to think of it.

TOUR MANAGER

💰 MONEY: From around £500 per week when you're starting out, to £1000 a week for a well-established tour manager, and around £2000 for really, really big tours.

⏱ HOURS: 24 hours per day for the length of a tour: you're always on call to sort out a mishap.

➕ HEALTH RISK: 7/10. Ver Road might take its toll a bit. Eat fresh vegetables.

✍ PRESSURE RATING: 10/10. Tough. You have to move a small army of music types (notoriously unreliable) around the four corners of the earth amid language barriers, changing currencies, and different people with confusing customs.

🍸 GLAMOUR RATING: 3/10. Waking up pop stars and trying to get them on a coach is not the most illustrious of tasks. Ringing up railways stations and airports isn't the most glimmering pleasure either.

✈ TRAVEL RATING: 10/10. You get to go everywhere! Places you'd planned, and sometimes places you didn't expect. Oh, and a lot of service stations.

The tour manager sorts out all logistical problems during a band's tour. That is, booking crew, trucks, hotels, and extra transport, and sorting out the budget and any other day-by-day requirements that your spoilt pop star might have (i.e. paying for wrecked hotel rooms).

Nobody ever really grows up wanting to be a tour manager. Imagine you are a nanny taking the kids on holiday, a holiday where the kids try to get as drunk as possible every night, snog strangers, and ruin the camper van. But also take into account that the kids have to work every night, and need to be kept as well as possible despite the ice cream and chip diet.

Being a tour manager is, frankly, a mug's job. It is only for the very most Mary Poppins of people, who has a strong constitution and an unshakeable calm in the face of inevitable disaster. Consequently, frightening people do the job because they are good at getting people out of bed in the morning, imposing fines for oversleepers, and taking what they call 'no shit' from anyone. As you can imagine, once you get yourself together and manage a few high-profile tours, the money becomes very good. There is fun to be had, you can be a roaming Jack Kerouac-style free spirit – you don't have to have permanent accommodation back at home to do it, unlike most jobs. But it is a lot of hassle.

Tour managers normally start through helping out friends, managing bands themselves, or moving up from being part of a touring crew – sound, lighting or **backline crew**. Obviously, you have to have some interest in music and not mind going to bed late. You also have to be able to organise yourself out of a civil war, if the need arises.

You start when you're asked by the artist's management or record company to do the job, as their band has just announced a tour which they've put together with a booking agent. Obviously, this can range from ten dates in Britain to a year-long trek round the world. You're given a **budget** and from there you contact everyone involved, including backdrop companies and stage-set designers, if you have that sort of cash for a big bonanza tour.

You find a production manager, lighting and sound engineers, and backline persons. These are most often people you've worked with before, or types recommended by people you've worked with before, just so you know they won't sulk in a corner when everyone else is playing charades. You have to negotiate the wages for all these people – you have to say a lot of 'I'm not paying you that!'s. You book the hotels and flights for everyone, with the help of a travel agent – and there are music travel agents who are used to this sort of thing and pick out

brring!

TOUR MANAGER

the hotels that have late bars and are more tolerant of pop-starry behaviour. You'll need at least one tour bus, and one with beds if not everyone is staying in hotels.

Then you may have to hire trucks – there are certain music-biz transport companies that have the right insurance – book equipment for when you're there, and contact venues to check they've got a stage, lights, etc. (sometimes they haven't). You also have to make sure your band gets their rider in the dressing room: from ten cigars to eight individually monogrammed pyjamas. You have to arrange the **per diem**s for everyone, too.

Steev Toth has tour managed Nitzer Ebb, Erasure, Spandau Ballet and Alice Cooper, plus other top names. He started as a sound engineer. He did school gigs then promoted gigs in his home town in Somerset. He did the sound for an Erasure concert, then started tour managing the band he was managing, Nitzer Ebb.

'Once you've got the information, you put it in an itinerary, which is known in the trade as **The Book Of Lies**,' says Steev, who got his real name – 'Steve' – changed by deed poll because he thought it wasn't exciting enough. This 'book' is doled out to the band, crew, management, record company, press office, and wifey and husbandy-types who need to know where their loved ones will be for the next few months. You should also have your tour **laminates** to bung about, too.

Hey! You're on the road! Here's where the proper work starts. You have to do the accounts, unless you're going with a dead famous band, who'll have the money to bring a special accountant along with them. Tour managers pay for everything as they go along: bus drivers, hotel bills, even little plastic souvenirs for the folks back home. If a show is cancelled, for instance, you'll lose thousands of pounds; if a bus breaks down, you have to get it fixed, so you have to put a bit aside for emergencies. After every gig you sit down with the promoter and work out how many people came along, what the promoter's advertising costs were, and, if the band are at a reasonable level, you split the chunk of profit between promoter and band. There's a guaranteed minimum fee for each show, and you almost always get paid in cash. After the tour is over you have to go back to the artist's management or accountant with a set of accounts.

Sounds OK so far? Not too bad, is it? Well, there's more. You have to sort out different currencies (there are fourteen in Europe) and look after the well-being of everybody – people get sick or homesick or start to hate each other. Then you have to liaise with the record label, as they are sure to arrange on-the-road press and promotional schedules for the artist. Making sure the band get to these contractual commitments on time, like in-store record signings, radio and TV interviews, is obviously pretty darn important. Then explaining the fact

that they nicked half the record shop's stock of Alternative Rock because they were bored is another thing. This is why a lot of tours are like a chaotic kids' holiday, where the children are **fined** for being late and are literally carted around being told what to do.

Steev Toth is very matter of fact about it. 'You get to have a method, and you do all tours the same. You find a good way of doing it. Bands *do* make the tour manager wake them up, to get to the airport on time. It's a bit "Let's see how far we can push him". I do issue warnings: the band must remember you're the boss – they must respect that.'

The job isn't for the weak of heart. You can be detained at customs when you touch down in a new city because they know you're with a rock band and that rock bands are renowned for taking drugs. You have to arrange work permits for everyone to enter some countries, and your promoter may forget to get them, or the authorities may not give them to you. There're all these things at stake. It's a rough ride and only for the insane, in all honesty.

'Two weeks in Russia in '92 was the most depressing tour of my life,' says Steev. 'Nitzer Ebb went to Siberia. There was no toilet roll or food – just vodka. It was a culture shock because we'd just arrived straight from America. You had to book a telephone call two days in advance. My wife desperately tried to get food and water out to us but failed. It was really frightening, so we trashed a hotel room out of frustration and had to pay for it. It was $80. A year's salary to them; to us it was pocket change. The whole bathroom, toilet and bed went out from the eighth floor. I thought that was quite a bargain, really.'

Steev can recall times when he's had to separate warring members of bands who are waging fist fights just before they're about to go on stage: 'Renegade Soundwave had a fight before a performance in Macedonia in

A TELEVISION ACCIDENTALLY
'FALLING' OUT OF A WINDOW.

front of fifty journalists. It makes a good story, but they were trying to kill each other.'

And, of course, there are also groupies to fend off. 'They get tedious,' he laments. 'They'll always be so sycophantic because they think music is a glamorous industry, and so will spend their time just hanging around. It's not just females – it's males as well. In the early days of Erasure, there were all these spotty youths hanging around trying to ask what kind of keyboard Vince plays. You become hardened and can be quite rude. And I do find I end up having to lie for the artists. Lying to wives isn't my favourite part of the job.'

And, to top it all, bands never make much money touring. The **shortfall** is picked up by the record company. You have to be playing arenas and stadiums

to start raking it in, and, if you want a light-show extravaganza or someone dressed as an anteater dancing to the left during the encore, you've blown your budget. The merchandise sales provide revenue, but the record company has nothing to do with this side so it can't pay for the tour.

But! There is a good side. You get to hang out with pop stars in strange hotels getting drunk on dodgy liquor. You get to cross people you don't like off guest lists – even famous people. You get to spend your PD on sweets and crisps. You can go on business-class flights, stay at the fanciest hotels, and you're not actually spending any money. All your wage goes in your bank account as everything on tour is paid out of the tour budget. And, if you can do the job properly, there should always be work.

'Most bands prefer a British tour manager,' says Steev. 'Americans insist on them because they're used to festivals and different types of venue. We tend to be more used to different currencies and languages. American tours are a piece of cake – it's either a club, an arena, or a shed. Over here you have to be a lot more versatile.'

GLOSSARY
● **Backline crew**
The guitar and drum technicians who you see faffing about with pedals and leads before a band goes on stage. They always look grumpy.
● **Budget**
All tours are based on a budget, which doesn't alter. It is set by the management and record company and allows for the fact that the tour might not break even. The budget is

rarely optimistically extravagant, thus ensuring that the shortfall should be as little as possible.

● **Per diem/PD**

'Per day' – amount of money every member of the tour contingent gets for sweets, pipe cleaners, and copies of *That's My Plectrum!* magazine. Sometimes spent in the pub. No, not sometimes. Always.

● **The Book Of Lies**

Contains every date, venue, telephone number, hotel detail, stage size, etc. Given to everyone. Except fans, that is.

● **Laminates**

The magical laminated cards on strings which get you access to parts, or all, of backstage. Eagerly sought after. They now have pictures on them so you can't nick one and pretend to be the sound engineer.

● **Fined**

A lot of bands have to be threatened before they'll behave themselves on tour. They are fined for being late in a lot of cases, because it wastes everyone's time, doesn't it?

● **Shortfall**

The money owed at the end of the tour – that falls short of the budget. It is always paid by the record company. They might ask for it back in some cases, if the band suddenly makes a lot of cash through record sales.

SKILLS YOU'LL NEED

Common sense; 'people management' skills; a desire to look after other people all the time; a bloody good organisational mind; ability to get going even when feeling a bit peaky; diplomacy, plus being dead strict, too. Sort of headmistressy skills, really.

TIPS

● Get to know about tours, by helping out friends in bands.

● Engineers often get into it. Plus truck drivers. Any job involved with touring will help you to do it.

● You have to start at the bottom. The Rolling Stones may employ four tour managers, but they've all had masses of experience. Patience, patience.

● Don't even bother if you're a bit of a dosser. It's a complete nightmare of unearthly hours and hard work. The tour manager is not a job for slackers, quite frankly.

TOUR PROMOTER

MONEY: From around £10,000 a year starting out at a big firm, to tens of thousands for dealing with stadium-style tours.

HOURS: 9.30 a.m. to 6 p.m., then the gigs start at 7 p.m.

HEALTH RISK: 5/10. Might be run over by the catering lorry.

PRESSURE RATING: 8/10. Arranging the unarrangeable, in some cases. Everything can get very last minute. A lot of decision making and crisis management.

GLAMOUR RATING: 6/10. It's mainly an office job, with lots and lots of paperwork. You might get to see one of The Tindersticks soundchecking, or someone from Dodgy at an aftershow party, but it sure ain't limos and champers all the way.

TRAVEL RATING: 7/10. Dudley or Aberdeen: going to see the acts you have fixed up to play is essential, but not terribly glitzy.

The tour promoter's job is to try to sell as many tickets as possible for a given artist's live performances. Promoters deal with the advertising and organisation once the tour is booked.

Ah, the world of touring. It is a veritable monster and many music-industry jobs are connected solely to this netherworld. The tour promoter is an essential prop to the industry, and no signed band can even remotely begin to survive without one. The tour promoter takes over once the booking agent has arranged a band's jaunt around the country, and sets about telling the world about the dates until, hopefully, they are totally and utterly sold out.

Promoters occasionally work with bands who are not yet even signed, but it's more normal for them to become involved when an artist has signed a record deal or is on the verge of doing so. Surprisingly, promoters can become just as involved in bidding wars as record labels and publishers, as competition to promote tours by much-touted upcoming bands is very fierce.

Essentially, the tour promoter buys up all the tickets for a date cheaply, and then tries to sell them on to the public at a higher price. Promoters can deal either with one show or the whole tour. However, it's very rare for a promoter to attempt to cross international boundaries: virtually all promoters below the absolute giants of the industry work dates only inside their own country.

Ticket sales are the key to making money on tours, or at least breaking even (tours, like singles, are generally regarded as promotional devices for albums, not money-making entities in themselves). The main task of the promoter is to ensure that the publicity reaches the right people: there would be little point in advertising Cliff Richard in *Kerrang*, or Oasis in *The People's Friend*. The tour promoter, rather than the band, loses money if tickets for a tour don't sell. Although, if a record company loses money on a tour which is particularly unsuccessful, the band may well find themselves having to recoup the loss from their advance. This, however, is another story.

There are venues to accommodate all audiences, from small pub gigs like the Camden Falcon, through medium-sized clubs like the legendary Buckley Tivoli and Dudley JB's, up to Wembley and the Docklands Arena. Before the promoter becomes involved, the booking agent (see 'Booking Agent' chapter) should have carefully estimated the likely appeal of the tour and chosen venues accordingly. However, bands do sometimes upgrade or downgrade at a late stage if ticket sales have been much higher or lower than anticipated – the latter scenario, which was wonderfully depicted in the seminal *Spinal Tap*, is deeply humiliating for the artist concerned, and will unquestionably be accompanied by loud crowing and sneering from the music press. On the other hand, extra nights may be added if **demand** is overwhelming. Sometimes venue ownership and tour promotion overlap – the mighty Mean Fiddler group own five venues in London and promote all gigs staged there themselves, as well as the Reading and Phoenix Festivals and a host of other events.

So, let's say you have a moderately successful band who would like to do a twenty-date tour of Britain in about four months' time. The booking agent arranges the venues and then the promoter steps in. The promoter, who is aware of the tour budget, firstly contacts all the venue managers, confirms that the venue is hired, and pays a fee to do so – which can be anything from a couple of hundred pounds to thousands of smackers, depending on the venue size and the date of the gig.

The next task for the promoter is to arrange the printing of tickets (although very occasionally individual venues may handle this task) and place adverts in newspapers, magazines and periodicals to promote the shows. Naturally, the *NME* and/or *Melody Maker* are pretty much essential for any tours of an indie or slightly alternative nature, and advertising space may be booked in these mags as much as ten weeks consecutively to publicise one tour. The prodigious cost means that television advertising is effectively a no-no for any act smaller than Kenny Rogers or The Rolling Stones, but radio stations such as Kiss FM are handy for dancier gigs. Most promoters also make use of **flyers** and will employ a host of students and part-time workers to stand outside gigs freezing their socks off and giving out bits of paper to drunk fans rolling out at midnight.

Flyposting is still technically illegal but all the major record companies and promoters do it and hold huge accounts with the poster companies. It's a vital part of the publicity process and can really boost a promotional campaign. Few offenders ever actually get pulled up by the police, unless their unfortunate operatives are caught red-handed. Like prostitution, flyposting is generally tolerated due to the vague belief held by the authorities that, were they to clamp down, something far worse would probably replace this fairly minor misdemeanour.

The next stage for the promoter is to liaise with the artist's tour manager to discuss stage size, lighting, the **PA**, forklift-truck hiring, security, etc. Normally the tour manager is the first port of call here, although extravaganzas such as U2's PopMart tour or The Rolling Stones's Voodoo Lounge monstrosity will have their own production manager, who in turn will have a host of staff. The promoter and tour manager will discuss finance, and also the sacred **guest list**.

Here is an example of how the finances of a typical date work. A band may be performing at The Forum, north London (there are, as you might imagine, quite a lot of indie venues in north London), which has a capacity of two thousand people. Selling tickets at £10 each means the promoter makes £20,000 if the show is sold out. After VAT, £17,000 or so is left. The combined costs of venue hire, promotions via press adverts and flyposting, ticket printing and insurance are likely to total around £9,000. The band themselves will receive in the order of £6,000, out of which they pay for

their crew, equipment hire, etc. The promoter is left with a profit on the night of approximately £2,000.

Paul Hutton is a director at Metropolis Music, one of the major promoters in Britain. He started, as many do, as social secretary at his university. Then he went on to stage gigs, with a couple of friends, in the Fridge club in Brixton and at the long-defunct Hammersmith Clarendon (which is now a Tesco's).

'It's hard for promoters to make a large profit,' he says. 'You are certain to promote some dates which lose thousands of pounds. Ask any promoter. If you made up a business plan based on promoting gigs and went to your bank manager, I'm certain he'd say, "No, no! Think of something else!"'

Most promoters begin at the lowest level, probably putting on gigs in pubs and small clubs as a hobby. Chances are you can meet an indie band you like, attract forty or fifty people, and earn about £60 on the night. The Camden Falcon have a club night called The Barfly which is run by a couple of people as a labour of love. Some of these people go on to be full-blown, large-scale promoters, but just as many head into being venue, band or tour managers, A&R people, or (more rarely) music journalists.

Promoters can find they

TOUR PROMOTER

spend half their life at rock gigs. The hours are very long, as it's important to be **on the circuit** and see not only your own shows but ones staged by rival promoters. You're always bumping into people at the bar, gabbing about The Next Big Things, making contacts and networking. The social side of the industry overlaps with/is indistinguishable from work, as per usual. You even have to enjoy talking to people about points on albums, in this line.

There's a danger you may be made the scapegoat for a tour when the band have failed to attract the level of ticket sales they expected. Artists on the slide will often give their promoter or booking agent the boot after a flop tour rather than look at their own waning star as a reason for the poor attendances. The band manager will also look to dump someone else before being dumped him/herself. Paul Hutton summarises the worst elements of the job as the hours and losing money.

Tour promoters may find special, one-off gigs in unusual venues an interesting challenge. Some bands are minded to play art galleries, circus marquees, or Battersea Power Station. Metropolis put on an Aphex Twin show at The Clink, an ex-prison in south London, but these kinds of event have their own problems. 'You have to remember that Johnny Punter can't always find his way to a lot of out-of-the-way places,' says Hutton. 'And one-off concerts cost a lot and rarely make money, so the record company has to be very much behind the band.

'I wouldn't necessarily recommend the job to anyone,' he summarises. 'You've got to be sure that you want to

do it. I set out thinking: I don't want to have a nine-to-five job. But sometimes I sit here and wish I had one. Basically, you just have to have a bit of an entrepreneurial streak.'

GLOSSARY
● Demand
The number of tickets that are wanted. Demand is always 'overwhelming'. If it is underwhelming, it is simply not mentioned: it doesn't exist.

● Flyers
Pieces of paper which advertise forthcoming gigs, given to people coming out of similarly styled gigs. Flyers are also used to promote club nights, theatre events, etc. No one is sure why they are called flyers, but they fly away in the wind if you let go of them.

● PA
Public address system. You can address your public in a musical stylee through the big speakers which sit on either side of the stage.

● Guest list
The most important word on a ligger's lips. The guest list is a terrifying list of all the people who are getting in free to a gig, or at a reduced price. These are all industry good-for-nothings who won't watch the bands and sit at the bar drinking cocktails and looking for famous people to talk to. Mostly.

● On the circuit
The 'rounds'. The endless toil of live gigs around the capital. Once you've been circuiting a while, you see the same faces everywhere. It is, as they say, a small world.

SKILLS YOU'LL NEED
The spirit of the entrepreneur; sociability, being able to organise, ability to do things at the last minute, friendliness, bossiness.

TIPS
● Many promoters start out at university student unions, where you learn the skills but are using other people's money.
● Some companies might take you on for work experience. Write to them.
● Local venues are often willing to put on gig nights for local bands. This is a good way to start and gain experience.
● Organise your friends to play in someone's garage, publicise it, and see if anyone turns up.

USEFUL ADDRESSES
● Harvey Goldsmith Entertainments, The Glassworks, 3–4 Ashland Place, London W1M 3JH.
TEL 0171 224 1992. **FAX** 0171 224 0111.
● International Talent Booking, 27A Floral Street, London WC2E 9DQ.
TEL 0171 379 1313. **FAX** 0171 379 1744.
● MCP Promotions, 16 Birmingham Road, Walsall, West Midlands WS1 2NA.
TEL 01922 20123. **FAX** 01922 725654.
● Metropolis Music, 491A Holloway Road, London N19 4DD.
TEL 0171 272 2442. **FAX** 0171 263 2434.
● Miracle Prestige International, Bugle House, 21A Noel Street, London W1V 3PD.
TEL 0171 434 2345. **FAX** 0171 494 3847.
● Riverman Concerts, Top Floor, George House, Brecon Road, London W6 8PY.
TEL 0171 381 4000. **FAX** 0171 381 9666.

VIDEO DIRECTOR

MONEY: For a video shoot where the budget is around £35,000, you'll be handed a tidy £3,500, 10%. You can make two promos per year, or two hundred (weather permitting).

HOURS: Anything from an afternoon a week to every day of the week, either doing the video thing or going to see clients, pitching storyboards, hanging out around idiosyncratic scaffolding for inspiration …

HEALTH RISK: 9/10. Trying to get anyone to stand still is difficult. And then matching them drink for drink afterwards is worse.

PRESSURE RATING: 8/10. You have to deliver a promo that band, record label, management and *The Chart Show* and MTV will like. And you have to make ugly people look good on a depressingly regular basis.

GLAMOUR RATING: 9/10. Those above will love you for it. Video directors get given flash awards nowadays as well, and get to go to Rotterdam to receive them.

TRAVEL RATING: 9/10. Yes, if you hook up with a glossy boy-band-type who likes to lord it about in the Bahamas with nothing but a billowing pair of trousers to their name, ready to **lip-sync** at the drop of hat.

The video director comes up with the idea for, and is in charge of producing, a feisty little film to go with a band's track. Shots of the bassist are optional, nowadays.

In the early eighties there were a certain number of snarling indie stars who liked to anticipate the demise of the pop video while spitting into their lager and lime. Such Luddite thinking proved to be hopelessly inaccurate and the use of the video as a promotional tool became more and more widespread. The birth of MTV meant the non-believers were scuppered. A new industry was born in which jobs were made, egos were expanded, money was spent on penguin costumes and careers were made or ruined by a little three-minute film.

A cheap video costs around £20,000. Yup, that's a cheap one. Around £100,000 is what you can pay if you're a swinging hellcat of a major band and have sold a fair few units in your time. For a promising, hit-friendly single in the UK, £40,000 is a respectable amount. In the US it can be much more expensive: $200,000 and upward.

Someone called a 'video commissioner' at the record company will be aware that a band needs a video made for a top new single due out in a month or so, and will commission (hence the name) a director to work on it. Directors will either be known by the commissioner through their previous work or else he will have seen their showreel, which is full of their best work. The most suitable person, within the band's budget, will then be chosen.

Note: Bands do not generally enlist the help of a director who's made videos in which bloody chicken heads dance around plates of rotten sprouts if the band is a Gaelic folk trio with a song about knitting.

AN IMAGE NOT ACCEPTED BY MOST POP BANDS.

Often, several directors will pitch for an idea after hearing the tune in question. The idea that suits band, management and record company will be chosen and the director duly employed. Once commissioned, the director will shout 'Yippee!' then get on with the task in hand. They'll have a **recce** with a location manager in the glamour spots of the world for starters. They'll often find themselves in Berwick Street Market in Soho, London – trillions of videos have been recorded next to the artichokes there. If you see a cheeky stallholder winking at **Kenny Thomas** as he's singing, you can bet they're in Berwick Street. Potters Bar is far too far to travel for London media-types.

The producer will be recruited and will work out a budget, and together with the director will find a crew and a casting director. The casting director is employed to get hold of any **models**, children or comedy fat/short people who may be needed. This process is all pre-production, which also includes meetings about what sort of lamps need to be used and how to make the triangle player look less morose.

Production is usually a one- or two-day shoot where the video is actually shot on film rather than video tape. The negatives of the film are then telecine-ed on to video; off-line editing begins, and it all gets very technical. Luckily, your editor will sit in the editing suite with you and help you to pick the best bits. Then, once this process is completed, the finished article goes back to the record company. They may well make you do a different edit if the original has, for example, **cats on fire** in it.

There are many and varied routes for people to become video directors. Film school is an obvious in – the London College of Printing and Harrow College are just two places that provide degree courses in film-making. Walter Stern, who's made promos for bands including The Prodigy, The Verve and Massive Attack, started at Bournemouth College. He wanted to direct his own films from the start, but wryly says that the chances of that happening immediately were 'slim'. So he made some short films, and as a result filmed a commercial for *Time Out* listings magazine in London. 'I thought: At least if it's rubbish, it'll be short,' he remembers. 'Then a friend took my showreel around a few small production companies without telling me. Someone liked it, and thought I should go into music videos.'

Most music-video directors work alongside a production company and sign a contract so they don't flee to rival companies. The companies deal with getting the **showreel** shown around and sometimes fixing up editors and other **technicians** if necessary. On average, the director gets 10% of the budget. The production company takes 15-20% of the video's budget and the producer gets around 5%.

Stern's first promo was for the re-release of 'Rock On' by David Essex. Well, we all start somewhere. He then made a video of some friends of his, a pub-band affair, which was more his style. 'As soon as I'd done one thing that represented my tastes, during the following six months my jobs got better and better,' he says.

One of his favourite jobs was doing the video for The Verve's 'Bitter Sweet Symphony' – although his original version, in which **Richard Ashcroft** gets beaten up, was rather different from the final cut which was shown on TV. The tale of how the vid for 'Bitter Sweet Symphony' developed is a good example of the way things work.

Walter initially wrote a **treatment** that was too expensive, so the record company told him to drop the idea and come back with another one. He then remembered a short film he'd wanted to make at college about a man trying

to walk down the street in a straight line. 'Luckily, it fitted in with the band,' he says. 'Richard Ashcroft said that he didn't want to do any acting and wanted to keep the filming very low-key and private – just him, me and the cameraman – so he wouldn't be embarrassed. He agreed to my idea then, the next thing he knew, he was surrounded by loads and loads of people – the exact opposite of what he'd wanted.'

Pop stars are difficult at the best of times. Getting them in a recording studio can be hard enough. Getting them to a film location on time is harder still. Then there's keeping them there. 'Drugs is the obvious problem,' says Stern. 'I've had bands leaving in the middle of a shot because they're out of it. My biggest nightmare – for a different reason – was with a band

VIDEO DIRECTOR

called World of Twist, who had previously made all their videos themselves. They didn't want an outside director but the record company insisted.

'They were very nervous of the camera so I had to shoot them secretly from a long way away. One band member left after the first day so the stuff I'd shot I couldn't use. They also kept wandering off all the time. What they really wanted was to film some guy in a bedroom listening to their track. I said this might get dull after a minute or two but they were saying, "No! You can zoom in on his belt and film a flare coming off it!" In the end I said, "Look, here's the camera, *you* finish it!" At which point they did. They were actually really nice people – but not to work with.'

Walter reckons promos use fewer effects now because they date quickly – and are now more story led. When you make a video you need to please the band, management, record company *and* television companies. *The Chart Show* are notoriously picky. They particularly don't like flames, guns, smoking or drinking. For example, if you saw the Blur 'Beetlebum' video on telly you will have noticed the 'fuzzy' hand of bass player Alex James. That was a censored cigarette. Coke cans and other commercial products also get wobbled out of view.

Video director Chris Cunningham filmed home-made mechanical masks in his garage with a school video camera, became a comic artist for *2000AD*, then went back into films, working for Stanley Kubrick, amongst others, on special effects. At the time he was into bleepy electronic music, and approached the band Autechre at a party and persuaded them to let him make a video for them. Since then he's directed promos for The Auteurs, Aphex Twin, Placebo and Dubstar. He found doing the latter rather difficult, because he decided he'd make a video that the record company and *The Chart Show* would both like. This highlights the director's dilemma.

'I was sent a tape of their music and it wasn't really my cup of tea so I thought I'd try to make something really really commercial as an interesting experiment. I wish I hadn't done it now. People were thinking, "He's lost it – he makes really *normal* videos now." I also did a Gene video for their single 'Fighting Fit' but unfortunately it was crap because I was only given one day's notice so didn't have a chance to get my head together. With Aphex Twin I had the trust of the record company to do something I wanted and it ended up taking a month and a half.'

'You're only as good as your last piece of work,' says Walter Stern. 'I'm careful of my own image. Pretty much 99% of what I'm offered I turn down.'

It is true that videos are often used to break in records. That (let's face it) awful 'Sledgehammer' video for Peter Gabriel was made in order to promote what the record company thought was an average song. Walter reckons that the promo for 'Bitter Sweet Symphony' broke The Verve in the States: they hadn't toured there for years or had much TV exposure. He also reckons that the same happened with The Prodigy's 'Firestarter', which didn't get exposure until Walter's video was shown repeatedly.

There can be bizarre problems which come along with this sudden wealth of acclaim. As ever, fame has its downside. 'There's a mad woman in Sweden,' says Stern. 'She rings up every time a Prodigy video comes on MTV and warns me that she'll do something crazy, something to do with Satan. 'Firestarter' surprised people, which is what we wanted to do.'

The people who succeed in video directing believe that, if you try hard enough, you'll get there in the end. It seems it really is as simple as that. 'There's no big mystery,' says

Cunningham. 'Any kid can buy or borrow a camera and make a film. You can edit it to a piece of music and next week you're doing a Prodigy or Kula Shaker video.'

However, don't expect to swap tips with any rival video directors when your career takes off. They simply don't mix. 'I've got a couple of friends who do the job,' says Chris Cunningham. 'But I'm not massively interested in what they're doing. I'm not being rude but I genuinely haven't the time for it. I don't want to be distracted. Anyway, I think that 95% of video directors are shit.'

GLOSSARY

● **Lip-sync**
Miming along to the soundtrack, while being filmed. Look closely at videos. Some pop stars are useless.

● **Recce**
'Reconnaissance' or 'reconnoitre', both French words for surveying, as in looking at interesting locations, such as the Berwick Street Market.

● **Kenny Thomas**
Loveable cockney soul singer who troubled the charts in the early nineties with pop-soul stuff about loving his baby. Still going, apparently.

● **Models**
Thin types. Often replace backing singers and lip-sync really badly.

● **Cats on fire**
Strictly not allowed. Neither are bleeding chicken heads.

● **Showreel**
The collected works of a director on video tape. A 'best of' for potential clients, i.e. record companies.

● **Technicians**
Lighting crew, stage-set hands, camera crew, dolly grips, etc.

● **Richard Ashcroft**
Lanky 'I am mad' singer with The Verve.

● **Treatment**
A short written outline of the overall video narrative – i.e. the plot, if you can call it a plot. NB: A storyboard is the plot, shot by shot, drawn roughly on TV-like squares.

SKILLS YOU'LL NEED

An eye for a good visual image; being a bit pushy – one has to admit; liking your music and being prepared to work on some ropey things before you hit the big time.

TIPS

● Start filming *anything*. The less you try to copy someone else, the better it will be. Video directors can be commissioned after someone's seen a piece of work that may not even have music on the soundtrack.

● The London College of Printing and other colleges do film courses for aspiring directors. However, they can be anti-promo and more full-length-movie based.

● An art course can be just as good as a pure-film course. And all colleges have camera equipment to borrow, if you suck up to the teachers (it has to be done sometimes).

● If you need to get to know the ropes, a lot of production companies take on youngsters to copy tapes, gofer, and make cups of tea. As in any job, this is a good foot in the door.

● Walk around holding up your hands in a square, as if you're looking through a camera lens. Directors do this in real life, and they say it helps. No, really ...

WIFE/HUSBAND/LODGER

> **Money:** Not a lot. Or loads. Depends on the state of your marriage, really.
>
> **Hours:** 24 per day, seven days per week.
>
> **Health risk:** 10/10. You may end up with the same set of addictions as they have.
>
> **Pressure rating:** 7/10. Depending on how famous your spouse is.
>
> **Glamour rating:** You may become mates with the bassist's partner as well, unless you're married to Diana Ross, who obviously knows presidents and statesmen and business moguls and stuff.
>
> **Travel rating:** 9/10. You can swirl around any place your beloved swirls, e.g. recording studios, rock venues, aeroplanes and posh hotels (when things are going well); transit vans and B&Bs (when they're not). The Caribbean is a regular haunt for the Imans of this world. You know, David Bowie's bird.

The husband or wife is the sturdy rock of support for the fragile, tortured artist who is allowed to sulk about there being no milk in the fridge because they have been on Richard and Judy. Once.

Rock wives don't get a very good press. You're seen as a glamorous addition whose only role in life is to phone Selfridges on your mobile to see if they've got any chocolate-covered shrimps. You pout and preen on your spouse's arm and glow in reflected glory. But that glory means nought, because everyone hates you. Especially the fans. Rock wives are portrayed as bimbos and money-grabbers who start nosing around in professional matters when they should be inventing new ways of cooking with broccoli.

Yoko Ono was charged with splitting up The Beatles by pulling her besotted husband John Lennon under the influence of her cruel womanly wiles. Patsy Kensit was accused of forcing Liam Gallagher to stay in England to househunt when he should have been promoting his band across the pond in the States. Nancy Spungen was accused of egging on Sid Vicious in his heroin-taking and general deviant behaviour. Yasmin Le Bon was just left to do shampoo ads: no one worried about her because she was a model – and they're not threatening because they're thick.[1]

Rock husbands don't have so much bother. More often that not, they have some power. They often tend to be managers, record-company people, footballers or fellow pop stars. There are a few trophy husbands, just there to look dandy and hold cigarette lighters aloft for passing tabs.

1. According to folklore.

But some rock spouses are fine people. Ozzy Osbourne's wife and manager, Sharon, brought the alleged bat-eater back from the edge of alcoholism. Belinda Carlisle's hubby helped her to stop taking cocaine. Gloria Estefan, on a more individual note, states that her husband gave her the freedom to be free, lose weight, or some such thing. These alliances *can* be fruitful.

Amelia is married to a musician, Clem, who was the singer of a band who had a moderate amount of success in the early eighties then were dropped and split up, although he's now '**working on a new project**'. She found little stress in rock-wifedom. 'I

wasn't that friendly with the other rock wives of the band,' she says, 'although I did spend a lot of time at home playing Sega with the girlfriend of the guitar tech. We'd hire games and sit and get the buns in. I also knew a "rock lodger" who lived with other members of the band so, instead of moping around on our own when the others were away on tour, we'd drink lots of red wine.'

The rock tour doesn't hold that much interest for peripheral people. There's either nothing to do at the soundcheck etc., or then there's unwanted attention after the gig. Being 'the girlfriend' is not all glamour. You end up trawling around record shops to see if their single's been placed in a prominent position, going around distribution warehouses putting flyers for the fanclub in record sleeves, and having to listen to your other half witter on about middle eights.

Furthermore, you're always your spouse's **plus one**, and this can be wildly infuriating. Rock husbands/wives get fans coming up to them, but so that they can get close to their famous partner and not because they actually want to chew the cud with *them*. These accessories have to talk to the geeks whom Mr/Ms Pop Star can simply waft away with a snooty flick of the hand. Plus, pop stars never get their round in because they're worried about looking 'flash'.

GUEST LIST
Mr Popstar Plus One
Ms famousey Plus one
A band plus four
A journalist

BOUNCER

WIFE/HUSBAND/LODGER

Either that, or they're mean.

'People would just be asking me questions about b-sides all the time,' says Amelia of the rock-touring lifestyle she ultimately decided to eschew. 'They assumed all the songs were written about me. Clem wrote a song based on a meat commercial which was about ballroom dancers who argued a lot and the fans assumed it was about our relationship! I'd just tell them, "Leave me alone!" I didn't know what most of the songs were about anyway ...'

Amelia says her bloke didn't get all high and mighty when he signed a deal with a major record label – just a lot porkier. 'We suddenly had a lot more money so we went out and ate loads. We definitely drank a lot more – it was an **F Scott Fitzgerald and Zelda** type situation for six months. I'm sure if Clem hadn't been dropped from the label he'd now be writing crass novels and I'd be in a sanatorium. But, actually, the fundamentals of life didn't change that much. There wasn't much scope for excess in Leicester. A six pack and a balti every night was about as far as we could go.'

Poppy has been going out with a pop star we'll call Ted for seven years. She started seeing him when she was in the sixth form, so she reckons her life changed but would have done so around that point anyway. She is just as feet-on-the-ground about it all as Amelia. 'I would never hang around the studio: it's dead boring and you just get in the way,' she reflects. 'And, if the

YOU FIND YOURSELF DRINKING A LOT OF FOREIGN LAGER. GLAMOUR, THAT IS.

band go away, they take lots of other people who are now my friends, so I have people to talk to even if Ted isn't there.'

Poppy doesn't worry about the groupie situation and neither does Amelia. 'There weren't any!' Amelia splutters. 'And, anyway, I trusted Clem. I once heard that there had been a woman interested in him and he literally ran away – his coping mechanism was to just go and hide. In any case, at the level he was at it just wasn't glamorous. Girls who went backstage would find themselves surrounded by men drinking strong lager, which is not exactly conducive to romance. I never found the lifestyle glamorous. If we ever went to record-company parties the bassist would normally end up in a fight with someone and we'd have to leave. I went to Switzerland and Germany and it is more glamorous abroad, but only because you're drinking the foreign variety of strong lager.'

Clem once got annoyed because he was slagged off in an interview by another band, who claimed they'd seen him and Amelia in a clothes shop and she was saying, 'Darling, you'd look great in that jacket on stage.' They called her a floozy, or something. That's as difficult as it got, and Amelia wasn't terribly bothered. She was more irritated by flying out to see the last leg of the band's American tour and finding the journey took 24 hours each way because she'd made a late booking. People did occasionally find out their phone number and call up but would invariably put the phone down without speaking rather than saying, 'Hey, bitch! That guy's for me!' Oh, and a Japanese stalker once tried to find Clem, who by now was living in Brighton. She found out where he hung out and spent a few weeks hiding behind lampposts because she was too shy to speak to him. He got a bit worried that she might find his house, but she eventually got bored and went away.

Poppy is also in a band herself, as yet unsigned, but doesn't feel there's an awful rivalry there between her and her boyfriend. 'His money pays our rent, and that's good,' she reflects. 'My sister's famous, so you get used to it. I hope one day to be successful myself so I'm not so bothered. The only thing that's a pain in the neck is when Ted goes away to Japan and he phones and either he's drunk or I am! I think sometimes I would prefer it if he had a nine-to-five job.'

There aren't many rock husbands who are not in bands or other such glamorous jobs. Most female musicians seem not to find lowly real people attractive, but perhaps this is something to do with the eternal balance of power – it's very difficult for a successful woman to go out with a less successful man. It is, after all, still a man's, man's, man's world.

Paul went out with a singer in a band for a few years but, for him, the relationship wasn't as settled as the previous examples. 'I think people in bands crave attention, on the whole, but also I went out with a particularly extreme example,' he says. 'She was a junior Courtney Love. Singers' egos are incredibly fragile and hers

certainly was. I can't say I'd recommend it. I don't think I've recovered yet, years on.'

Paul says that, in his case, his partner's lifestyle affected their relationship in a negative way. Birds of a feather, in this case, certainly do hang out at the same nightspots. 'They go on tour and it's amazing the way a lot of people in bands get satisfaction seeking the attention of other pop stars,' he claims. 'This may be a sad thing to say, but stars are very clannish. Oh, it was bloody awful. When I started out I didn't care what she did because I was in love with her, but over a long period of time it ground me down. There are long spells of boredom for musicians and then there's the thrill of doing something completely exciting – a show – and it only lasts an hour! After that you don't want to go to bed; you want to celebrate and get hammered. These people are living a graveyard life.'

Furthermore, when the press gets involved and splashes your personal life on their grimy pages, the game changes. Your private life becomes their private life and suddenly your godmother knows where your boyfriend's been before you do. Your mum will ring up and ask who the kiss-and-tell former girlfriend is, and the people in the corner shop will ask you about your holiday even if you haven't got a tan. It gets to the point sometimes where the spouses who try to act normally and want their private life to remain secret have to move house, or leave their jobs, or both, if any scandal is revealed. It can be tough at the Very Famous level. But, to be honest, most people don't get that far: there aren't that many pop stars who approach tabloid potential.

A lot of hangers-on and groupie-types do often go out with, and even wed, the stars, but a lot of women who couldn't give a toss about whether David Bowie is coming around to tea also become rock wives. However flippant this might seem, rock wife or husband is a job: you're permanently associated with the famous, and it's not an easy ride. Before you marry that megastar, make sure you realise what you're getting into.

GLOSSARY
● **Working on a new project**
What ex-pop-stars do next. It can span from 'being in the pub by midday' to inventing quantum leaps in techno music under an assumed name.
● **Plus one**
As on a guest list, e.g. 'Lord Famous Person, plus one'. This chapter could have been called 'plus one' because that's essentially what we're dealing with.
● **F Scott Fitzgerald and Zelda**
F Scott Fitzgerald, author of *The Great Gatsby* and his wife Zelda sank into an alcoholic abyss intensified by their habit of holding week-long parties. Zelda was finally certified insane.

SKILLS YOU'LL NEED
Getting on with your chosen one, not minding if they go out a lot, having a life, being able to bear hearing their songs over and over again, being a plus one.

TIPS
● Don't do it unless you really do want to hear those b-sides in full, each day every day for months.
● Don't do it unless you are completely *not* in awe of the other person or else they'll make you go to the shop for them all the time.
● Don't do it unless you want to be hanging around horrible cold and empty venues in Wolverhampton listening to roadies shouting 'Two! Two!' at soundchecks.
● Don't do it unless you don't mind your name being unofficially changed to P One (see glossary above).

* All names have been changed.

A MUSICAL SHREW.